WAKEFIELD PRESS

I0025600

QUIET CITY

Carol Lefevre has published novels, short stories, and journalism. She is a Visiting Research Fellow at the University of Adelaide, where she completed a doctorate in creative writing. *Quiet City* is her first full-length work of non-fiction.

BY THE SAME AUTHOR

Nights in the Asylum
If You Were Mine

QUIET CITY

Walking in
West Terrace
Cemetery

CAROL LEFEVRE

Wakefield
Press

Wakefield Press
16 Rose Street
Mile End
South Australia 5031
www.wakefieldpress.com.au

First published 2016
Reprinted 2018

The line from Virginia Woolf's *The Waves* is quoted with permission from the
Virginia Woolf Estate.

The research and first draft of this work was completed with the assistance of a
grant from Arts SA.

Edited by Julia Beaven, Wakefield Press
Cover designed by Liz Nicholson, designBITE
Typeset by Clinton Ellicott, Wakefield Press

National Library of Australia Cataloguing-in-Publication entry

Creator: Lefevre, Carol Ann, author.
Title: Quiet city: walking in West Terrace Cemetery / Carol Lefevre.
ISBN: 978 1 74305 387 4 (paperback).
Subjects: West Terrace Cemetery (Adelaide, S.A.)
                Cities and towns – South Australia – Adelaide – History.
                Cemeteries – South Australia – Adelaide – History.
                Adelaide (S.A.) – History.
Dewey Number: 994.231

CORIOLE

McLAREN VALE

Australian Government

Australia Council for the Arts

Publication of this book was assisted by
the Commonwealth Government through the
Australia Council, its arts funding and advisory body.

Come view with me the last long home
Of those who share the common lot;
With chastened footsteps, pilgrim, come!
And tread with me this hallow'd spot

'Fragmentary Lines
Written in the West Terrace Cemetery, Adelaide'
– Caroline Carleton, 1860

There is the story of the boot boy, the story of the man
with one eye, the story of the woman who sells winkles.

The Waves
– Virginia Woolf, 1931

Contents

A Poetic Place

For years I lived in Adelaide without visiting West Terrace Cemetery. I had passed its western flank countless times on the train, but it wasn't until I was halfway through writing a crime novel and decided to set a scene there that I resolved to take a closer look. It was a hot afternoon in late February, one of those days of flawless sky and scouring light that defines an Adelaide summer. As I turned in through the main gates a seemingly limitless ocean of pale monuments shimmered before me. Angels with lichen-spotted robes stood vigil; stone doves watched over the well-trod paths. In places there were vestiges of plant life from before white settlement, and while a stern sign warned that picking olives was prohibited, olive trees quietly ripened fruit and pines released a medicinal scent into the heated air. Aside from the occasional train arriving into Keswick station, the work-day clamour of the city was muted.

I had been reading the diaries of author and printmaker Barbara Hanrahan, and in them she remarked that West Terrace Cemetery was the most poetic place she knew in Adelaide. On walking through it that first time, I agreed with all my heart. To my novelist's eye it was crammed with characters, and their life stories were as fascinating as any fiction. Many of the headstones hinted at adventures and misadventures that would not ring true in a novel, and although I had come to gather details for my work-in-progress I saw that this populous yet profoundly quiet city deserved its own book.

One of the first memorials to catch my eye belonged to a nine-year-old child who, in 1916, had been accidentally shot while playing soldiers. From the inscription I learned that the boy's father had been killed the year before at Gallipoli. The angel that watches over this grave is one of the loveliest in the cemetery, its beauty enhanced by the delicate mottling that has settled on it over almost a century of South Australian weather. I fell to wondering how such a shocking accident could have happened, and almost before I knew it I was at State Records in Leigh Street with the coroner's report for that year open in front of me.

The heavy pale-blue paper was filled with the elegant copper-plate handwriting of the investigating police officer, Constable McCabe. On duty in the City Watch House, equipped with inkwell and dip pen, I imagined him sitting on a hard chair to methodically record the painful details. And somewhere between the perfect slope and loops of Constable McCabe's letters and the barely muted grief of the memorial inscriptions on the boy's grave, a moment from the past in this city I call home opened up to me. I understood what had happened – the when, the where, and even something of the why of it – and I saw that stories like this one would eventually be lost unless they were written down.

The lives of the first wave of settlers who came to South Australia were, without exception, extraordinary. They had embarked on an adventure of a scale that for most of us is beyond imagining. For in its finality, and in its stretches of time without communication with loved ones left behind, the voyage to the colony must have seemed like a leap into the darkest of dark unknowns. Many were buried at sea, and others quickly succumbed to the hardships of their new lives. There were the dangers of childbirth, and a range of common diseases that stalked households everywhere before the discovery and availability of reliable medicines. Women and children were the most vulnerable. From the very beginning there was an urgent need for a cemetery.

The Adelaide Public Burial Ground as it was first known appeared on Colonel William Light's 1837 survey for the city, an oval shape covering thirty-two acres in the south-western corner of the parkland belt. With no formal management in place, and no official records until July 1840, people died and were hastily buried on the site. The colonial chaplain, Charles Beaumont Howard, assumed a measure of responsibility for recordkeeping, thus the funeral services held at Trinity Church would become the earliest of West Terrace Cemetery's records. The first burial in the church register is of Eliza Stace, aged twenty-one years, on 9 February 1837. Unfortunately, the site of her grave is not recorded.

In 1839 Governor Gawler appointed an Adelaide Cemetery Trust, but while government and settlers struggled to establish the new colony, little energy was given to cemetery management. Yet pioneers continued to die, and as many as 500 are thought to have been buried on the site before James Laffen, on 6 July 1840, became the first recorded burial.

The history of West Terrace Cemetery is woven into the social, political and religious history of South Australia. The hardships and perils of pioneer life are everywhere evident, and the site records our changing attitudes towards death and dying from settlement to the present day. I have returned many times since that first visit, and in walking its paths and noticing the names and the inscriptions on headstones I have learned something about the lives of both its well-known and more obscure inhabitants. I have become an admirer of the skills of the early sculptors, stonemasons, and foundry workers, as well as a collector and interpreter of the symbols of sorrow and mourning they so subtly translated into stone and iron. In the course of my research I have stumbled across people, previously unknown to me, to whom I am related by blood or marriage, and my own sense of belonging has deepened through tracing their stories.

My walks have carved a meandering path both through this heritage-listed site and through South Australia's history; I have paused by the graveside of many a prominent citizen, but as their lives have been so thoroughly documented elsewhere they have not been the focus of my research. Instead my passion has been to discover something about the people whose names are slowly slipping from living memory, the ones who can now only be found in the files so meticulously preserved by the State Records Office, or among the treasures held by the State Library, or in the pages of old newspapers.

Like Barbara Hanrahan, I believe West Terrace Cemetery is the most poetic place in Adelaide, a place where the beginnings of the colony are still within reach, and where the people who in myriad ways shaped our understanding and experience of South Australia still have much to show us about our own history.

⚜

West Terrace Cemetery is a city of few roads and many pathways. Its narrow roads can be accessed by car, while its pathways are only wide enough for foot traffic. There is a map that shows the main divisions. The site is not as neatly laid out as Colonel Light's grid system of the city and there are areas where paths peter out into haphazard patterns. Not everyone buried there has an accurate address, but many do, and it is possible to find them.

I began by wandering, but soon started to search people out. If I heard of someone from the past who had done something extraordinary I would find out whether they were buried at West Terrace, and whenever I had a spare hour I would go and look those people up. It came to feel a bit like calling on a friend, and often it was clear that I had been their only visitor in a long while.

All the sections of the cemetery have their own atmosphere, from the restraint of the Quaker and Jewish graves to the often chaotic alignment of headstones in the Catholic Old Area. Whether in sunshine or rain, or even the dry, penetrating chill of a desert winter, I hope my walks will inspire you to plan walks of your own. In a site so crammed with history, what I have seen will not necessarily be what you see, for this is a personal sampler of the lives that have interested me, and you will doubtless be tempted, as I was, to make many detours. Let me also admit that I am not a historian but a writer with a love of stories. Neither am I a walker in the sense of one who puts on special boots and takes a rugged path, though I will ramble all day long until the light goes when carried along by story; time and discomfort dissolve when something catches my eye.

I was often drawn off course by the lure of an immortelle – a circular arrangement of porcelain flowers with cut tin leaves, nestled under a glass dome. Many include birds, anchors, or joined hands. Based on varieties of everlasting flowers in the natural world, immortelles became popular as funerary ornaments from the late nineteenth century. In the language of mourning they promise perpetual remembrance, though their deeper message is of the denial of human decay. Always fragile, their age means that many of their glass domes have been smashed and the flowers broken or scattered; each one that has survived intact is something of a miracle, and it has been my mission to photograph them.

Young as cities go, Adelaide is unique in Australia for having been founded on utopian ideals by free settlers. Within the boundary walls of its oldest burial ground, in a landscape culturally created through a many-layered process of ritual and mourning, there is much to be gleaned about memory and identity, about public and private emotion, and about the ways in which we have arrived at where we are now.

1

Under Summer Skies

It is one of those blue mornings when the air feels thin, a luminous morning on which all seems more or less right with the world. I turn in through the cemetery's main gates, and immediately find myself in a calmer, less hurried place. The small red-brick curator's cottage stands to the left of the entrance. Built in 1907, this is the third dwelling on the site, the earliest being the 1843 timber cottage in which the cemetery's first sexton John Monck lived with his wife, Catherine – poor Catherine Monck, who birthed and buried five children here before expiring herself. The Dead House, or morgue, was once close by. It stood just south of the caretaker's cottage where the eastern road from West Terrace meets the path junction in the area known as Plan Z. But it was always vulnerable to vandalism, and with the development of the private funeral industry its use declined and it has been demolished.

The poet Caroline Carleton also occupied that early cottage, which by 1857 had become so ramshackle it was replaced with a new lodge. From 1855 until 1861 Caroline lived here with her husband and children, and if you were raised in South Australia, or went to school here for any length of time, then you can probably recite at least one of her poems.

⚜

In 1859 the Gawler Institute celebrated its second anniversary by running a competition for the lyrics of a patriotic song. The closing date was 14 October of the same year, and the substantial prize of ten guineas stirred public interest. Competitors were instructed to write 'Poem for Prize' on the envelope, and to address their entries to George Isaacs, Gawler. Rather than submitting under their real names they were to choose a motto, and from ninety-three entries the judges settled on a poem by a writer with the pen name '*Nil Desperandum*'. Its author was Caroline Carleton.

Her pseudonym carries more than a hint of desperation, as well it might, for Caroline wrote the sunny lyrics generations of schoolchildren would sing at morning assembly while living with her ailing husband and their five children in the superintendent's house at West Terrace Cemetery. When a subsequent competition selected a melody by the German composer Carl Linger, 'The Song of Australia' would become an enduring symbol of home for those raised beneath South Australia's 'summer skies'; in the 1970s it would even jostle, without success, for a place as the national anthem. But while the lyrics are still familiar to many South Australians, few now could name the poet.

Caroline was born at Bonnar's Hall in Middlesex, the youngest daughter of a bookseller, William Baynes, and his second wife, Mary Ann. Her grandparents were French aristocrats who fled to England at the time of the French Revolution. An intelligent and well-educated young woman, Caroline spoke French and Italian and knew Latin; she played both the pianoforte and the harp. With these accomplishments, and her youth and beauty, a bright future seemed assured when at eighteen she met and married Charles James Carleton, a medical student at Guy's Hospital.

Charles had a family connection with the Earls of Dorchester, and has been described as 'of artistic temperament, somewhat delicate health, and sweet disposition'. While Caroline clearly had a bookish upbringing and wrote poetry, Charles was said to enjoy making pen and ink sketches. Around 1832 he wrote and illustrated a medical book with the intriguing title *Paintings of the Anatomy of the Brain, Explained in a series of Paintings from the Subject*. It seems likely that their mutual interest in the arts drew the couple together.

Unfortunately, Charles never completed his medical degree, and his employment history would always be one of sudden shifts of direction. But he charmed Caroline Baynes; they married and had two children, and it might have been the pressure of providing for his young family rather than any weakness of resolve that forced Charles Carleton to quit his medical studies and look towards the new colony of South Australia.

In the summer of 1839 Charles and Caroline Carleton, with their two tiny sons, sailed aboard the *Prince Regent*. Other than in the experience of refugee people fleeing war-torn homelands, the quayside scenes at such momentous partings are almost unimaginable in this age of jet travel. But while Caroline may have been venturing into the unknown, in her later poems we glimpse a free spirit who must have relished the grand adventure of the voyage, with its promise of reaching an exotic land.

Whatever dreams she may have cherished were quickly shattered, for the voyage on the *Prince Regent* was rough, and provisions ran short. Of the 199 passengers who embarked, there were twenty-three deaths. Charles acted as the ship's Medical Officer, but despite his efforts both Carleton children died. The phrase 'buried at sea' is one of those euphemisms so dear to the Victorians, an attempt to smother with language the horror of watching the bundled body of an adored infant being launched into the limitless and empty ocean, and of sailing on. When Caroline arrived at Holdfast Bay on 26 September 1839, childless and weakened by the deprivations of the journey, she must have wondered what she had done to deserve such a fate.

Although they had reached their destination there was to be more discomfort, for at disembarkation much of the luggage in the hold was found to be underwater and had to be stood on end to drain. Due to the tides, it was between seven and eight o'clock in the evening by the time the passengers had landed and been loaded onto the waiting carts. At least one driver declined to wait for baggage and, pleading the lateness of the hour, rattled away into the darkness with an empty cart. The remaining belongings had to be left behind overnight, and amid protests from disgruntled passengers the goods were made secure. During the night an unusually high tide driven by strong south-west winds caused further damage, and some of the items lost were a sixty-five-pound tub of butter, a canister of gunpowder, a carton containing assorted pieces of delft, and a box of books wrapped in a piece of carpet.

Letters written to family in England by another passenger on the *Prince Regent*, William Ewens, paint an optimistic portrait of Adelaide, and it must be assumed that the Carletons were likewise pleasantly surprised. For one thing, it was far more built up than had been expected, with houses and many other buildings. Ewens described the views of the country as more handsome than 'a Gentleman's park', with a range of beautiful hills as far as the eye could see. Flowers and birds were likewise pleasing, and the parrots made good eating, though he thought it a pity to kill them.

Vegetables were 'very Dear'. Candles cost 2 shillings and 6 pence, milk 8 pence a quart. A house with three little rooms could be rented for 1 pound and 4 shillings a week. For many people setting up in their first home, there would be dirt floors, packing cases for tables and empty barrels for chairs. Portable houses and tents were common, and despite Ewens's impression of a settled town, others complained of signboards in the scrub bearing the names of terraces and squares that existed only on a map or plan; they spoke of an imaginary town without buildings, where cattle rubbing against the posts were the only evidence of life. There were white ants to deal with, locusts, fleas and cockroaches, and the ever-present flies. This then was the reality of life in Adelaide at the time of Caroline and Charles Carleton's arrival.

Charles bought land at Glenelg and opened a chemist's shop, but the economic strain in the colony during the early 1840s found them on the brink of insolvency. Somehow they avoided that step, and soon Charles was making and selling cordials, castor oil, and other commodities. As an assayer, he accompanied the Inspector of Mounted Police, Alexander Tolmer, on an expedition to Mount Alexander, and on his return took up a position as medical dispenser for Doctor Nash, the colonial surgeon. During this appointment he and Caroline lived at the Adelaide Hospital with their young daughters.

After moving to Kapunda, and then back to Adelaide, Caroline gave birth to a son, Charles James. Meanwhile, her husband went to Victoria, perhaps as a medical officer at the diggings. On his return to Adelaide he advertised for sale *Carleton's Baking Powder*, and *Carleton's Farinaceous Food, Dysenteric Pills*, and other remedies bearing his name. By 1853 he was selling bottled English porter and stout at Blyth's Building, Hindley Street, and there is a sense of desperation surrounding the family at this point. At last, in 1855, Charles took up an appointment as superintendent at West Terrace Cemetery, and he and Caroline and their children went to live there.

Legend has it that Caroline wrote 'The Song of Australia' on a seat in the cemetery while her children played around her. On Sunday afternoons it was a popular place to walk, more park-like than the parklands; in the year before the Carletons took over, John Monck reported that in fine weather hundreds of people came to promenade among the groves of wattles and other trees. Even allowing for Monck's exaggeration, it seems likely that a significant number of people were drawn there to walk – comfortable with the proximity of death in an era when bereavement and grief had clearly defined rituals.

Caroline Carleton wrote poetry for pleasure, but in the Gawler poetry competition her eye would have been on the prize, for the cemetery was beset by financial difficulties and within only a few months of taking charge her husband faced criticism for his record-keeping, and eventually for exceeding the budget. Only an appeal to the governor prevented a sum of £55 being extracted from Charles's salary in compensation for this extravagance. By 1859 he was dying of tuberculosis and unable to work, and his wife had taken over the running of the cemetery.

Some readers of the *South Australian Gazette and Colonial Register* were stinging in their criticism of Caroline's winning poem. It was an 'ominous fact' that 'a lady gained the laurel' with a poem that had 'the sweet softness of the female mind, which characteristic almost unfits it for a patriotic song'. 'Cantator' of Goolwa wondered whether a pair of analytical chemists could throw light on the extraordinary combinations of colour depicted in the poem, singling out 'rosy light' and 'azure'. Another critic considered the poem to be 'calm, soft, gentle and feminine, suitable to be sung by a cluster of juveniles at a tea party'. A national song, it was proposed, ought to be 'short, bold, masculine and full of fire'. In a letter to the editor, 'T' moaned that the prospects of the colony were 'already sufficiently gloomy' that with 'ninety-three poets we are in almost a hopeless condition'. The writer, almost certainly a man, objected to importing poets rather than poetry. Settlers should not waste time scribbling poems when they could be getting on with their work, nor should judges waste money on 'the miserable cudgel-brained rhyming submitted to them'.

Finally, at the end of October, the paper published the following lines:

Epigram by the successful competitor of the Gawler Prize Poem
A thousand faults the critics find,
To shreds and tatters rend it;
One only fault she find with thou –
'Tis that they can not mend it.

In early November the newspaper pleaded a shortage of space and the 'immediate prospect of the English mail' as the reason they would not be printing any further correspondence on the subject of the Gawler Poetry Prize. When a year later Caroline Carleton published *South Australian Lyrics* a final carping note to the newspaper insisted that the author had 'scarcely done herself justice in this selection'.

With the loss of her infant children on the outward journey, and finding herself in residence at the cemetery, it is hardly surprising that death finds its way into a number of Caroline Carleton's poems. In 'On the Suicide of a Young Lady' her compassion for the victim is clear, as is her resignation in the face of prevailing social attitudes. 'To look on life – yet long to die' is the repeated refrain in another poem, and yet others lyrically praise the country's wildflowers, its radiant light and sparkling night skies.

In July 1861, Charles Carleton died of tuberculosis and Caroline appealed to the governor to appoint her as superintendent in his place. She had been running the cemetery throughout the final years of her husband's illness, but the response from the chief secretary declared that the position 'required an oversight and decision, such as no lady of education could be expected to possess'. Caroline pursued the matter but her appeal was rejected, and from fifteen applicants Henry Edward Brookes was chosen for the position.

Left without an income, Caroline Carleton took almost the only option available to educated women in straitened circumstances and opened a school on North Terrace. This was the first of a number of schools she ran, but none made a profit and with debts amounting to £107. 6s. 4d, and no assets, she was declared insolvent. Caroline retreated to Wallaroo, where her daughter, Amy, ran a school.

At Matta House near Kadina, she caught a fatal chill. The house was owned by the mining magnate William Horn, who probably knew Caroline Carleton through poetry circles in Adelaide. Despite his business interests Horn enjoyed poetry, and on his return to England he published *Bush Echoes* and *Notes by a Nomad*. Horn seems to have been of a benevolent nature, and the statue of Venus by the Italian sculptor, Antonio Canova, was one of three sculptures he donated to Adelaide. Matta House is now a museum.

Caroline's only son, who had hoped to establish a business selling lemon syrup in the Northern Territory, became lost in the bush and perished shortly after his mother's death at Kadina. He was twenty-two.

Members of the British royal family, including Queen Victoria, were presented with a copy of the music of 'The Song of Australia', and King Edward VII also requested a copy of Mrs Carleton's book of poems. A recording of the song, made by Peter Dawson, would be played by ABC Adelaide each day to open its morning session.

A year before the Carletons moved to the cemetery the current system of rows and roads was drafted. Leaflets in a display case near the entrance contain a map. For a lunch-hour walk there are two spots within sight of the curator's cottage where it is pleasant to sit and eat a sandwich. The picnic table beneath the big pine tree to the right of Road 1 is pleasantly shaded on a warm day, and as the tree also shelters one of my relatives by marriage I often linger in the vicinity. Maria Dailey became the second wife of my great-great-great grandfather, Elias Battley, and she is buried in the Dailey family plot on the north side of Road 1, on the corner of Path 4. I often wonder how Maria felt about her husband choosing to be buried at Clarendon beside the wife who had made the journey with him from England, but perhaps that was what second wives expected in the Victorian era.

It is a gentle stroll down Road 1 to where it eventually turns south, and on Path 38, beyond the first bend, stands an impressive sandstone memorial to the composer of the melody of the 'The Song of Australia', Carl Linger. Surrounded by an expanse of grass, adorned with commemorative plaques and a flagpole, the 2.5-metre-high obelisk is at the centre of what appears to be the largest single plot in the cemetery. The monument was erected in 1936 on the site of Linger's neglected grave, the funds having been raised by public subscription. It was unveiled by the premier, Richard Layton Butler, before a large crowd, but in the years that followed it must have fallen into disrepair, for a further plaque notes that in 1995 it was restored with government assistance.

Carl Ferdinand August Linger was born in Berlin in 1810, the son of an engraver. He had won a reputation as a composer by the time he, his wife Wilhelmine, and his brother sailed for South Australia aboard the *Princess Luise*. The ship, under Captain Bohr, had been chartered by the Berlin Emigration Society, a group founded by brothers Richard and Otto Schomburgk, who were anxious to escape the unrest that had spread across Europe following the French Revolution. The passengers who embarked in Hamburg, although refugees, were drawn from the professions, and included intellectuals and skilled artisans who would make a lasting contribution to the colony. Dr Richard Schomburgk would become the director of the Adelaide Botanic Garden from 1865 to 1891; another passenger, Hermann Buring, established a well-known Australian wine business. The *Princess Luise* arrived at Port Adelaide in 1849, Wilhelmine Linger having given birth to a daughter during the voyage.

After a disastrous attempt to farm eighty acres at Munno Para, during which time Carl Linger fell into debt and out of favour with his neighbours, the story goes that the composer came to Adelaide with only two shillings in his pocket, and took up work tuning pianos. But his skills were such that it was not long before he was welcomed into the homes of well-to-do colonists as a music teacher. Soon his fortunes improved, and he was drawn into the musical life of the young city. By 1852, Carl had paid off his debts from the farm and bought an expensive piano. In 1859 he conducted Adelaide's first philharmonic orchestra in its performance of Handel's *Messiah*.

As with the Carletons, tuberculosis would make its presence felt in what had otherwise become a rewarding and comfortable life. Wilhelmine died of the disease on 7 April 1860. Strangely, the West Terrace Cemetery archive records the death of Wilhelmine Linger on 9 April and gives her age as three years; the location of the grave is unknown. Very soon after the loss of his wife, Linger married Christiane Hogrefe, and a child was born to them the following May. But by then Linger was in poor health, and he died from dropsy on 16 February 1862, just a year after the widowed Caroline Carleton and her children left West Terrace Cemetery. Like Wilhelmine Linger, Charles James Carleton was buried in an unmarked grave in the cemetery he had once supervised.

⚜

Tuberculosis will surface often in these walks through Adelaide's history, for it took so many lives, including that of the first surveyor general, Colonel William Light. Considering its awful symptoms, the 'hot cough' and the blood, it is difficult to understand how it came to be regarded as 'the poet's disease', with the accompanying notion that sufferers developed heightened sensibilities and spirituality.

It is, perhaps, the oldest disease, with traces being found in human remains from the Neolithic period. It has also been identified in Egyptian mummies. Nefertiti and her husband are both thought to have died of tuberculosis, and Egyptians established hospitals to treat the disease as early as 1500 BC. In the ancient world, it spread from Europe though India and China, even reaching South America. But it was during the nineteenth century that tuberculosis hit epidemic levels and became known as the white plague.

Its slow progress fitted neatly with the Victorian notion of the 'good death', which meant having time to put one's affairs in order and to make one's peace with God. Novels were written with consumptive heroines; Lord Byron announced that it was his preferred way to die, which immediately bestowed a poet's blessing.

Strangest of all the myths surrounding tuberculosis was the superstition that it could be cured by the Royal Touch. Both French and English monarchs were reckoned, by the authority of the divine right of kings, to have the power to heal. King Henry IV of France kept a regular appointment with sufferers, seeing them once a week after taking communion. One suspects that constant exposure must have fortified the royal immune system, although his eventual assassination saved him from the disease that had become known as the *mal du roi*, the king's evil. By the reign of Louis XIV the Royal Touch had become sessional; times when the king would be available were widely advertised. Across the channel, touching ceremonies were almost as formal as baptisms. The English monarch, seated on a canopied throne, would make contact with the afflicted person and press a coin against their neck. In Oxfordshire, parish registers recorded eligibility for the Royal Touch alongside births, deaths, and marriages. Needless to say both French and English royal advisors ruthlessly manipulated the recovery statistics.

Eventually a Prussian physician, Robert Koch, discovered the cause of tuberculosis. Once its contagious nature was understood, sanatoriums sprang up to isolate and treat victims. In 1882 Koch noted that one in seven people died of tuberculosis. In our own time there is a perception that tuberculosis is a disease of the past, one that better hygiene and the development of drugs eliminated. Unfortunately, that is not the case, and a rise in drug-resistant strains means that each year there are as many as half a million new cases worldwide.

2

A Walk to the Wheelhouse

Of the first nine ships that carried colonists to South Australia, two of their captains are buried at West Terrace Cemetery while a third, Colonel William Light, may have been briefly interred here in the days after his death and before his burial in the city square that bears his name. A comparison of the passenger lists of those ships with the cemetery's archive turns up the names of many of the first colonists and ships' crews. In order of their arrival, the ships were *The Duke of York*, *Lady Mary Pelham*, *John Pirie*, *Rapid*, *Cygnet*, *Emma*, *Africaine*, *Tam O'Shanter*, and the *Buffalo*. The latter was under the command of the colony's first governor, Captain John Hindmarsh, and its figurehead was a water buffalo. I imagine this creature scudding over the waves, stubbornly covering nautical mile after nautical mile, its carved profile not unlike that of the governor's. The crowded *Buffalo* carried 173 passengers, and as well as its crew there was a rowdy contingent of marines who were to keep law and order in the colony. The decks were cluttered with livestock, including two mules, Minna and Brenda, acquired in Rio; there was Hindmarsh's dog named after the *Beagle*, which he had once captained, and stowed deep in the hold was his wife Susannah's piano.

While the *Buffalo* brought the vice-regal colonising party, the *Rapid* and *Cygnet* carried the men who would survey the land. Colonel William Light captained the *Rapid*, a two-masted brig with the figurehead of a greyhound. His watercolour of the ship riding out rough weather at Rapid Bay reveals how frail these craft appeared in even middling rough weather, let alone when set against the wilderness of the great oceans. It is a tribute to the fearlessness and skill of the mariners that all nine of the ships that left England arrived safely in South Australia, though the John Pirie under Captain Martin came so close to disaster that when completely engulfed by seawater even its dauntless captain doubted it could rise again.

After leaving Falmouth the *John Pirie* was caught in a savage storm. The first casualties were the sheep in pens on the deck, washed overboard; the captain's cabin was flooded, with the subsequent loss of instruments and maps, and hay and other cargo had to be jettisoned. When after six days they were able to shelter at Dartmouth a number of the crew deserted, apparently too traumatised to continue the voyage. Aside from the unfortunate sheep, the *John Pirie* carried pigs, turkeys, and rabbits – the latter, it must be assumed, survived to populate the countryside. The *John Pirie* was described by one of its passengers as 'only a washing tub with a tiller', but its staunch captain claimed he had never seen a better sea boat.

The *John Pirie* weathered the elements, but the remainder of the voyage, though calmer, did not lack drama. A passenger, Elizabeth Chandler, the mother of four children and wife of Charles Chandler, a thirty-year-old ploughman, threw herself overboard and had to be rescued. Hauled back on board, she railed at Captain Martin for saving her and later refused to take food. After a few weeks Elizabeth Chandler died and was buried at sea, her youngest child Harriet abruptly weaned by her mother's demise.

Captain George Martin had a large family; he and Mary Brett had married in 1817 and by the time he sailed on the *John Pirie* she had given birth to eleven children in places as far flung as London, Rio de Janeiro, Hobart, and Sydney. In 1823 he and his family had settled in Hobart, but although he owned land there they later moved to Sydney; for all his steady hand on the tiller, on land George Martin appears to have been a rather restless spirit. Mary stayed behind in England when he left for South Australia.

In her shoes, I might have looked upon the separation as a welcome respite from childbearing. Her husband took two of their sons with him on the South Australian adventure – eleven-year-old Robert Terence, listed as an 'apprentice seaman', and six-year-old George. Childhood was shorter then, yet an education was sometimes gathered along the way: both George and Robert Terence were taught to read and write during the voyage by ship's mate Henry Simpson. Mary followed later with the rest of the family.

The first weddings in the colony were both held on board the *John Pirie*. On 28 August 1836, just twelve days after the ship arrived at Kangaroo Island, Captain Martin read the marriage service for Samuel Stephens, the manager of the South Australian Company, and Charlotte Beare, sister of the company's superintendent of buildings. Neither bride nor groom had travelled out on the *John Pirie* and their marriage caused considerable gossip, not only because Stephens was thirty and Charlotte fifty-six, but because it was said they had been shamelessly cohabiting during the voyage. The second wedding was between William C. Staple, one of the *John Pirie*'s seamen, and a fifteen-year-old passenger, Mary Ann Powell – another instance of a childhood curtailed.

Captain Martin was by all accounts a religious man and he is recorded as donating £1 to the public subscription for Trinity Church. His death was described in the newspaper as 'lamentable' and there is no doubt that it was a sorry ending for a man of his gifts. It seems that by 1842 he had ended up in the Adelaide Gaol as an insolvent debtor. Depressed by a reversal of fortune and by a verdict against him in the Magistrate's Court for £20, Captain Martin took his life at his premises in Currie Street, which were in use as a store for agricultural produce. The deed was done with a pistol. Mr Solomon from next door was the first on the spot and found the captain expiring. A coroner's inquest returned a verdict of 'Temporary Insanity'. His widow and children were left with nothing, so a subscription was got up to help them.

But this story takes its strangest twist after Captain Martin's burial, when the Colonial Secretary, Robert Gouger, went for a stroll in the cemetery one afternoon with his wife and a visitor and came across Martin's headstone.

Sacred to the Memory of
Captain Geo Martin
February 24th 1842
Age 59 years
His death was accelerated
by disappointment
They have spoken against me with
a lying tongue and fought against
me without a care
CIX PS part of the 2nd and 3rd verse

The reading from Psalms, which Mary Martin intended people to look up, expressed her bitterness and her opinion of the reasons for her husband's suicide.

For the mouth of the wicked and the mouth of the deceitful are opened against me: They have spoken against me with a lying tongue. They compassed me about also with words of hatred; and fought against me without a cause.

On seeing the inscription, Gouger (who presumably knew his Psalms) flew into a rage and attempted to wrestle the offending headstone out of the ground. Later he would describe it as 'indecorous, malicious, and in all respects unchristian'. Gouger's guest, Mrs Alfred Watts, recorded the incident in a letter in which she also claimed Captain Martin had been dismissed from his employment with the South Australian Company for misappropriation of funds and chronic intemperance. It seems likely that she acquired this information in conversation with Gouger. The latter part of the inscription she described as 'a string of curses from the psalms'.

⚜

Robert Gouger is recorded as the first colonist to acquire a plot in West Terrace Cemetery and all too soon he had a use for it. His wife Harriet had left England in a state of anguish, having taken badly the parting from her family; her grief was doubtless heightened by being both pregnant and suffering from consumption. Their child, a son, was born in December 1836, on the day after the proclamation of the new colony. In the following March, Harriet lost her battle with consumption, and Henry Hindmarsh Gouger, an infant of only eleven weeks and one day, died the day after his mother.

It is rumoured that Robert Gouger buried them on private land, but that after his permanent return to England he fretted about what would happen to their graves. So he arranged for them to be exhumed and interred at West Terrace Cemetery. There is no record of any Gouger in the West Terrace Cemetery archives and no way of knowing whether the plot associated with Robert Gouger's name holds their remains, although it probably does. Why would he have bought it, only not to use it? Poor Harriet and her son perished in the time when records were poorly kept, but for the woman dying of consumption and homesickness, it was the least of her worries.

⚜

In perhaps the only episode of censorship by the trustees in the history of the cemetery, Captain Martin's headstone was removed due to outrage at its angry inscription. A few years later the trustees received a complaint about the missing memorial and voted to erect a replacement, minus the inscription, at their own expense. Whether that ever came to pass is difficult to tell, for today George Martin's address is Road 2, Path 10, Plot 11 on the eastern side, and there is nothing to mark it.

⚜

Captain John Finlay Duff, a native of Dundee in Scotland, captained the *Africaine*. But when the ship sailed from London on 28 June 1836 Duff, due to be married on the following day, was not on board. He and his new bride Anne Eliza Turner joined the *Africaine* two days later off the coast of Kent, and the voyage became the couple's honeymoon.

Captain Duff was a well-respected mariner and he handled the myriad difficulties that arose during the voyage with diplomacy. In 1839 he returned to England, and on the return voyage aboard the *Asia*, George Mayo the ship's doctor recorded in his diary a tiny sketch of him.

> *Captain Duff at 39. He is rather a pleasant mannerly man, not very much to say for himself except when shipping or anything on that subject is broached.*

Later he added:

> *Captain Duff is a very pleasant man when you come to know him, no nonsense about him and I do not think him capable of saying anything to hurt a person's feelings.*

Mayo was a little less complimentary about Duff's wife and the couple's baby.

> *Mrs Duff is nice lively woman, like most women rather vain, she is not very pretty, but there is a very neat style about her. She comes from Chepstow, partly educated in Bath, she prides herself I think on her knowledge of music and dancing and even in the languages, has rather a pretty voice, her baby is like her husband therefore not very beautiful . . . Mrs Duff is an awful talker, and when people talk so much they must sometimes talk foolishness, poor Mrs Duff has the great weakness of speaking so much of herself . . . When Mrs Duff is talking to one she rolls her eyes about so much, I have come to the conclusion that she thinks it looks interesting.*

When they were 200 miles east of one of the Cape Verde islands, shots were fired across their bow and a brig came close and ordered them to heave to.

> *Duff ran forward with trumpet and said we had 200 convicts on board, he then went off close to the wind. Captain Freeman*

thought the Brig was going to clap us alongside. I ran into the
Cabin for an instant and there saw Mrs Duff and Mrs Garratt
on their knees in an agony of terror. The four guns were shotted,
and the muskets and boarding pikes got ready. When I went below
many of the women were very much alarmed, and hoped their
husbands would not be cowards. Some of the Scotch women were for
dressing in men's clothes and I was to head them.

A later diary entry made in Adelaide notes that Mayo went with Captain Duff to visit Colonel William Light. Perhaps the good captain took Mayo there in a professional capacity because Light was dying of tuberculosis. It is almost certain that Mayo met Light's housekeeper Maria Gandy on that occasion. Maria had travelled with Light on the *Rapid* and nursed him in his final illness. After Light's death Mayo would marry Maria, and it looks very much as if Captain John Finlay Duff can be credited with having introduced the couple.

Perhaps weary of fending off pirates and bundling deceased passengers into the sea, Duff remained in South Australia, buying land and operating a business selling imported goods with a partner, John Hallett. After Anne Duff died in 1854 he eventually married Mary Schroeder.

⚜

Captain Duff's address is Road 1 South, Path 28, West 4th, Plot 37. As I wander west along Road 1, I marvel at those wooden ships, and the passengers and crew who endured months of confinement. The *Buffalo*, at thirty-six metres in length, was the largest of them; at only nineteen metres the *John Pirie* had barely enough room to swing a cat, and perhaps it was the lack of space to walk, to think, to talk in private or even to suffer and die in private that drove Elizabeth Chandler to fling herself into the sea.

Captain John Finlay Duff was also among the original subscribers to Trinity Church, and he donated an acre-and-a-half in Magill for St George's Church. St George's was opened in 1848 by the newly arrived Bishop Short, who, less than a fortnight later, would bury his own infant daughter in its cemetery.

The captain's funeral procession left Glenelg for West Terrace Cemetery at two o'clock on a May afternoon in 1868. The Reverend Thomas Field of St Peter's, Glenelg, read the Church of England burial service, and there were many old friends and others from the first ships present at the graveside, including Charles Everard who had been ship's doctor on the *Africaine*.

Duff's headstone, a little weathered now but still beautifully clear, is engraved not with an anchor but with an olive branch and a four-petalled flower. In the language of flowers favoured by the Victorians the olive is said to symbolise peace; I am uncertain whether the flower is a rose, but if it is it may be a token of love from Duff's second wife. Mary Schroeder was twenty-seven when they married in 1862; Captain Duff was fifty-one. Although not commemorated on the headstone, their two-day-old infant Charles George was buried here in 1864. Another child, Edward Duff, died in 1863; he was a year old, and may have been Mary and John Duff's firstborn son. Unfortunately, the location of his grave is marked as unknown in the archive, but it seems probable that these infant deaths established the gravesite.

After her husband's death, Mary, who was still only thirty-five, married a widower, Henry Hamilton, one of the state's pioneer vignerons. Having outlived him, she later moved back to Glenelg, where her first husband had been harbourmaster. At her death in 1919 Mary left two Duff sons, Joseph Stilling and Stuart Duncan; Joseph died in Wellington, New Zealand, a year after his mother, though he is listed on the headstone with his parents. Stuart and his wife Mabel Annie are buried alongside Mary and Captain Duff. Unable to locate a record of her burial, I am unsure what became of the excessively talkative first Mrs Duff.

Of the other captains, Hindmarsh was a naval officer who went to sea at the age of fourteen with his father, a gunner on HMS *Bellerophon*. At the battle of the Nile he was commended by Nelson but lost the sight of an eye. Hindmarsh had met William Light in 1834 while travelling to Alexandria on a ship captained by Light. When he heard that Light was to be recommended for the post of governor of the new colony of South Australia, Hindmarsh rushed to London and pulled strings to secure the position. Later he graciously suggested Light for the post of surveyor general.

Left to Hindmarsh, Adelaide would be a port with streets named after long-lost naval heroes. But the street-naming committee vetoed many of his choices, and his governorship lasted less than two years. His recall to London has been well documented – fortunately the British Empire was an overcoat with many pockets and after leaving South Australia Hindmarsh went on to govern Heligoland, a German island in the North Sea. A summary of his career recognised his 'extraordinary gallantry as a sailor' and his 'very bad fortune as a governor'. He died in London on 29 July 1860.

The remaining ships were commanded by Captain John Rolls (*Cygnet*); Captain Robert Clarke Morgan (*Duke of York*); Captain John Nelson (*Emma*); Captain Robert Ross (*Lady Mary Pelham*); Captain Whiteman Freeman (*Tam O'Shanter*). They all left South Australia.

3

Above Stairs, and Below

Whenever I think of the *Buffalo* I see it afloat at dusk on a calm sea. The agile voice of an Irish fiddle weaving through jigs and reels drifts across the water, and while the music does not soften the wooden grimace of the water buffalo on the ship's prow, and the stern-faced captain does not smile, restless children are lulled to sleep and Irish toes are set tapping. I feel fairly sure the image is a true one, for Charles Beaumont Howard, South Australia's first colonial chaplain, was an Irish-dancing enthusiast who played his fiddle on board ship. Although rudely treated by Captain Hindmarsh during the voyage, upon arrival Howard assisted with swearing-in officials at the proclamation of the colony.

The Reverend Howard was accompanied by his young wife, Grace Montgomery Neville – unflatteringly described by Hindmarsh as a 'handsome' but 'insinuating, tale-bearing woman'. The couple's young daughters travelled with them, and also Grace's sister, Rachel Neville. Seventeen-year-old Margaret Shines and twenty-three-year-old Catherine Kenna accompanied the family as domestic servants; they were listed as coming from Portsmouth but both were almost certainly Irish. John Luke Monck – who appears on the *Buffalo*'s passenger list as 'labourer' – was also in the chaplain's service.

Howard preached the first service of worship at Holdfast Bay on New Year's Day, 1837. In February of the same year he appointed Monck as sexton of the cemetery. Monck was also clerk of Trinity Church, probably named by Howard as a salute to his years at Trinity College, Dublin.

For both the Howards and their servants, 1837 was a momentous year. Charles established his ministry and personally erected a six-roomed Manning house on the church town acre on North Terrace; Grace gave birth to a son, Charles Neville, who died after three days and was buried by his father, and both servant girls were married at Trinity Church. In May, Margaret Shines (of Dublin) wed one of the marines Hindmarsh had brought with him on the *Buffalo*, Corporal Richard Mew; on 12 October, Catherine Kenna became the wife of John Luke Monck and they set up house at West Terrace Cemetery.

Grace Howard had a reputation for being 'fond of dress and showing it off'. At the first baptism at Trinity Church we see her in 'stiff corded black silk, her hair tied with cherry ribbon', a stand-out figure among the other women in their white, lemon, and pale-green frocks. Her sister Rachel Neville wore violet silk, a colour consistent with Victorian half-mourning, so it can be assumed they were still formally grieving for the loss of baby Charles. But when I think of Grace I see that flash of cherry ribbon, and it hints at a nature that at times might have struggled with the constraints of being a rector's wife.

Meanwhile, John Monck was given the daily management of the cemetery. In his years there he would become notorious for his slapdash recordkeeping, for pursuing a lucrative sideline as a monumental mason, and pressuring people to avail themselves of his wares. Sunday burials attracted unauthorised charges, indeed charges in general were fluid under John Monck. In 1854 a select committee was appointed to examine the workings of the cemetery, and the most shocking revelation to come out of this inquiry was that a drain down the centre of the cemetery had been used for destitute burials. Without funeral rites of any kind, undertakers had lowered coffins, two abreast, into the drain, where they were covered. Water continued to flow through the drain, for the cemetery had always been subject to flooding, and argument flared that the site was hazardous to public health. Monck had also decamped to the Victorian goldfields for a time, leaving his father in charge of the cemetery.

The denominational divisions in the cemetery – for by now there were separate Jewish, Anglican, and Catholic sections – would only make life after the committee findings more difficult. To avoid dismissal, Monck tendered his resignation, and then promptly obtained the support of Bishop Short to stay on as sexton of the Anglican burial ground. This embarrassed the government, but they were forced to bear up. It was around this time that the Society of Friends applied for a small portion of the cemetery; apparently they were not deterred by the awful stories then circulating.

Catherine Monck died in December 1857. Although the cemetery's archive lists the site of her grave as unknown, her name – misspelt – appears on the side of a substantial tomb that includes the Monck's five infant children, John Luke Monck, and his parents; it must be assumed that Monck knew where he had buried his wife. Considering its age, their tomb is in remarkable condition – perhaps it is Monck's own work, including the spelling of his wife's name: *Catharine*. There is no official record of her death, and I wonder if this is also Monck's doing. He is described in stone as *an affectionate husband and a kind friend*.

Their address is Road 1 South, Path 22. Plot 8 is on the western side and is visible from the road, being surrounded by unmarked graves.

When Monck finally relinquished his role at the cemetery, he moved to Glenelg and made a little money by renting out his house in the summer. He would show visitors a book from his days at West Terrace – it is tormenting not to know what the book contained, perhaps the exact locations of various burials, or the sums of money he made on the side during his residency – but it is said to have had the following self-penned verse:

John Monck is my name,
England is my nation;
the cemetery is my dwelling place,
and Christ is my salvation.

By 1840 the Church of England membership had swelled, and Charles Beaumont Howard sought the assistance of fellow Irishman and Trinity College graduate, James Farrell, incumbent at St John's in what is now Halifax Street. Grace had given birth to two more daughters, Henrietta Hindmarsh in February 1839, and Elizabeth Susannah in January 1840.

In the winter of 1843, Charles Beaumont Howard caught a chill and died. He had entrusted the welfare of his wife and children to James Farrell, though had he foreseen the scandal that was soon to transpire he might have made other arrangements. In February of 1845, James Farrell was prosecuted for indecent assault of a fourteen-year-old-girl, Sarah Charlesworth. The case was brought by Sarah's father, a shoemaker; Sarah was in the employ of Grace Howard.

Despite the summer heat the court was packed for Farrell's trial, with the crowd overflowing outside to peer in the windows. As this inauspicious moment in Grace Howard's life played out it was revealed that she, with Rachel Neville, the four Howard children, Sarah, and Farrell, had been squashed into a four-roomed cottage at Glenelg. Perhaps Grace had rented it for the holidays. As second colonial chaplain since Howard's death, Reverend Farrell had his own residence at Trinity Church, so it was awkward that he should be caught sleeping on a sofa in the parlour that opened onto Grace's bedroom.

Sarah Charlesworth testified that she had woken up to find Farrell, clad in his nightshirt, pulling back her bedclothes and that one of his hands was on her left breast. She asked him to leave, which he did, but later, in the parlour, he pinched the back of her neck and asked her where she was from. When she told him, he remarked that she should have married before she left Kent. At only fourteen, Sarah protested in court that she had been a very young child when she left England.

Grace Howard came to Farrell's rescue, testifying that she had asked him to wake the girl, who was slow to rise in the mornings. Sarah was extensively questioned, and after many hours in the witness box was on the point of collapse. Along with the serious charge against Farrell, the newspaper coverage notes a further dispute between servant and mistress, for the widowed Mrs Howard had tackled Sarah about spreading a rumour that she would soon have a baby. In court, Grace accused Sarah of having rummaged in her drawers and found some baby clothes that had been a present to her from 'Mrs Grey'. Given that the case occurred in the middle of George Grey's governorship, it seems certain that the gift of baby clothes must have been from his wife Eliza after the death of her own infant son.

Farrell was eventually acquitted for lack of evidence, but the taint of the scandal was slow to evaporate. He and Grace married quietly on 12 November 1845; the marriage was solemnised in the stringybark church of St Mary's-on-the-Sturt, but from all accounts their union was not without conflict. It was the beginning of the end when, in 1866, instead of medicine Farrell accidentally swallowed a liquid containing arsenic. Two years later, still ailing and in search of a cure, he sailed alone to England, where he died while taking the waters at Malvern, Worcestershire. He is buried in Malvern cemetery. Interestingly, the bulk of his considerable estate went not to Grace but to St Peter's College.

Charles and Grace's address is Road 1 South, Path 23; Plot 6 is on the western side, where it resembles its own small section of the cemetery. A headstone surmounted by a cross was raised by the couple's daughters, Grace and Henrietta, and their initials are inscribed underneath their mother's name. An obelisk on the site was erected by members of the Manchester Unity Oddfellows in 1921 to replace the original monument.

4

A Walk Beyond the Pale and Back

One of the chief fascinations of walking these pathways is coming across graves that date back to the colony's beginnings. Rather than a straight line through time, history begins to resemble a complex web of relationships, and I realise how closely woven were the lives of the first shiploads of immigrants; in 1836 Adelaide was so small that everyone knew everyone else. The great adventure had begun the moment they sailed from England, and being thrown together for months in a confined space – often in terror of sickness, or storm – forged alliances and antagonisms that directed future marital, financial, and social status; for women, especially, it often dictated their deaths. I think of poor Harriet Gouger and wonder whether she would have lived a little longer and whether her tiny son would have survived, had she not been dragged across the world to live in a tent at Holdfast Bay: she died three months later at the end of her only Adelaide summer. At its outset, South Australia was no place for the faint of heart or the physically frail.

If I could choose to meet just one of these pioneer women and have her tell her story it would be Maria Gandy. (In the family her name has always been pronounced 'Ma-rye-ah'.) For while Colonel William Light remains a presence in the city he laid out so meticulously, the woman who shared the last great adventure of his life, and who nursed him at his death, is visible only in rare glimpses. This extraordinary act of erasing springs from the moralising nature of the young colony, where Maria Gandy and William Light were judged to be cohabiting without the sanction of marriage. At the time, and ever since, people have been quick to refer to Maria as 'Light's mistress', although officially, and very possibly, she was never more than his devoted housekeeper.

Maria was born in 1811 in the English village of Twyford, Hampshire, not far from Southampton. She was the eldest of the eight children of William Gandy, a labourer, and his wife Mary Anne. It happened that around 1834 William Light was also living in Twyford, and Maria, a seamstress, went to work for him as his housekeeper. Although Light's relationship with the Gandy family is unclear, from records of small payments made by him to various family members it appears he had known them for a number of years.

Maria's father died in April 1836, and with Light about to depart for South Australia we must suppose that it came as an enormous relief when he invited her and the two Gandy boys who were still at home to sail with him on the *Rapid*. William Gandy, a lad of nineteen, was listed as an emigrant labourer, while Maria and ten-year-old Edward were two of the seven 'persons of a superior class' whose passage was not defrayed by the Emigrants' Fund. The only other female on board was Sarah Bradley, the wife of one of the seamen. When the *Rapid* arrived in South Australia, Maria was twenty-five and William Light was fifty.

⚜

Mary Thomas, a passenger on the *Africaine*, recorded in her diary a description of the colonists' first Christmas Day. Divine service was held in the rush hut of the principle surveyor, and was followed by an afternoon walk around the lagoon. Though home was now a world away and conditions were not conducive to cooking elaborate meals, Mary notes that they did their best to stick to comforting and familiar customs, eating plum pudding after a main dish of ham and the rather less traditional 'parrot pie'. Later they would discover that one of their neighbours had lunched on a large piece of roast beef. It transpired that when the *Africaine* had landed at Glenelg one of the passengers had taken charge of Captain Duff's cow and calf, and the cow, which had been tied to a tree near the lagoon, slipped over the bank. The animal was so injured that it had to be killed, thus supplying some colonists with Christmas lunch.

Light kept a diary but he did not record what he ate for lunch on Christmas Day or on any other day, being completely absorbed with choosing the best site for the capital. But on Christmas Eve he left his ship and 'walked over the plain to that part of the river where [the deputy surveyor, George Strickland] Kingston had pitched his tent with a small party of the surveying labourers'. Light returned by six in the evening to make final arrangements for leaving the ship, which he did on 28 December, setting his tent close to Kingston's on the banks of the River Torrens.

There is a drawing by Light of a woman on horseback that is generally supposed to be a sketch of Maria. It shows a slender young woman, probably tall and willowy when standing; sitting side-saddle, she slouches casually, her legs hidden under voluminous skirts. Her wavy hair is gathered loosely at the back of her head; her strong profile would not be out of place on a coin. While she rests one elbow on a knee and gazes into the distance, the horse waits with its ears pricked as a dog darts between its front legs.

It is, above all, an affectionate portrait, a sure rendering of a familiar and easy relationship between sketcher and sitter. The viewer is drawn into their intimacy with a feeling that at any moment Maria might slide down from the horse and stroll over to flop down for a chat – Maria would slide rather than leap from the saddle, if there is a saddle; she is not a brisk, nervy, creature, but a calm, self-possessed woman. At least that is how I read the body language of the only possible portrait we have of Maria Gandy. And it must be her, for what other woman could Light have been in a position to draw in such an unguarded moment? Further, I am guessing it was made before his house at Thebarton was built, at the time when he and Maria were living in a wood and reed hut around the junction of North and West terraces, the place where Light began his survey of the city.

In 1838 Maria's brother George arrived from England with his wife Mary Jane – George was the brother closest in age to Maria, and she must have been overjoyed at his arrival. A brick-maker, George soon set up in business, advertising bricks to be delivered to any part of South Australia for £3 per thousand. He is thought to have built Light's house at Thebarton, and while it was being completed, Light, Maria and her brothers continued to live in the hut. Then, on 22 January 1839, at about two o'clock in the afternoon while they were finishing a meal, Light heard the rumbling of a fire in James Hurtle Fisher's Land Office next door. In less than ten minutes both buildings were razed, with the loss of Light's papers, including an account of his life, his sketches and paintings and everything of value.

The youngest man on Light's team of surveyors, William Jacob, had been asked to remove a keg of gunpowder to safety, and returned to find Light battling the flames; Jacob reported later that Light was so exhausted he had to make him come away. Light wrote in his diary that the only clothes he saved were those he was wearing, and it must be assumed that Maria also lost all her belongings.

⚜

As surveyor general, Colonel William Light's life has been written of at length elsewhere, usually with much space given to his differences with Hindmarsh and others over the best site for the city of Adelaide; it was a drawn-out disagreement, which ended with Light's resignation. Unfortunately these battles divert attention from his brilliance, for William Light was a man of many talents, described by a friend as 'a man of extraordinary accomplishments, soldier, seaman, musician, artist and good in all'. However in love and in health he was not so lucky, and he seemed to understand this about himself. In a letter from Light to William Jacob we hear a rather wry voice: 'I have been accustomed to make leeway all my life and such a thing as rounding a cape of good fortune never enters my head.'

Light's first wife is supposed to have died, and his second – Mary Bennett, the illegitimate daughter of the Duke of Richmond – set up house with another man while Light was away in Egypt and eventually had three children by him. Had Light been divorced there seems little doubt he would have married Maria Gandy, if only to still the gossiping tongues and quench the hostility shown towards them in the colony. Together with the tuberculosis that was killing him and the days of unendurable heat documented in his diary, Maria's ostracism must have weighed heavily. Only two women summoned the strength of mind to walk beyond the pale and visit her in Thebarton – they were Caroline Woodforde, who in 1838 had married Dr John Woodforde, surgeon aboard the *Rapid*, and Anne Finniss, wife of Light's assistant and staunch friend, Boyle Travers Finniss.

As Light lay dying, Finniss tried to persuade the colonial chaplain, Charles Beaumont Howard – at that time the only Anglican clergyman in the colony – to visit him. Described in the *Australian Dictionary of Biography* as 'tolerant and kind', Howard refused, giving as his reason that Light would not repent and end his scandalous liaison with Maria. In the final weeks of his life, William Light must have worried about Maria's ability to survive without him, and after making a will leaving everything to her, which included not only his land but his debts, he asked his friends to stand by her when he was gone.

Light knew that he would not live to see the city grow. Shortly before he died he discussed its future with William Jacob who, together with others of Light's team, formed the private survey partnership of Light, Finniss & Co. after Light's resignation as surveyor general.

'Jacob,' Light said, 'if you live an ordinary life you will see these plains enclosed.'

William Jacob did live an ordinary life, and in 1901 at the age of eighty-six he expressed his pleasure and amazement in an interview with the *Register*.

Little did we dream then that they would develop to what they are to-day and be connected with a railway. I may claim to have lived an ordinary life, but what has transpired has been far beyond my expectations.

William Light expired of tuberculosis on 6 October 1839. On the day of his death he was sketched by the artist John Michael Skipper. The work in pencil, pen, and wash, shows Light's head and shoulders propped against pillows. His eyes are closed, his exhaustion complete; in truth, he is probably already dead. The torn page is signed and dated, as if Skipper wished to make a record of this historic event.

Shunned in his dying days, except for a few close friends, the colony took Light's death to heart and he was given a bells and whistles state funeral. By order of Governor Gawler, shops and businesses were closed and government officers were ordered to attend. The hearse left Thebarton just before noon accompanied by Light's friends, and set out towards Adelaide and Trinity Church. Minute guns were fired and the flag at Government House stood at half-mast. The procession grew in numbers, being joined by the governor, government officers, and 'four-hundred-and-twenty-three gentlemen, all in deep mourning'. The colonial chaplain, his conscience apparently clear, led the procession. Light's friends, including Captain Duff, Dr Woodforde, and Boyle Travers Finniss, walked on either side of his coffin. The 'servants of the Colonel's household' followed, ahead of the government officers and other officials. The governor brought up the rear, leading the colonists, 'two and two'. After the service, William Light was buried at Light Square with several thousand mourners in attendance.

What must have been going through the Reverend Charles Howard's mind as he glanced across the soaring, whitewashed space of his church to where Maria Gandy sat? In July the following year, on a Tuesday morning, George Mayo and Maria were married; Reverend Charles Howard officiated.

Marriage rescued Maria and brought her back from beyond the pale, for Dr Mayo was highly respected – he is listed as number eight on the Medical Register of South Australia. Perhaps he took the view that Maria had been adequately chaperoned by her brothers. In England some forty years earlier, Dorothy Wordsworth, when reprimanded by her grand-aunt Mrs Crackanthorpe for staying in a house belonging to a young gentleman, had tartly responded that she regarded her brother William's presence as sufficient protection, and Maria Gandy must have felt the same. With no illegitimate offspring to taint her reputation, mealy-mouthed matrons who had been loath to mention her name just a year earlier would have been forced to acknowledge her socially, although Mayo was described as a reticent man and perhaps this, together with their dauntless temperaments, stood the couple in good stead. Maria was closer in age to Mayo than she had been to Light: he was thirty-three and she was twenty-nine when they married. They lived for a time at Light's house at Thebarton, until Mayo built Nibley House in Morphett Street. Between them they paid off William Light's debts.

Maria Mayo died of tuberculosis, probably contracted when she was nursing Light. She was buried at West Terrace Cemetery on 14 December 1847. Her children were all so young at her death that there are few stories of Maria within the family. The eldest child, Mary-Jane, kept a diary, and her seven leather-bound books produced by Letts of London are held by her descendants. They have beautifully marbled endpapers, and ribbon markers, and record Mary-Jane's life after her mother's death. She often accompanied her father on visits to patients, and her diary notes that she walked with him from Morphett Street to see the new asylum at Parkside, and climbed to the top of the tower. She became adept at applying leeches, on one occasion placing seventeen on her father's back, and he applied two to her face for a painful abscess; both treatments successful. A memorable day in Mary-Jane's life was 14 November 1870, when she reported that 'Mr Reid came to see Papa. He proposed and our engagement was announced'. Mary-Jane married James Farrell's successor at Trinity

Church, the Reverend Richardson Reid; the couple lived at the rectory.

As a young married woman, Mary-Jane recorded her daily life in thick black ink. She usually noted the weather, and who came to visit, and many entries detail the marriages, christenings, and burials performed by her husband – in one especially hot summer there were over thirty funeral services through January and into February. Names throughout the diaries read like a rollcall of old colonists, many of whom came to dine at the rectory, including Bishop Short, who brought his dog. While they were dining the dog killed all of Mary-Jane's rabbits, bred for the table.

Mary-Jane's diaries, and Light's drawings, are more or less the only surviving links with Maria Gandy. The house at Thebarton has long since been demolished, as has Nibley House where George Mayo lived until he died in 1894. He was eighty-seven.

❦

Maria's address is Road 2, Path 10; Plot 26 is on the western side of the path. George and Maria's youngest child, ten-month-old Maria Louisa, was buried here in November 1847; when Maria gave birth to her she must have been very ill with tuberculosis. This is the Mayo family plot, and both George Mayo and Ellen Russell, the wife he married while on a trip to England in 1852, are buried alongside Maria in Plot 25.

When I walked here for the first time I had trouble locating the site because there are no headstones. Maria's grave seemed to belong to that of the Knabes next door. A marble skirting and low iron rail encloses the plots. To one side, a gum tree sheds leaves, and pine needles drift across from the tree on the corner of Road 3. The absence of headstones is strange, since Ellen died in 1901 and Maria's brothers all outlived her.

As for the Gandy boys, William was another victim of tuberculosis; he was buried in Melton, Victoria in 1862. George died in 1893 and was buried in the North Road Cemetery in Adelaide. Edward, a boy of ten at the start of the great adventure aboard the

Rapid, followed a number of careers, including stockman, cattle dealer, and hotelier. His first wife Agnes was of Scottish birth; she was the widow of John Miller, and after her death from tuberculosis she was buried with him here at West Terrace. Edward Gandy's second wife, and the one who is buried with him, was also a widow. Marie was the daughter of John Bailey the colonial botanist; she was only five when she sailed from England with her family, and grew up in the gardens her father established in the Adelaide suburb of Hackney.

Edward and Marie's address is Plan 3, Row 3, Plot 30. After leaving the Mayo plot I walk to the end of the path and turn left onto Road 3, then follow the road towards West Terrace. Almost opposite the junction at the top stands a marble cross on the grave of George Napier Birks, and crossing into the Plan 3 area beside it, I walk as far as the second path and turn right at Frances Westall's headstone. From here, Edward and Marie Gandy are seventh on the right.

Their plot is surrounded by a low iron fence. Marie died first, so Edward must have chosen the headstone. Restrained in design, still it expresses his affection for her with a circular flower motif, its stem bent, and a single flower on either side. A snake's head, though worn, is still identifiable above each of the side flowers, its body scalloping the top of the stone. In the early Victorian period snakes and serpents were common mourning motifs, the symbol of wisdom and eternity. Marie died at the end of the High Victorian era, but the mourning symbolism being used in the colony then probably dated from closer to white settlement, the years designated Early Victorian. Hooped snakes, or snakes eating their tails, represent eternity, and together with the other symbols on the headstone this two-headed snake appears to speak of a long-standing affection between Edward and Marie.

By the time Edward Gandy died in 1902 the Victorian era was over. His headstone claims he was eighty-three but this does not tally with the family's record of his christening, which establishes his birth on 1 December 1825. Taking the family's christening record as the more reliable, this puts his age at death at seventy-seven. What is certain is that as a sturdy young boy he witnessed the birth of the new colony, that he outlived almost everyone who had shared the adventure with him and that, as it says on the headstone, Edward Gandy was a colonist of sixty-six years.

When my own grandfather was born in 1895, both Edward Gandy and William Jacob were still alive. Although only a lad of seven my grandfather could have heard them spoken of, perhaps even learned something of their stories in his earliest schooldays. Realising this overlap pulls what we used to call 'the olden days' in close, until I feel as if I were sitting in history's lap.

5

Nature Walk
No. 1

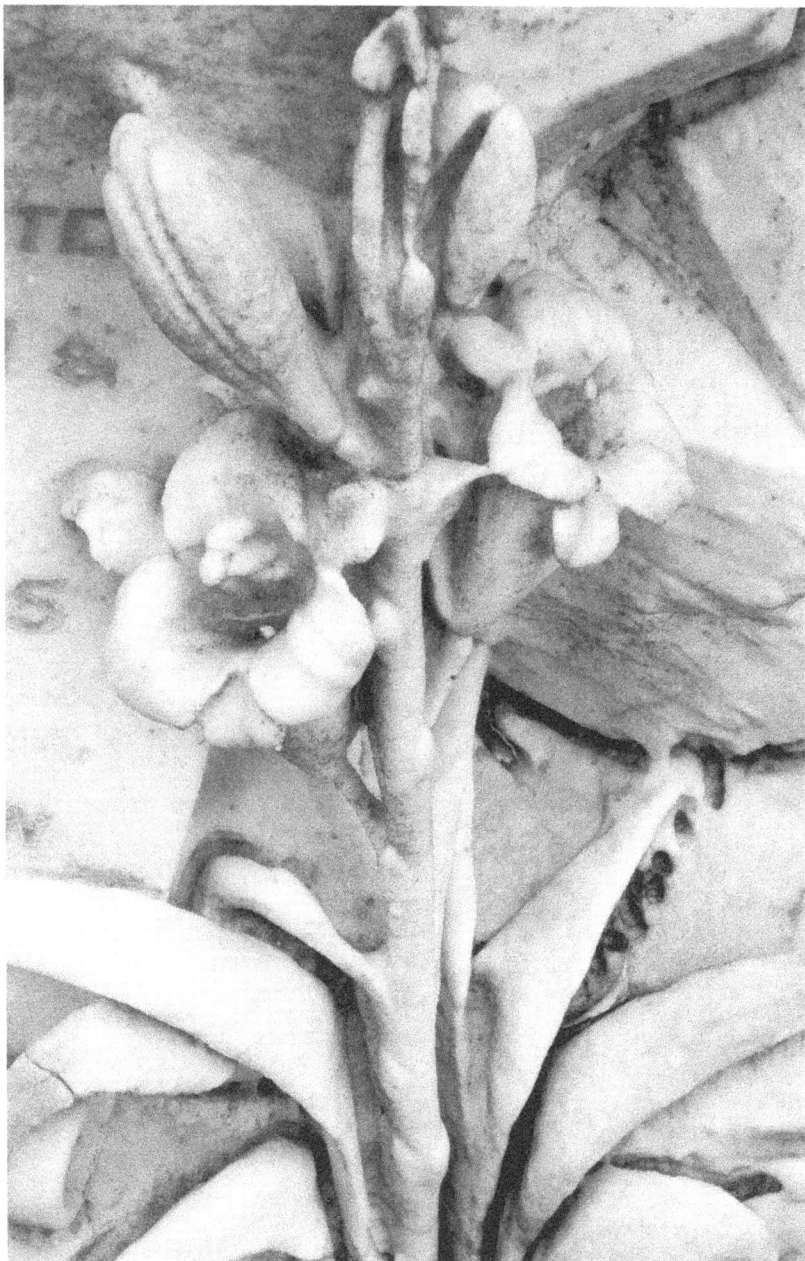

Oh say not that no perfume dwells
The wilding flowers among,
Say not that in the forest dells
Is heard no voice of song.
'Wild Flowers of Australia'
– Caroline Carleton

It is one of those clear autumn mornings when the ghost of the moon lingers in the western sky. Beside the entrance gates the frangipani tree stands in a shower of its own creamy petals. I have arrived early before the day warms up, for this nature walk will be a longish one, with visits to some passionate plantsmen, gardeners, and botanists, and an artist renowned for her exquisite botanical illustrations. I want to see, too, some of the rare and endangered flora that has found a safe haven here, pockets of vegetation, now protected, remnants of the landscape of the Adelaide plains prior to European settlement.

The nature walk calls for a backpack stocked with sandwiches, a water bottle, notebooks, maps, and a camera. For safety's sake I am wearing heavy boots, since one of the groundsmen has warned me that snakes abound here in hot weather. It is probably a little late in the season, but if there are any about my guess is that they will favour the stands of native vegetation.

South Australia's first colonial botanist, John Bailey, arrived in South Australia in 1839 aboard the *Buckinghamshire*. His wife Maria and five children came with him. Three years earlier they had thought they would go to New Zealand where Bailey had been selected for the role of colonial botanist. However, the bill to colonise New Zealand failed to pass through the British Parliament, and Bailey's disappointment was later recounted by his son, Frederick Manson Bailey. His father, Frederick said, was unsettled by the collapse of his plans to go to New Zealand and instead turned to South Australia, where he had thought he would farm.

Governor Gawler appointed Bailey as colonial botanist. He had worked for twenty years at Conrad Loddiges & Sons at Hackney, a firm that specialised in Cape bulbs, shrubs, and plants from 'New Holland'. As an expert nurseryman, Bailey was a good choice, and together he and Gawler chose a site in the north parklands where he would curate a botanic garden. His salary was to be £80 per annum.

John Bailey's passion for botany would be handed down through the generations, to Australia's lasting benefit. His son, Frederick, a lad of twelve when the family arrived at Holdfast Bay, was already nurturing a consuming interest in plants; he would make important contributions in the fields of horticulture and botany, and establish a botanic garden in Queensland. Frederick's son, John Frederick, would follow in the family tradition, travelling extensively to remote parts of Australia, and documenting the botanical identity of many North Queensland timbers. John Frederick spent much of his career in Queensland, but in 1917 he took up the post of director of the Adelaide Botanic Garden close to the site where his father and grandfather had once rolled up their sleeves to dig and plant the first planned garden in the north parklands.

⚜

Queen Victoria presides so prominently over the city's heart that it is natural to think of Adelaide, in its earliest form, as a Victorian city. Yet the first settlers had already arrived when Victoria was crowned and the city's founders were really products of the late Georgian era. I confess I am not an expert, but a quick look at the dates shows that John Bailey, though only a child, was alive at the time of the Battle of Waterloo. War was a feature of the Georgian era, but it was also a time when the British Empire was having a growth spurt. Botanists went along on the expeditions of explorers like Captain James Cook, and brought back specimens and drawings and lucid accounts of everything beautiful and strange and rare in the New World. But by then the world was both expanding and shrinking, and the rise of non-conformists and religious dissenters during the same period paved the way for Edward Gibbon Wakefield's plan to begin afresh in South Australia.

This thread of knowledge unwinds in my thoughts as I walk down Road 5 in search of the grave of John Bailey's youngest son, John Manson Bailey. At the bottom of the road where the small octagonal shelter stands, I turn right onto Path 34. There are three gravestones here, and beside Hannah and William Bradfield is an unmarked grave where John Manson Bailey was buried in 1888; if there was once a headstone it has not survived.

John Manson Bailey, a lad of fifteen when the family left England, is entered on the ship's passenger list as an 'agriculturalist' engaged by his father. While his brother Frederick grew up to establish a career as a botanist in Queensland, John seems to have stuck close to the family.

Many of the graves in this row are early ones. I consider how far back their history takes me, and in an instant the four Georges who were kings of England, and England's prolonged struggle against France during the Napoleonic Wars, the battles of Trafalgar and Waterloo, with Jane Austen scribbling furiously and never mentioning the war – all of these events gather and twist into a skein of history that frays into my own time, into the here and now, and this morning of glittering calm in West Terrace Cemetery.

Stories, I realise, join up the dots, they make sense of who we are; the stories of earlier lives, like those of the people I have visited here, set our own lives in context, they hook the broader bough of history and pull it within our reach. Of course, we will catch and hold our history, we will pick a handful of plums, but we will never understand it as it was lived, for – as Henry James once said of the flaw inherent in writing historical fiction – we can never recapture that earlier innocence.

One of John Bailey's great-grandsons, also a botanist, has shared a story that must have been passed down through the Bailey family. It tells how when wheaten flour was very expensive in Adelaide in the early forties, Maria Bailey ground the grain of sorghums in her coffee grinder for the making of johnny cakes and damper. He also recollects that lighting oil was scarce, so the younger children were sent out to gather twigs and bark and then coaxed to feed it continuously into the fire so the older Baileys could read in the blaze of the firelight.

Unfortunately for Bailey the young colony was in financial strife, and Governor Gawler was recalled to England. Gawler left in June 1841, at which time he was presented by the colonists with a purse containing £500. According to Mary Thomas he left the money to be invested in land on his account, and to keep a link between himself and the colony. But the ex-governor had other more personal links here, for he had buried his infant son just a few months earlier at West Terrace Cemetery. Edward Cox Gawler died on 20 February 1841 aged eight weeks and three days. In 1894 Gawler's eldest son Henry would be buried in the same spot; he was sixty-seven. The Gawler grave is marked by a monument in the style of a pile of boulders. It may be ugly, but at least it has endured. It is one of only three sites linked with South Australia's governors, and the address is Road 2, Path 9; Plot 29 is on the eastern side behind an iron fence.

Gawler was replaced by George Grey, who had undertaken to slash expenditure. An early casualty of Grey's austere regime was funding for the gardens, and Bailey was forced to abandon them. He established a private nursery on seven acres he had bought at the corner of Botanic and Hackney roads, and for a long time afterwards the area was known as Bailey's Gardens.

The next tenant of the Old Botanic Garden site was George Stevenson. When he sailed from England on the *Buffalo* as private secretary to Governor Hindmarsh, Stevenson brought with him English trees in pots, a large collection of camellias and several glasshouses in which to nurture them. He was one of the most accomplished gardeners in the colony, and as well as a beautiful garden at his house in Finniss Street he developed a site of sixty acres at his mother-in-law's property *Leawood*, which lay at the turn of the road to Mount Lofty at the infamous Devil's Elbow.

What gifts of knowledge these early botanists and gardeners brought, and how we have benefited from their adventurous spirits and indefatigable energy. While they carried plum and almond and fig and apple trees, those with different interests arrived laden with trunks full of linen, sheet music, watercolour paints and brushes; they brought surgeon's scalpels, and mortar and pestle, pen and ink and new account books. Tradesmen brought their tools. I try to imagine a life where no replacement is available when something breaks, and begin to understand how resourceful so many of them were, how patient, and inventive. My thoughts slide off into something I've read about generational memory, and how the experiences of our ancestors may be passed to us through our genes. I think of the people I relied on when I was very young, country folk with practical skills, and recognise the same 'can do' spark that burned in these determined early gardeners.

⚜

Maria Bailey died in April 1853 at the age of sixty-six. Her death certificate gives the cause of death as 'debility', which may mean that she was worn out by the toughness of a life spent in establishing gardens from scratch. John Bailey closed his Hackney Nursery in 1858, auctioning off his stock, which included more than 15,000 olive trees. He travelled to England in 1859 for an extended visit, but after his return two years later his health deteriorated and he died in the Adelaide Hospital of Bright's Disease on 25 May 1864. At his death his 'trade or profession' was simply listed as 'gardener', his days as colonial botanist apparently forgotten.

I have not been able to find where he and Maria are buried. It is possible that they rest here at West Terrace in the same plot as their son, and that the cemetery's archive – notorious for being poorly kept under John Monck, and again in the first years after the Carletons left – has not recorded it. If John Bailey is buried here it is a poor, bare, plot to mark the final resting place of a gifted gardener. It seems the first wave of settlers like Bailey often lived and died hard, leaving future generations to harvest the rewards.

George William Francis was one of the original members of the Botanical Society of London, and as well as being a man of learning and achievement Francis nurtured a great yearning to establish a botanic garden. In 1842 he had applied for the post of Professor of Botany at King's College, London, but lost to another candidate by a single vote. This appears to have been the tipping point in his decision to emigrate, for suitable positions at places like Kew Gardens and Regent's Park had already been filled, and times were hard in England. Or perhaps news had reached him of the failure to establish a botanic garden in the new colony, and he saw a chance to realise his dream.

In that same year he published four new books: *Illustrations of British Mosses and Hepaticae*; *A Flora of Britain*; *A Companion to the Little English Flora*, illustrated with woodcuts and engravings; and *Chemical Experiments*. George William Francis was an energetic and productive man. Before leaving the northern hemisphere he went to France as master of a boy's boarding school in Boulogne, and there he became acquainted with methods of distilling essential oils and perfumed waters. He had published another book, *Favourites of the Flower Garden*, before departing for France, and on his return in 1846 there was yet another book with an intriguing title: *Manual of Practical Levelling for Railways and Canals*. All of these works were written, researched, and published, with a young family underfoot. Francis's botanical knowledge and practical skills would prove invaluable in South Australia, however it would take him a while to become established, and in Adelaide he would be forced to support his family for some time on the income from his many books.

They sailed from England in 1849 aboard the *Louisa Baillie* and arrived in September. Spring in Adelaide generally supplies radiant weather, and George Francis would have been enchanted by the new and interesting flora and fauna.

The governor at the time was Sir Henry Fox Young, and it was with him that Francis would do battle to establish a botanic garden. Fox Young was dismissive of his ideas, but Francis doggedly persisted. Correspondence flew back and forth, until finally in 1850, after much wrangling, he was granted the lease of the Old Botanic Garden once tended by Bailey, at a rent of £35 per annum. Then began a long dispute over fence repairs, for the site was routinely overrun by cattle, and by police horses making their way to the river. Francis complained that the animals ate his hay and other crops, and 'destroyed my melons and seedling plants, and seriously damaged the garden by trampling over every part of it, and breaking the vines and trees'. A season's labour could be lost in a single night. But His Excellency, having agreed to fix the fence on one occasion, was not sympathetic to further appeals.

George William Frances began to understand the forces that had beaten his predecessors, and he made up his mind to treat the land as his place of residence while he looked around for other employment. Even with all of the difficulties, he still managed to harvest the first crop of olive oil to be grown and pressed in South Australia, which gained him an honourable mention at the Great Exhibition held at the Crystal Palace. Thereafter, he made little headway with the gardens, and entered a period of serving on committees and sub-committees, consolidating his position in the colony while pursuing his dream behind the scenes. Today we might describe as 'networking' his early membership of the Freemasons. Prominent men belonged to the Lodge of Truth, and Governor Sir Henry Fox Young was the first president.

The stalemate over the garden site was broken when salvation arrived in the unlikely form of the Adelaide City Council. Francis was one of the men appointed by the governor to preside over the first election of councillors. A month later, the Old Botanic Garden came under the Council's control, to George Francis's immense relief.

In 1854 tenders were invited for the laying out and planting of Victoria Square with trees and shrubs. George William Francis's tender was accepted, and he was further contracted to plant the smaller squares – Whitmore, Light, Hurtle, and Hindmarsh. He also planted Brougham Gardens and Palmer Place, North Adelaide.

The proposal for a botanic garden on a new site fronting North Terrace was gradually making headway, and Francis offered himself as superintendent. The matter ground on until March 1855 when Acting Governor Boyle Travers Finniss appointed a management committee, which included among others Dr William Wyatt. Eventually the committee appointed Francis superintendent at a salary of £300 per annum.

It had taken him five years to get the go ahead, and now he set to work with characteristic zeal. He had six men working for him at seven shillings per day, yet ended up doing much of the spade-work himself. When the garden opened in 1857, George William Francis became the first director.

Long thin shadows stripe the roadways, and a magpie flutes its cool clear song from the topmost branches of a gum. The sky is a bowl of sheerest blue; the air is silky. It is a perfect, still, Adelaide morning as I amble west along Road 2, and turn left along Path 16 to find the place where the quandongs grow.

Quandongs, *Santalum acuminatum*, are sprawling and untidy in habit, propped up in some cases by the wrought-iron work surrounding these old graves. This is reckoned to be one of the last remaining examples of fruiting quandongs in Adelaide, and an information plaque at the site tells me that they are semi-parasitic trees, which in order to survive extract nutrients from the roots of host plants, such as wattles. When they germinate from seed they will use grasses and ground covers as hosts, before fastening on a tree or shrub as their long-term source of sustenance. I am guessing this means that the quandong roots spread until they find something suitable to latch onto, but it sparks an entertaining image of young quandong trees lurching about the cemetery like the plants in John Wyndham's novel *The Day of the Triffids*.

Quandongs have twice the vitamin C of oranges; Aboriginal people ate both the fruit and the kernel, while the early settlers made the fruit into sauces, pies, and jams. The trees shelter many types of wildlife (I am keeping my eyes peeled for snakes) but the rare wood white butterfly relies on the quandong as a host plant for its caterpillars. The quandongs at West Terrace Cemetery are healthy, and in August the trees are decked with scarlet fruit, like early Christmas baubles. They are protected here and look a little as though they are allowed to do as they please. Unfortunately, they have colonised and semi-destroyed some of the early graves.

The gossamer thread of a spider stretches from one mottled headstone to the next, and from there to a wrought-iron railing and finally to the large and beautiful monument to a woman called Emily Starr; Emily died in 1941, and a lovely angel stands guard over her grave at the corner of Path 14. I wonder whether her mother might have been an avid reader of L.M. Montgomery's trio of novels, the favourites of my own girlhood, *Emily of New Moon*, *Emily's Quest*, and *Emily Climbs*.

⚜

The magpie's song is all joy, and when I look up to see where it is perched there is the chalk mark of a jet trail on the perfect sky. George William Francis's address is a little further down Road 2 at Path 20; Plot 1 is on the western side. The corner of the path is marked with an obelisk commemorating James Jepson. Francis's grave, and that of his wife and some of his children, is on the right as I turn in from the road.

The headstone is modest, but it notes his role as founder of the Adelaide Botanic Garden. He died on 9 August 1865, a mere sixteen years after his arrival in Australia; it is astonishing to realise how much he accomplished in a relatively short time. His wife Ann lived to see the century turn and died a year after Federation, aged eighty-seven. Their youngest son Arthur is also buried here, and their daughter Annie. A separate headstone marks the burial place of the couple's eldest son, George Francis, and another son, William Augustus Francis, who together with Annie outlived both parents.

I have fallen a little bit in love with George William Francis, with his simple, heartfelt poems, with his joy in the natural world that also insisted upon scholarly precision. Who could not love a man whose knowledge bank included canal systems and obscure British mosses alongside the humbler arts of bottling fruit and making jam? In the modern city of Adelaide, Francis is not as well-remembered as he deserves. There is a native shrub named after him, *Hakea francisiana*, and an obelisk to his memory in the Botanic Garden at a site that is thought to mark the place where his pet monkey is buried. The well that he dug remains useable, and the pepper tree he planted, now huge and gnarled, guards the North Terrace entrance gates, but his two-storey house was long ago demolished and built on by the Royal Adelaide Hospital.

His successor, Richard Schomburgk, is credited with establishing *Victoria regia*, the giant water lily, but a conversation with one of George Francis's descendants uncovers the story that it was Francis who had arranged with Schomburgk's older brother, an explorer whose expeditions took him to the Amazon, to send seeds of the water lily to Adelaide. One of Francis's friends living at St Peters had dug a swimming pool, and had agreed to accommodate the water lily in it until the Botanic Gardens could afford to build a glasshouse. Unfortunately, Francis died, and Schomburgk gave the *Victoria regia* specimen or seed to his brother, Richard, who cultivated the plant and reaped the glory. Another story goes that Francis had seen the plants growing at Kew Gardens when they were grown there for a short period in 1846, and that a packet of the seeds was sent to him from Kew. It is true that the first specimen to flourish in the Adelaide Botanic Garden was under the directorship of Richard Schomburgk.

In 1859, Francis published a *Catalogue of Plants* then under cultivation in the garden. It listed 2878 species, with a further 200 not named, and around 500 florists' varieties. After only three years of planting, it was an enormous achievement. He had also distributed many seeds to the public, and written extensive articles aimed at fostering knowledge of economic plants among the colonists on topics as diverse as cultivating and curing tobacco, preserving milk and potatoes, making wine and cider, jelly, cheese, and marmalade.

A delivery of six cases of cork oaks arrived in Adelaide from Kew Gardens aboard the *Orient*, and six more by the *Coratto*, and when those needed for the gardens had been subtracted, the rest were distributed. Each governor of the Botanic Garden received 100 trees, and the rest were sent to people in outlying areas who agreed to report on their success or failure.

When he died in 1865, George Francis had not been able to compile a further catalogue, but he had kept a careful register of all plants cultivated in the interim period, and by 1860 at least another 3000 had been added to the original number. Most of the forty-acre garden was under cultivation at his death. He had also collected many animals and birds, including the English songbirds much missed by the early colonists. I am not sure whether I have George William Francis to thank for the blackbird who visits my garden, but its song is one of the delights of early spring, and I can understand the nostalgia that saw pairs of the birds carried across the oceans.

By the close of 1859 his animal collection included six white swans donated by Queen Victoria, and a pair of emus that would cause him great regret. Quiet at first, once the emus had settled in they proceeded to pick off all the buds within reach of their long necks, both of trees and flowers, Francis reported. 'In one week they very seriously injured the Garden.' He also despaired over an eagle and the danger it posed to young children. 'Had I known or considered the habits of this animal, I certainly never would have allowed it to have been left in the Garden.' There would be further trouble over a tiger, and a bear. The feeding and housing of the animals, especially the exotic and unmanageable specimens, became an increasing burden. But their cages in the garden attracted many visitors, and they would become the basis of the Adelaide Zoo.

⚜

In 1987 I lived for a short time in the gatehouse of the Rockford Estate at Mylor, South Australia. Though mildly infested by rats, the house's great charm was its period style; it had been decorated and let as a furnished cottage by the elderly and eccentric owner of the estate, Mrs Little. That lady would sweep past the gatehouse in her rattling old car – her grand but crumbling house, screened by trees, stood further up the hill at the end of a potholed drive. She habitually wore one of a collection of once-elegant pastel hats, and white cotton gloves, often a bit on the grubby side. Glancing towards the gatehouse as though we had been awaiting her arrival, she would wave like the Queen, and pass on. The reason I tell this story, aside from the fact that the late Mrs Little was, and remains, a legendary character in Mylor so that even minor memories of her should be kept somewhere, is that the first thing she pointed out to me in her beautiful, wild and rambling garden was the Spanish cork oaks that grew beside the creek.

According to Mrs Little they were over a hundred years old. She might have said more about their provenance, but I wasn't paying close enough attention. Back then, the trees were a spectacular sight, and it happens that this year I have visited them again on a day when the gardens were open. Now that I do the maths, I am certain they must have come from the consignment of trees that were sent to George William Francis from Kew Gardens. Perhaps the Rockford estate was owned at that time by one of the governors of the Botanic Garden, otherwise they must have been of the stock Francis sent to outlying areas to see whether they would survive. He would be pleased, I think, to know that they are not only still living but transforming this spot beside a creek in Mylor into a place of extraordinary beauty.

⚜

After Francis's death, Richard Schomburgk took over as director of the Botanic Garden; Schomburgk and his brother Otto had come to Australia in the same ship that brought Carl Linger. He at once set to work to transform what still appears in the *Australian Dictionary of Biography* under his name as 'a sterile waste', a description that would have distressed the Francis family.

Schomburgk compiled a second catalogue and it was printed in 1871. In the foreword he stressed the labour he had put into it, and remarked in an offhand way that the catalogue of the late director had enumerated only about 2800 species, while his contained around 6000. Not only had Schomburgk inherited the post without his predecessor's long struggle for approval, and with the benefit of his ten years of unstinting labour, but his summary of Francis's catalogue was inaccurate.

The long waiting times for seeds and plants to arrive from places like Kew Gardens that had strained Francis's patience, the scarcity of funds that saw him feeding the animals out of his own pocket, were not a feature of Schomburgk's reign. The colony had weathered its economic crisis and eventually even the shipping times grew shorter as the century waned.

Richard Schomburgk remained in residence until 1891 when he died at his house in the grounds. He is buried at North Road Cemetery. Under his management the Botanic Gardens gained a palm house, a hothouse for *Victoria regia*, and the beautiful Museum of Economic Botany. He planted Wellington Square, North Terrace, and the gardens at Government House and Marble Hill.

⚜

To find the native apricots that grow here, I walk along Road 3 to Path 32. They flourish in the filtered shade of a tall eucalyptus tree, which sheds its bark all over the path. As with the quandongs, the plants have colonised the graves, although some survive with their intricate wrought iron still in place.

In a letter to the *Register*, George William Francis expressed his concern at the careless naming of native plants. It was a habit he thought both misleading and potentially dangerous; the popular names, he said, led people to believe that South Australia had indigenous fruits; they gave children erroneous notions. 'The Native Orange is not an orange; the so-called Native Pear is not a pear; the Native Peach is not a peach' and he included flowers, insisting that 'Sturt's Pea is not a pea', and that the fuchsia, honeysuckle, she-oak, lilac, and willow in no way resembled the plants for which they were named. Francis would not have approved of the tendency, both then and now, to refer to *Pittosporum angustifolium* as the Native Apricot. It was his belief that if we would just use the Latin words they would soon become as familiar as those already in our vocabulary, like crocus, geranium, and ranunculus.

Pittosporum angustifolium grows between two and seven metres tall, with a greyish trunk and weeping branches of long thin leaves. Its egg-shaped fruit splits to reveal multiple sticky seeds; honeyeaters and wattlebirds eat them, and when the seeds have passed through their bodies they germinate. As George William Francis pointed out, the popular name makes the fruit sound edible by humans, and it is not. However, Aboriginal people found uses for it, with the fruit being employed as a purgative, while a substance – possibly derived from the seed – was used as a poison to stun fish.

⚜

There must have been a moment in her long career as an artist when Rosa Catherine Fiveash painted both quandongs and native apricots. She was the foremost Australian botanical artist of her day, illustrating scientific papers for the renowned naturalist Edward Charles Stirling, and also for museum curator and zoologist, Edgar Ravenswood Waite. Her thirty-year-long collaboration with orchidologist Richard Sanders Rogers produced a remarkable body of work, much of which is in the collection of the State Library of South Australia and the South Australian Museum.

Rosa was the daughter of Robert Archibald Fiveash and Margaret Rees. Four of their eight children had died in infancy, and Rosa was the youngest of the four who survived. Robert Fiveash had arrived in South Australia in 1839 on the *Planter* and became superintendent of the Blinman and Yudanamutana copper mines. The Fiveash family home was Gable House in North Adelaide, and apart from two years spent overseas, where she must surely have visited the great European art galleries, Rosa lived there all her life. Both she and her older sister Mary were devout Anglicans, and neither of them married.

Rosa Catherine Fiveash's address is Road 1 South, Path 21; Plot 3 is on the eastern side as you turn in from the road. It is marked by a simple but solidly imposing marble cross, which looks as if it was raised for Robert Fiveash at the time of his death in 1872. His wife Margaret followed in 1885, and their four infant children are remembered below. The names of Rosa and her sister Mary ('Lil') occupy the northern face of the plinth.

⚜

West Terrace Cemetery has become a valuable seed bank for rare native plants of the Adelaide Plains, with seed sent to the International Millennium Seed Bank at the Royal Botanic Gardens, Kew. Seed collected here is raised at Provenance, a specialist nursery, and is both reintroduced into the cemetery and used for other re-vegetation projects in Adelaide. Coaxing these plants to germinate can be tricky, with some species requiring a drop in temperature and others immersion in hot water; germination in fire-adapted species may be encouraged by the use of smoke-water – this can be made by a process of bubbling smoke through water, or simply by including smoke-infused vermiculite in the potting mix. Quandongs are renowned for being difficult to germinate. Where emus were once the main processors of quandong seed, Provenance now achieve good results by cleaning the seeds thoroughly, cosseting them in sphagnum moss, and maintaining them at a constant temperature over the summer months. Only plants raised from seed gathered on the site are returned to the cemetery.

The common names of our native shrubs and grasses are so beautiful, it is surprising that they are not more widely grown if only for the opportunity to say the names out loud on a regular basis: nodding chocolate lily, and windmill grass, bottle-washer, silky blue-grass, pale rush, sea rush, and sword rush, punty bush and gold dust wattle. That they thrive in full sun and on short rations of water comes as a bonus to their etymological beauty. Special plants that can be seen at West Terrace Cemetery include the native oxalis (*Oxalis perennans*), wingless blue-bush (*Maireana enchylaenoides*) and Australian bindweed (*Convolvulus species*). The latter can be found entwined in some of the wrought-iron fences.

6

A Walk with Friends

by a few old

Alison Marjorie Ashby was a home-grown South Australian botanical artist and plant collecter, noted for her precise watercolours of native flora. A one-time student of Rosa Catherine Fiveash, Alison was the youngest daughter of one of the early champions of South Australian native plants, the ornithologist, passionate gardener, and Quaker, Edwin Ashby.

Ashby arrived in Adelaide in 1888 and two years later married Esther Coleman. The couple had two sons and two daughters at Trumara in Melbourne Street, North Adelaide, and in 1902 they moved to Blackwood and established the property Wittunga. Although Ashby worked as an estate and land agent he was an avid naturalist, collecting birds, butterflies, and shells, in particular chitons, on which he became a world authority. His collection of the latter was regarded as the best of its kind when he donated it to the South Australian Museum.

At Wittunga he gradually increased native plantings, experimenting with methods of cultivation and watering. It was here that Alison Ashby developed her love of native plants, and where she learned from an early age how to collect and dry specimens, and to draw them. The species *Acacia ashbyae* and *Solanum ashbyae* were named in her honour, while *Banksia ashbyi* commemorates her father.

In 1920 the Ashby family suffered a private blow from which they never really recovered. Alison's brother Ivan, a talented medical practitioner of only twenty-seven, died of diabetes, and

67

afterwards Esther Ashby became bedridden and had to be nursed by Alison. Fortunately, the second brother Keith was able to take charge of the farm.

After both her parents had died, Alison transferred her portion of the estate to the National Trust and today it is one of South Australia's most treasured botanic gardens.

⚜

Edward Gibbon Wakefield, the Englishman whose promotion of colonisation led to the settlement of South Australia, was born into a Quaker family. It is difficult to reconcile Wakefield's elopements with wealthy young women – the second of which landed him a spell at Newgate Prison – with the Quaker qualities of simplicity and truth, but although the prison sentence left his reputation tarnished it did not diminish his ability to influence and inspire others. Yet Wakefield was a theorist, and it would take the energy of people like Robert Gouger and George Fife Angas to make the dream a reality.

While Wakefield never actually set foot in Australia, the history of The Religious Society of Friends intersects with that of the colony through his involvement, as well as through the Quaker families who crossed the seas to make South Australia their home. In 1855 the colonial government granted the Quakers a piece of land at West Terrace Cemetery. This followed upon other demoninational divisions, with the Jewish community being the first in 1843, followed by the Roman Catholics in 1846, and the Church of England in 1849. Quakers needed their own cemetery, for as they do not baptise they were refused burial in consecrated ground. Early on, a piece of land in Pennington Terrace, North Adelaide, was set aside for that purpose. Then in 1840, when their meeting house arrived from England in sixty-nine flat packages, and hauling it by bullock cart up into the hills proved impractical, the Friends put it together on the land in North Adelaide, where it stands today. The unassuming yet lovely little building relies for its beauty on the austerity of its design. It was the work of London architect Henry

Manning, who made his name with what might have been the first pre-fabricated structures.

Today, all but two of the early graves have been relocated to West Terrace Cemetery, and the Quaker burial ground can be found by walking west along Road 1, and turning in north at Path 26. It is the pleasantest place in the cemetery, and after a long walk I often head for the small stone seat tucked into a dip in the pathway fledged with grasses. After scouting for snakes, I can rest my legs and reflect for a few moments.

Further along from the seat, Edwin and Esther Ashby lie side by side with their children, their graves inscribed only with names, date of death, and age. Other headstones have a similarly quiet feel, the very opposite of the visual clatter of the elaborate, flower-decked marble tombs elsewhere in the cemetery. The reserve of this burial ground is perfectly in tune with Quaker ideals. Here, broken headstones have been carefully repaired, and there is a sense of protection and enclosure, for the area is ringed with native vegetation; a curved memorial wall offers a second shady resting place. The motto of their founder George Fox urges Friends to *Walk cheerfully over the world, answering that of God in every one.*

Native plants flagged here are black-anther flax-lily (*Dianella revoluta*), native lilac (*Hardenbergia violacea*), and wattle (*Acacia species*), no doubt favourites, all, of the Ashby family.

⚜

When Quakers meet for worship they do not sing hymns or say prayers but wait together in silence. They believe in living simply, in non-violence, in tolerance for others. In death, both burial and cremation are permitted, but funeral services are noted for their lack of pomp and ceremony. Quakers value silence, finding in it a release from pressure and hurry and trivial chatter, though unlike solitary meditation it is routinely undertaken as a shared experience.

I have sat in silence among Quakers at the beautiful old meeting house at North Adelaide. Hidden away up a small lane, and in the shadow of St Peter's Cathedral, during the hour I sat with the

Friends I heard the intermittent groan of the cathedral's pipe organ, and eventually its bells. Silence is rare in our stressed-out world, particularly since the invention of the mobile telephone. While I prize it as a creative tool, the Quakers see silence as a way to commune with God, and they are good at it. Twice a year I go to a writing retreat where speaking during the day is discouraged, and I am always surprised at how difficult others can find this.

Adelaide is known as the City of Churches and over the years I have been to many of them – sometimes out of curiosity, sometimes in the course of freelance work. Quakers, I found, believe in being open to differing opinions. As the day heats up around me with the medicinal scents of pine and eucalyptus, I wonder how often other people step outside their familiar routine to investigate unfamiliar ways of thinking, other religions.

It is the Quaker movement's lack of dogma and my own love of silence that draws me to them, though I would have to work harder at 'walking cheerfully' to earn a permanent place among their congregation. Still, if I had to choose a spot in which to be buried at West Terrace Cemetery it would be here in the quietest corner of the quiet city, sheltered from the hurrying, worrying world by hedges of native trees and shrubs.

7

Visiting a Victorian Novelist

It is a mild Sunday afternoon in autumn when I visit Maud Jeanne Franc for the first time; I should be at home nursing the beginnings of a cold, but instead I gather camera, notebook, pen, and map into my backpack and set out. Once inside the main gates there is a choice between the scenic route and the more direct way. There is not much between the two in terms of distance, but the scenic route borders some interesting areas, and that is the path I choose – following Road 1 where it turns south past the Kingston Allotments and the Jewish Section, and on to its intersection with Road 4. At this point it would be easy to peel off on a side trip into the Afghan plots, but I resolve to leave that for another time and push on; Matilda Evans, who wrote under the pen-name of Maud Jean Franc, died 127 years ago, and with these early sites I am always anxious in case there is nothing left to see.

As a writer of novels, I feel a small sense kinship with Matilda. We have inhabited the same city, albeit in different eras, and our lives and writing have nothing in common except that she has sat for many hours at a stretch, as I have, filling blank pages with words, conjuring plots and characters in her head. Like most of the writers I know, or have heard speak, she will have had her writing routines and theories, and will have gone to sleep each night pondering the strengths and weaknesses of her latest work-in-progress. I imagine she woke up thinking about it too, because the sustained creative effort of writing a novel hasn't changed all that much in the last century and a half. She probably wrote her drafts by hand with a dip pen and a bottle of ink, her middle finger on the right hand acquiring that slight indentation that comes from gripping the wooden barrel of the pen, of pressing it to make the downstrokes heavier, the upward strokes lighter, acquiring ink-stains on skin and on clothing, spoiling a page when the nib splutters. I can be fairly certain that this image of her is a true one, having learned to write in primary school back when every desk had its porcelain inkwell and the whole class would compete each week to be the ink monitor. I still own a dip pen and I use it sometimes to practice what I continue to think of as proper handwriting, but it is inconvenient for all of the above reasons and I am deeply attached to my Mont Blanc fountain pen.

Fountain pens were around towards the end of Matilda's life, so it is possible she used one. Their arrival followed at least a thousand years of quill pens, and it was the natural reservoir formed in the hollow channel of a feather that prompted sharp-eyed inventors to try to produce something similar. Early models were not all that successful, and probably left the writer's fingers every bit as inky as the quill or the dip pen. In 1883, American insurance salesman, Lewis Waterman, produced a fountain pen to sign an important contract, but the pen leaked and spoiled the document and he lost the sale. Perhaps it was this moment of humiliation that prompted him to perfect a practical fountain pen. By 1888 he had opened a factory in Montreal. I like to think that Matilda Evans, or Maud Jeanne Franc as she appeared on the spines of her books, was sent a fountain pen by her English publishers. They were Sampson Low, Marston, Searle, & Rivington, of Fleet Street.

Matilda's address is Road 4, Path 33; Plot 24 is on the eastern side. There are no trees here, so the sun must beat down relentlessly in the height of summer. I wander along but am slow to find the name of Evans. Instead, it is Congreve that catches my eye – her maiden name – and I find myself staring at the headstone that commemorates her father, Henry Congreve, and her mother Elizabeth, who in 1852 died at sea on the voyage to South Australia. Underneath Elizabeth Congreve's name is the inscription

I am seeking. The reason I did not spot it immediately is that Matilda Jane is not buried under her own name but by her married title, *Mrs. E. Evans*, with *Maud Jeanne Franc* in brackets. Her sister Emily's name appears underneath. The plot is surrounded by a low iron railing of modest design. Their headstone is simple, yet after all this time its lettering remains clear. Matilda was fifty-nine and her sister, sixty-six.

They all died in hope of the glorious resurrection.

⚜

Matilda Jane Evans was born on 7 August 1827, at Peckham Park, Surrey. She was the eldest of Henry and Elizabeth's two surviving daughters. Brothers Henry and William had migrated in 1849, so when her father lost a lot of money in unfortunate circumstances, the rest of the family, which included younger brothers James and Frederick, sailed out to join them. Elizabeth Congreve perished on board.

The family arrived in Adelaide in July of 1852, but by December their father was dead. What a shock it must have been for the young Congreves to lose both parents in such a short time, and so far from all that they had known. At her father's death, Matilda was left to take responsibility for her younger siblings. Fortunately, she seems to have been a very able young woman, having already opened a school in North Adelaide, and later one in Mount Barker. It was during these early years, driven by need, that she began to write under the name of Maud Jeanne Franc. Her first novel, *Marion; or, The Light of Someone's Home*, was published in 1859, and although she wrote thirteen more it remained her most popular, being reprinted many times.

At the time of my visit to Matilda, I am reading her novel *No Longer a Child*, one of the few of her titles held by the Barr Smith Library that is not squirrelled away in their rare books collection. It was published in 1882, and its opening pages carry the reader along with a wedding party travelling in a horse-drawn waggon through the Adelaide Hills. There is plenty of pretty detail – muslin dresses and beribboned horses – but what fascinates all these years later are the glimpses of the hills only fifty years after settlement, the nestled farmsteads, with haystacks and barns, the 'lean-to' or 'skillion – beautified by the glamour of distance, or leafy drapery, or the effects of light and shade'. She writes of the places where human hands have cut great slices from the flanks of the hills, and of shrubs and vines and trees and flowers.

Pasted inside the front cover is a notice from the Adelaide Circulating Library, to which the book once belonged. It advises that a subscription costs seven shillings per quarter, or twenty-six shillings per annum, payable in advance. It adds that each subscriber is allowed to borrow three bound works and two periodicals at one time, and that the library is open daily, except for 'Sundays and Holidays'. As well as this useful information, the leaflet carries a warning about what will happen if the book is not returned at the expiry of the seven days allowed for reading. In semi-legal language it states that there will be a fine of two pence per day for every day the book is retained, and that lending it to a non-subscriber, or someone who is not a member of the subscriber's household, will result in expulsion. It is signed: *Chas. M Reid, Secretary and Librarian.*

Considering the labour intensive households of the era, seven days barely seems long enough to read a book with more than 300 pages. It suggests that people read more back then than they do now, our interest in books having been distracted and diffused by the range of entertainment available to fill our leisure hours. With the bulk of my own life having fallen in the twentieth century, there was a time in the mid-sixties when at night I would read aloud to my mother while she sewed. We lived in the country, and had radio but not television. That image of my mother's head bent in concentration over her needlework while I hunched over a book seems to me quaint and dated, yet how much more companionable it was than when, not many years later, the two of us sat passively facing a television screen.

As with a glut of anything, the oversupplied object drops its value. But the threat of expulsion from the library pasted into the front of Jeanne Maud Franc's novel signals the relative scarcity of books available for borrowing, and I imagine people took a novel home and devoured it within seven days, perhaps reading aloud to each other, as we once did. Half-read books did not accumulate in dusty stacks on bedside tables, if only because people could not have afforded the librarian's fines.

The Adelaide Circulating Library was based in the Institute Building on North Terrace and is part of the lineage of the present State Library. But as it turns out, South Australia is literary to its bones, being unique among the states for having planned a public lending library even before settlement. As soon as the British Parliament passed the *South Australia Act* in the summer of 1834, a group of prospective colonists led by Richard Hanson and Robert Gouger formed the South Australian Literary Association. Members donated useful books, which formed the basis of the colony's first library, and two years later the collection was packed into an iron trunk and loaded aboard the barque *Tam O'Shanter*.

The ship had been privately chartered by Osmond Gilles and others, and as well as the cargo of books it carried the timber for Government House, building materials, provisions, many iron bedsteads and seventy-four passengers. Under the command of Captain Phillip Mitchell, it left Plymouth in July of 1836 in company with the *Buffalo*, and arrived four months later at Kangaroo Island. Its journey from there to Port Adelaide was not without difficulties, and the precious trunk carrying the seeds of our library system fell overboard from one of the ship's boats and had to be hauled up out of the Port River. Although a little the worse for being dunked in saltwater, the books reached their destination. About forty of them still survive and are held as the Gouger Collection by the State Library. Matilda Congreve would have been a borrower and a reader, and as Maud Jeanne Franc her own novels circulated through the library system.

On 16 February 1860, at Zion Chapel in Adelaide, Matilda married a widowed Baptist pastor from Nuriootpa and became Mrs

Ephraim Evans. When her husband died three years later, she was left with four small children – two from her husband's first marriage, and two of her own tiny sons. Ever industrious, she opened a boarding school in Angaston and later a similar establishment in Buxton Street, North Adelaide. She was living there in the year *No Longer A Child* was published, and in her later years she became a deaconess at the North Adelaide Baptist Church in Tynte Street. Matilda died of peritonitis before her sixtieth birthday. The Reverend Rice performed the burial service in rough weather, choosing for her a text from Revelations. 'They shall see his face.'

The church still stands, a solid edifice said to be in the Venetian style with a vertiginous sloping floor that gives the congregation a clear view of the altar and the pipe organ. The walls are punctuated by stained-glass windows, and one of these was once dedicated to Maud Jeanne Franc. After her death a collection was made to finance the window, but six years later, when the window had still not been bought and installed, Henry Congreve wrote to the editor of the *Advertiser* pointing out the length of time that had elapsed since the funds were gathered. It appeared soon afterwards on the western wall. On a recent visit to the church to look for it, a volunteer explained that it had been removed a long time ago. She thought it probable that the window had been painted, and at some point the church council had ruled that all windows be traditional stained glass.

8

Death by 'Striped Beauty'

It is not often that you will stand at the graveside of a man who was killed by a tiger. In the normal run of life, I'd say most of us never will. Yet if you walk down Road 3 almost as far as the Afghan Section and turn onto Path 30, you will come to the last resting place of a young man who, in a moment of inattention, fatally turned his back on a tiger. John Isaacs, or Señor Gomez as he was professionally known, worked as a tiger tamer. It was a perilous way to earn a living, although among circus performers the job of the equestrian was said to be the most dangerous. Isaacs knew the tiger well, and he went into the ring with it many times each week. But at a Saturday afternoon matinee in Gawler, the two performed together for the last time, and as the ringmaster announced their act it would not have occurred to John Isaacs that he would never leave Adelaide.

Harmston's Circus arrived in Australia in 1898. The company had been on an extended tour of South East Asia, during which its proprietor William Batty Harmston had died (or perhaps met his death in a circus accident) in Singapore. Harmston's was an English outfit of considerable size, travelling with around fifty performing animals and a menagerie that included three lions, four tigers, four elephants, two panthers, three bears, fifteen monkeys, ten geese, two kangaroos, a llama, thirty-five cockatoos, fourteen horses, and nine ponies. Of their thirty performing artists, some, like the Clarke family, were associated with other old and established circuses. Along with Madame Minetta, the Lady with Teeth of Steel, Harmston's had jugglers and trick cyclists, Gus Burns the elephant trainer, and a strong equestrian contingent – William and Jane Harmston themselves were both equestrian performers.

The show opened in Brisbane on 1 March 1898, and the *Brisbane Courier* mentions, among other performers, Señor Gomez the Tiger Tamer. By April the circus had moved to Sydney, where it opened at Belmore Park. The *Sydney Morning Herald* reported on its dazzling array of costumes designed by Mrs Harmston Love (by that time the widowed Jane Harmston had married the circus's business manager, Robert Love) and their estimated value of £2400.

In a time when entertainment was scarce, touring circuses received a rapturous welcome in most Australian towns and cities. Saturated as we are now in arts festivals and fringe shows, and in the daily dose of glamour and glitz pumped out by the media, it is difficult to imagine a world devoid of even the smallest razzamatazz, a world in which the arrival of a circus, with its exotic animals and flying trapeze artists, seemed like a visitation from the gods. But if they appeared god-like under the big-top lights, touring Australia's harsh Outback roads over great distances was a tough life, though one that those born and bred to it rarely cared to shake off.

Aside from Harmston's, and the great circuses that visited from America during the goldrush years, many Australian circus families lived a nomadic existence, honing their extraordinary skills on the road, and passing them on from generation to generation. Wirth, Fitzgerald, Ashton, Sole Brothers, Bullen, and St Leon are circus names that even now trigger a ping of recognition, and most twentieth-century-born children have probably witnessed at least one Grand Parade. Marching ahead of a noisy brass band, circuses arrived in a flurry of prancing ponies, tumbling acrobats, and clowns; young women in sequinned dresses waved regally from the backs of elephants.

The golden era for Australian circus stretched from Federation to the mid-1920s. With the First World War and the Great Depression, many went under; television and cinema would eventually finish off the survivors. But in June 1898, Adelaide was in a fever of excitement with the arrival of Harmston's Circus.

John Isaacs had travelled with the circus for around four years. He was a well-built young man of twenty-five or six, a South African, with a mother and sister living in Cape Town. By the time he arrived in Adelaide he had been, for the preceding twenty months, keeper of an eight-year-old tiger by the name of Duke.

Duke was the offspring of a pair of 'striped beauties', Bruno and Kitty, who had produced twin cubs in Japan. But while his brother remained on display at the Royal Gardens in Tokyo, Duke found his way into the circus, probably picked up by Harmston's during their tour. He'd had a succession of keepers, three of whom he'd attacked. One of them was rescued by Isaacs after Duke sprang at him and broke his jaw. Duke had not begun to perform in public until the age of five, and considering that circuses started training both humans and animals as young as possible, it might have been this late start that made the tiger restless and unpredictable in the ring.

At the Saturday afternoon matinee in Adelaide, towards the finale of the show, John Isaacs entered the cage with Duke. Instead of carrying his usual whips he held a small riding crop, and a stick that was used to drive the circus's donkey. Perhaps he had mislaid his whips that afternoon, or perhaps his mind was on some young woman in the audience. Witnesses later testified that Isaacs was 'a great one for the ladies', and that if there was a pretty woman sitting ringside he would be looking at her.

At first he made the tiger run around the cage, and then stand up in the corner opposite the safety gates. Then he made him lie down until the fire gate was passed in. This was a gate bound in kerosene-soaked rag, which would then be set alight. The tiger would jump the fire.

At four-thirty on that winter afternoon in the middle of June, John Isaacs – for whatever reason – decided not to light the fire gate. The spectacle of it would have engaged Duke's attention, but instead the tiger's eyes were on his keeper. Isaacs hit Duke on the legs with the riding crop. Robert Love later speculated that this annoyed the tiger. Isaacs made him jump the gate twice, then he committed the fatal mistake of half turning his back to the animal.

'Look out, Johnny, he's going for you,' cried one of the assistants.

Before a shocked audience, Duke grabbed Isaacs by the neck and leapt over the gate.

The injured man was attended by Dr Dawe, and by Monday he had recovered sufficiently to be moved to the Adelaide Hospital. But once there his conditioned worsened, and at about five o'clock on Tuesday evening, he died. Whether or not the tiger knew what he had done, it was reported that on the night of the attack Duke ceaselessly prowled and roared in his cage.

The post-mortem examination confirmed three puncture wounds, one two inches deep. All were inflamed; one had fractured the spine.

The funeral procession left the hospital at a quarter to four on the Thursday afternoon with most of the circus performers and employees in attendance, despite heavy rain. The coffin was covered with floral tributes, and the man called Strieff who had once been saved by Isaacs from a similar fate to his own, marched beside the hearse. The Dramatic and Musical Society of Melbourne had arranged for a pillar of white flowers with *REST* picked out in violets. It must have been a colourful if damp procession along North and West Terraces to the cemetery gates.

⚜

As I dawdle along the path towards John Isaac's grave, imagining his coffin making the same journey – borne along by men who could dance the tango on a tightrope and throw backflips on the rump of a cantering horse – I wonder where Isaacs acquired his circus skills. It is a little known fact, and an astonishing one, that during the nineteenth century and the early part of the twentieth century it was commonplace for unwanted children to be given away to circuses to be trained as apprentices. All the touring circuses took them. Sometimes the children were as young as three years of age. Their training started young and covered all aspects of circus craft and life. Many children acquired in this way went on to become skilled performers; a few, like May Wirth the Bareback Queen, became international stars. Others ran away, or died in tumbling or riding accidents.

In 1908 a five-year-old boy, Charles Godfrey, died in suspicious circumstances in Broken Hill. He was the adopted son of a local acrobat, Jack Ice, who was training him to become a contortionist. Jack Ice testified to the coroner that he had got the boy in answer to an advertisement he had placed in the newspaper about two-and-a-half years earlier. Charlie's stepfather was an elderly man, a Mr R. Walker, who was employed in the Locomotive Department of South Australia. Walker had seen the advertisement and handed over his stepson, who at the time was less than three years old.

Jack Ice was charged to be tried for wilful murder, although the woman who lived with him, Eva Gregory, was acquitted as an accessory. Unbeknown to Ice, the child was suffering peritonitis, and when he failed to do a back bend correctly Ice struck him on the stomach with a broomstick. A post-mortem examination showed ruptured intestines. The litany of abuse that surfaced during the trial makes for sickening reading. Suffice to say that the matron at Broken Hill Hospital reported that, though Charlie's face was unmarked, a finger could not be placed on his body without touching a new wound or an old scar. Jack Ice had billed Charlie as 'The Boy Wonder', but all the wonder in this case is for how adult human beings could have set in motion the chain of events that led to Charles Godfrey's miserable life and cruel death.

I have read different accounts of how May Wirth the famous bareback queen became part of the Wirth's Circus family. One story goes that in 1888, when May was about two and her sister Gertie was five, their mother abandoned them in their father's absence and they were brought to the circus by a neighbour, who had found them scavenging among rubbish. The father was brought to the circus and gave his consent for the Wirths to take them. The other story goes that May was the natural daughter of a rather volatile gymnast called John Zinga. May's mother, of mixed ethnicity, was called Dezeppo Marie. May had already been taught the basics of tumbling work when her mother, unable to tolerate Zinga's violent behaviour, left him and took May to the circus. It was 1909 and there were no formal procedures for the adoption of children. May was somewhere between seven and eight years old.

Fortunately for May she was treated well, and with a trademark big pink bow in her hair, went on to become a 'circus queen', performing tricks on horseback that had rarely before been accomplished. In America she starred in Ringling Brothers Circus and has been rated by a number of circus historians as the greatest bareback rider in the world.

When describing their circus experience adult performers often remark on the harshness of their early training, though few of them linger over the details. After all, for most of them the circus became the only home they knew, and the circus folk who took them in became their family. As a child of seven, Mervyn King was taken to the St Leon Circus by the man he thought of as his grandfather. He was told that he was going on a holiday with the circus, but seventy years later Mervyn had still not returned home. Only a couple of years after being given to the circus he was performing as a top-mounter in the St Leon acrobatic troupe. He went on to become an outstanding acrobat, and was moderately skilled at most other jobs around the circus, including playing in the band. He regarded the circus as his home and Gus St Leon as his new 'grandfather', and spent his whole life on the road.

If circus families are reticent about training methods, eyewitness accounts in newspapers of the time provide odd glimpses into the lives of circus apprentices. In the same newspaper piece that reports on the sad case of Charles Godfrey and Jack Ice, the writer relates an episode in which a girl he knew went to a local circus to have riding lessons. She happened to be in the ring one day when the two daughters of the circus proprietor were being taught to jump through a hoop on horseback. The father stood in the middle of the ring with an enormous whip, which he cracked to keep the horses moving. But whenever one of his daughters missed the hoop, or fell off the horse, he flogged her with the whip until she could scramble back onto the cantering horse. The girl decided not to go on with her riding lessons, and the showman's wife confessed to her that on more than one occasion she had called the police. When her husband was angry he had been known to 'cut pieces clean out of the girls' with the whip.

In his book, *Children of the Circus*, Mark St Leon – a descendant of the St Leon Circus family – notes that apprentices were needed to replace ageing performers and keep travelling circuses alive and vibrant. Such was the stigma of illegitimacy that even well-to-do families were only too ready to offload an unwanted child. Aboriginal children were obtained from families living in poverty on the fringes of country towns. Most often they were of mixed blood.

But if their training could be punishing, there were compensations for children in the life of a travelling show. Circus people tended to stick together; they had to rely on each other, and there were many companionable occasions when, camped out in the bush, the band would play a concert, and performers and crew would sit around the fire and tell stories. Children gathered little formal education, but they knew the country inside out and they knew how to survive. Mervyn King probably spoke for many who grew up in this way when he said that it was better to be where he was wanted and needed rather than in a family that was prepared to give him away.

On 2 June 1898, Harmston's Circus invited fifty inmates of the Adelaide Destitute Asylum to watch their matinee performance. Acts of philanthropy, especially towards the orphaned and the down and out, were common among touring circuses through both good times and bad, and their generosity makes sense in light of the backgrounds of so many of the performers.

John Isaacs could have come to the circus as an apprentice, for he was South African born – possibly a man of colour or of mixed blood, given his choice of a performing name; he had no family connection with the Harmstons. Mark St Leon notes in his book on circus in Australia that from the 1920s tighter welfare and adoption legislation reduced the instances of young children being mistreated and exploited. Of course, that period coincided with the end of the golden era of the touring circus. Striped beauties, too, would soon be living on borrowed time.

9

Unhappy Women

No priestly requiem is heard,
Hush'd is the voice of prayer;
She lies in a dishonoured grave –
The suicide lies there!
'On the Suicide of a Young Lady'
– Caroline Carleton, 1860

In the opening lines of *Anna Karenina*, Tolstoy famously declares that all unhappy families are unhappy in their own way. However a search of police reports to the Adelaide coroner on the deaths of young women during the nineteenth and early twentieth centuries makes it clear that the unhappiness of women arose from relatively few sources. An inability to control their own fertility was a major factor, and many died as a result of abortions, sometimes self-induced. Lack of commitment from their menfolk held the potential for fatal misery, for when husbands drifted away – in some cases to start new families elsewhere – women were often left destitute, and some were desperate enough to take their own lives.

Around 1911, suicides by poisoning reached a record level, with Lysol being the chemical of choice. Before Lysol there was carbolic acid, and before that those intent on self-harm soaked match heads in water and drank the phosphorous-laden liquid.

Lysol was available from chemists and the only restriction on its sale was that the seller's name had to be on the label along with the word 'poison'. Made by dissolving certain phenols in liquid soap, its dark-brown colour turned clear when mixed with water. As a poison its effect was almost the same as carbolic acid – the mouth and throat were burned, and then the lining of the stomach. A teaspoonful of Lysol in water was more than enough to kill an infant. Death by Lysol was agonising but reasonably quick, with heart failure following soon after ingestion. The only remedies were alkaline solutions, but they were seldom effective because of the speed of the poison.

Phenyle was on hand in most households as a disinfectant. Occasionally, someone would drink a fatal dose. The label of a brand of phenyle called Everlasting claimed it would remove all unpleasant odours and that it had been 'tested bacteriologically'; when one part of phenyle was mixed with two-hundred parts of water it would 'kill the bacillus of typhoid in five minutes'. In case of poisoning it was recommended to send for the doctor immediately, and then, without delay, to give one ounce of Epsom salts in a tumbler of water. This was to be followed by an emetic, one teaspoonful of mustard or egg in a pint of warm water. Then, after the stomach had been emptied, it was recommended to give white of egg in milk, or olive oil, or liquid paraffin, and a further dose of salts. The patient was to be kept warm with blankets and hot water bags.

To disinfect dog kennels and fowl houses, two tablespoons were to be dissolved in half a gallon of water. In the garden, sawdust well-moistened with a weak solution of phenyle would prevent slugs and snails from attacking seedlings. It was also an ant deterrent. The distinctive blue and white label of Everlasting Phenyle had the words 'not to be taken' and 'poison' printed in red, though the letters were small. It contained 17.20% phenols.

Belladonna poisoning was nearly as terrible, with delirium and blindness thrown in. Unlike Lysol, *Atropa belladonna*, or deadly nightshade, has a long history of cosmetic and medicinal use, although Culpeper in his *Complete Herbal* published in 1653 offers no uses for it and remarks that many children have been killed by eating the berries. Culpeper also gives an account of the destruction of an army of Danes who invaded Scotland. The Scots mixed the juice of the deadly berries into drink they had been forced to supply them with under a truce, and as soon as the enemy soldiers were incapacitated, the Scots swiftly despatched them.

In the early hours of 10 August 1941, Constable John Swan went to a house in Carrington Street where he found a young woman lying on her bed, having swallowed belladonna. Annie Hooper refused to go to the Adelaide Hospital, although she later died there.

At the inquest into her suicide, Annie's husband Keith, a labourer, testified that he came home soon after midnight on Saturday to be told by his wife that she had taken belladonna. He saw that the bottle she used was empty, although it had been a quarter full; he also saw a letter she had left for him, though he would not say what was in it.

Mr Zeising, the acting city coroner, questioned Keith Hooper about the contents of the letter.

'Did you ever read the whole of the note?'

'No. I lost it when I went to phone the doctor,' Hooper said.

Annie's niece, Bernice Elliot, was in the house that night. It must be assumed she had been babysitting the couple's young child, for Bernice told the inquest her aunt had been out at a dance and that when Annie returned she said she'd had a good time.

'She did not seem worried,' Bernice added.

And yet Annie Hooper came home, wrote two letters and then drank the contents of the bottle of belladonna. Having kissed her niece and made her promise to look after the child, she then lay down on her bed to await the inevitable.

'It won't be long now,' she said. 'It will work soon.'

When Constable Swan asked Annie why she had swallowed the poison all she would say was that she had explained in the note to her husband. Hooper said he had destroyed the note because he did not want to get his wife into trouble, although at the inquest he denied telling the constable he had destroyed it. According to Keith Hooper, his wife had been given the belladonna at the Adelaide Hospital and it was intended for pain relief following an operation the previous December.

There is so much to wonder at in this story. Were Annie and her husband together at the dance? And if they went as a couple what happened there to make her decide to leave alone, come home, and take her own life? We can only suppose that Keith Hooper destroyed the note because his wife's explanation reflected badly on him. But what of the second letter? Who was it addressed to? And what became of Bernice – and Annie's child?

It is a raw afternoon in August when I walk down Road 1 and turn south into Path 32. Plot 43 is on the western side. Seventy-two years on, almost to the day, most of the graves that line this path are unmarked and Annie Hooper's is one of them. It leaves the visitor with the feeling that little care was taken over her burial. Puzzling over the possible contents of those letters brings on a frown. I wonder, too, about the symptoms of belladonna poisoning, how painful its effect on the body.

Since the quantity taken resulted in Annie Hooper's death, it is probably safe to say that she experienced a dry tongue and a burning sensation in the throat. There would have followed great difficulty in swallowing, and intense thirst. Drops of belladonna in the eyes have been used since medieval times to dilate the pupils and make the eyes look huge and alluring, but a quarter of a bottle probably brought on blindness, vertigo, and increasingly wild delirium. Medical sources describe great prostration, loss of control of bladder and bowel. For all the sweetness of its name, death by belladonna is not pretty.

⚜

By contrast with Annie Hooper's unmarked grave, the last resting place of Mercia Dunstan bears evidence of love, parental bewilderment, and grief. At the time of her death in 1937 Mercia had been a high-school teacher in Kadina, and the open stone book that marks her grave affirms that *she was loved by all her friends and pupils*, while the marble plinth below the headstone is engraved: *Beautiful Memories*.

The eldest daughter of John and Nena Dunstan, a farming couple from Penfield, Mercia had gained a BA and an MA and had taught at Adelaide High School, Burra, Woodville, and finally in Kadina. Her parents were clearly proud of their daughter's academic achievements, for they put the MA on her gravestone.

On 4 September 1937, Mercia had arrived at her parents' farm in a motorcar driven by Leslie Meyer. On the following day, Meyer drove Mercia and her mother to Adelaide, where three days later Mercia was to attend a lecture at the New Educational Fellowship Conference. The title of the conference was 'Education for Complete Living: The Challenge of Today', and it brought to Australia a large number of learned men and a few learned women from places as far away as Denmark and Japan, as well as a strong contingent from America and England. The conference opened in Brisbane on 3 August, and from there it had moved to Sydney, Canberra, Melbourne, Hobart, and Adelaide. The irony is that by the time the conference closed in Perth on 18 September, Mercia Dunstan was dead.

She had gone to the lecture on the morning of 8 September, and later that afternoon said goodbye to her mother at the railway station. Nena Dunstan testified that her daughter seemed cheerful and happy. She had not complained of feeling ill, although she had remarked that she was tired.

After seeing off her mother, at some time during the next thirty-six hours Mercia went to the house of a Mrs Challacombe in Angas Street. On Friday morning at around 10 am, Dr Wells of South Terrace received an urgent call to attend the house. Mrs Challacombe took him into a room with two single beds. Mercia Dunstan lay in one of them, blue in the face and without a pulse. When asked what had happened to her, Mrs Challacombe replied that 'a certain event' had taken place. She added that Miss Dunstan had arrived at her house that morning, saying she was ill and needed to lie down. She was in too much pain even to sit, she said, so Mrs Challacombe had given the girl her own room. She had gone to find a drop of brandy to give to her, and when she returned the girl's face was puffy and she had 'turned colour'.

'I wish I were dead,' said Mercia. 'I am very bad.'

Half an hour before the doctor arrived, a young man in a motorcar had come to the house in Angas Street; he had asked after Miss Dunstan. He was a schoolteacher, Mrs Challacombe said.

She'd told him Miss Dunstan was very sick, and that the doctor had been called, whereupon he remarked that that was the best thing to be done.

Dr Wells lost no time in informing the police.

Detectives Maddaford and Harris attended the scene. Mrs Challacombe told them that she had known Miss Dunstan for about four years and that she always came to see her when she was in Adelaide. She denied having given her anything other than a teaspoon of brandy with some sugar in it. Later, on hearing that a post-mortem had confirmed an illegal operation had been performed, the widow denied that she had used an instrument on Mercia Dunstan and suggested the police find out where she had been before she arrived at her house.

'I wish to goodness she'd never come near the place,' Mrs Challacombe cried. 'If anything has been done to her, it did not happen here.'

The police, however, discovered 'certain articles' in a cardboard box in a bedroom drawer.

The coroner found that Miss Dunstan had died of shock as a result of Mrs Elizabeth Ann Challacombe's attempt to bring about 'a certain event'. Both Leslie Meyer and Mrs Challacombe's daughter, Gladys, refused to answer questions on the grounds it might tend to incriminate them, and Mrs Challacombe was charged with murder.

At Elizabeth Challacombe's trial, the jury struggled to reach a unanimous verdict. After three-and-a-half hours they were divided as to who might have performed the operation and requested guidance from the judge. His Honour, Justice Napier, advised that if they could not be sure, then she must have the benefit of the doubt. They went out again, and after a further retirement returned with a verdict of manslaughter. Elizabeth Challacombe's defence lawyer pleaded for leniency, saying that the convicted woman had met Mercia Dunstan four years earlier at the Show, and that she had assisted someone she knew rather than acted as a professional abortionist.

This is, as far as I can tell, the only instance of the word 'abortion' being uttered during the entire saga, either by the police, the coroner, the doctor, or Mercia Dunstan's parents. This unwillingness to speak of what had happened, even during an official investigation, illustrates as nothing else could the buttoned-up nature of Australian society in the years prior to the Second World War. The stigma of pregnancy outside of marriage led to many painful and unnecessary deaths, of which Mercia Dunstan's was but one. In sentencing Elizabeth Challacombe to eighteen months imprisonment with hard labour, Justice Napier remarked that such crimes were rife and required the deterrent of stiff sentences.

I walk from the entrance gates along Road 1 and turn left where a big pine tree stands guard over the entrance to Path 5. A little along on the right is the grave of the young and beautiful Ballets Russes dancer, Madeleine Parker. I have almost reached the end of the path before I find Mercia Dunstan on the eastern side. Her parents suffered greatly over their daughters, for the spot also remembers Mercia's younger sister Josephine, who had not survived beyond the age of four.

Elizabeth Challacombe lived until 1952 and is also buried in West Terrace Cemetery. Her address is Road 5, Path 2; Plot 43 is on the western side. From her headstone I learn that her husband, Edward Thomas, had died just six months before Mercia Dunstan knocked on her door. I also learn that Elizabeth's name in the family was Bessie, for her husband is described as the *beloved husband of Bessie Challacombe*.

So what was it that threw her and Mercia Dunstan together at the Adelaide Show? Did they meet and become friendly over a floral display, or a sponge-cake judging? Was Mercia, with her farming background, drawn to the horses, the cattle, or the sheep, and did she somehow strike up a conversation with Bessie Challacombe that would blossom into home visits? And over the course of those visits, what hint did Bessie drop that she had the skill necessary to terminate an unwanted pregnancy?

None of this can now be known, but on Elizabeth Challacombe's headstone she is remembered as *A mother to all, never to be forgotten*. Now could it be that a habit of reaching out to others, of not being as strait-laced and judgemental as most mothers of that time, was the quality in Bessie that struck Mercia Dunstan and brought her to the door when she was in trouble? It could, of course, be read as a defiant affirmation from the family, for Bessie's time in prison would have cast a shadow over all their lives.

⚜

Of all the unhappy women in West Terrace Cemetery, Winnie Goater stands out. At twenty-one she was already the mother of a three-year-old child and by September of 1906 she was, secretly, 'in a certain condition'. At 2.30 on a Sunday afternoon, Winnie told her mother she was going out for a 'walk with Will' on the Unley Road and would be home in time for tea, and slipped out the front door of their house at 254 King William Street. It was the last time Mary Ann Goater would see her daughter alive.

At the beginning of September, Mary Ann had noticed that Winnie appeared pale and unwell and she had quizzed her about her relationship with the man she had been keeping company with for the past nine months: he was known to her as Will Cameron. Winnie had told her mother that there was no need to worry, that she was quite all right, but Mary Ann remained suspicious.

When Winnie did not return, her mother reported her missing. Mrs Goater had spoken to Will once when he called while Winnie was out, and asked him whether he had employment. Cameron had told her he was working for the government, fixing warning bells on the railways, so in the wake of her daughter's disappearance Mrs Goater enquired after him at all the government offices. Eventually she tracked him to a house in Pirie Street, and when he opened the door, according to Cameron, she 'started up at a terrible rate', demanding to know whether Winnie was inside and accusing him of having ruined her daughter. Will Cameron was adamant that Winnie was not there and that he had not seen her since 13 September, when he took her to the Show.

'But I'll help you look for her,' he said, 'because she's a nice little thing.'

William Cameron boxed clever, but Mrs Goater was having none of it. Somehow she forced him to accompany her to the 'Detective Office', where she insisted he account for his movements on the day of her daughter's disappearance. Once there, Cameron suddenly denied that he had even accompanied Winnie to the Show. A furious Mrs Goater accused him of lying, and 'ran him down to the lowest'. She would never give up the search, she said, until she found her daughter, dead or alive.

How those words must have later rung in Mrs Goater's ears, for by then her daughter was dead, and had been buried at West Terrace Cemetery under the name of Mary Elliot.

⚜

On 13 September, Winnie Goater had met Will, and eventually the information was extracted from him that he had gone with her to Parkside. They had walked together along Gilles and Hanson streets to Hindmarsh Square, and when Winnie said she thought it would be wet and sloppy at the Show, Will agreed and they decided not to go.

'I'd like to go out to Unley, if you'll come with me,' she said.

'What do you want to go to Unley for?'

'Oh, I want to see the doctor.'

In Cameron's account of this conversation he affected not to remember the doctor's name. It also transpired he was unemployed, and that his name was not Cameron but McDonald; he was unable to offer a satisfactory explanation for going under an alias with Winnie and her mother.

They had caught a tramcar and Winnie told the conductor where to stop. When they alighted she led the way along the left-hand side of Young Street, and soon afterwards they crossed over and paused opposite a church.

'Wait till I come back, Willie,' she said.

He saw which house she entered, and later admitted to Constable Hogan that it belonged to a Doctor Sheridan. Winnie was only gone for a few minutes, he said. She came back and told him she had seen the doctor.

When Mrs Goater got wind of this she went to visit Sheridan. Her daughter was short, she told him, less than five feet tall; she was fair-haired and blue-eyed. Sheridan said he had no one there answering that description. He showed her all over the house, all the while saying nothing of the young woman who had died there four days earlier, though he must have known by then that the girl who had come to him as Mary Elliot was actually Winnie Goater.

※

Francis John Sheridan claimed he was 'registered in the old country as MB, CM, of Aberdeen University, 1878'. He had no certificate of registration, but believed that since he was entitled to be registered in the old country it would be the same in South Australia. He had not studied in Aberdeen, but merely taken his examinations there. Sheridan was unaware, he said, that no one could obtain a degree from Aberdeen University without having studied there for a certain number of years. By good fortune, he had come into a bit of money, and since it was not his intention to practise medicine he hadn't troubled whether or not he got the certificate, indeed, he could not say whether he now had his degree.

Such was the shiftiness of the man Winnie Goater came to for help. If she was the first young woman to die in 'Doctor' Sheridan's care, which seems unlikely, she would not be the last, but although his story had more holes in it than a sieve, on this occasion he would get away with murder.

※

An inquest was held at the Elephant and Castle Hotel. Standing opposite the cemetery, as it still does today, the hotel's cellar is said to have often been pressed into service as an extension to the Dead House, or City Morgue, with bodies being stored there prior to autopsy or burial. It was established that Winnie Goater had been buried at West Terrace on 27 September, and on 3 October she was exhumed. Mrs Goater identified her daughter's remains.

Sheridan recognised the corpse in the morgue as that of a young woman who gave her name to him as Mary Elliott, aged twenty-three. She had called at his house on 13 September at about three o'clock in the afternoon. She said she was not feeling at all well, and was in trouble. She had asked him to examine her. Sheridan said he told her to go home and tell her mother everything.

'I couldn't; it would kill her,' Winnie answered.

The following Sunday the girl returned, and again asked to be examined. The witness repeated his advice, whereupon the young woman fell into a fit and began 'foaming at the mouth'. He and his wife carried her into a bedroom, where she remained in a comatose state all night. Her temperature was 101 degrees, and at seven o'clock the next morning Doctor Coombe, a legally registered medical practitioner of Hindmarsh, was called and arrived and examined her. Sheridan wanted the girl removed to the hospital: he must have been frantic at the prospect of her dying on the premises. Coombe said that her condition made any move inadvisable, although reading between the lines it was the questions that would be asked at the hospital that made such a move impossible. A couple of hours before poor Winnie Goater died, Sheridan asked Doctor Coombe what would be the best thing to do in that event and he replied that, as she was unknown to them, the best course would be to bury her.

Apart from her breathing, Winnie showed no signs of life, and on Monday 25 September, at about 7.30 in the evening, she finally expired. Sheridan could not write the death certificate, so Coombe had to attend to it. By the time it was produced in evidence it stated the cause of death as acute nephritis, uraemia, and miscarriage. The city coroner, Dr William Ramsay Smith, asked Sheridan if he could explain why there were different inks used in writing the certificate.

'No. Only that I had two inks on my table.'

The coroner then asked the jury to examine the certificate and consider why it was 'such a patchwork'.

And to Sheridan: 'Did you receive any payment for the girl who was in your house for eight days?'

'No, nothing. She only had 6d, tied in her pocket-handkerchief.'

Mrs Goater confirmed that Winnie's jewellery and her bankbook had been left in her drawer at home.

Sheridan had made arrangements with an undertaker at Bowden by the name of Elliot. The price was fixed at £7, and Sheridan requested that the funeral depart from the undertaker's house rather than his own. Frederick Thomas Elliott arrived at Young Street late at night and whisked Winnie's body away in a coffin. But even then her progress towards West Terrace Cemetery was not straightforward, for Elliot was spotted by a Constable McMahon around midnight; he was on North Terrace, outside the Terminus Hotel. Elliot told the policeman he had a corpse on board his four-wheeled trap, and that it was a typhoid case from the Parkside Lunatic Asylum.

Next morning, Dr Coombe delivered the death certificate to the undertaker's residence. Elliot explained this away by saying it was because the doctor was treating his wife. The funeral took place at 11.30 that morning and two ladies and a gentleman attended; one of the women was Mrs Sheridan. Eight days after Winnie Goater died, Elliot sent his assistant, Williams, to register the death and the receipt was sent on to the curator of the cemetery. The law allowed ten days in which to register the certificate, and the coroner remarked to the jury that it was a 'very unsatisfactory state of the law, which allows any undertaker to bury a body and not register the burial until ten days afterwards'.

Elliot said that on the day after the funeral, Dr Coombe called and asked him for the death certificate as he wished to add something to it. He took it away, and returned with it about half an hour later. The undertaker admitted he could not remember ever before being asked to return a certificate to a doctor after a burial. He could also not ever remember a case in which one doctor arranged a funeral while another provided the death certificate. The word Dr Coombe had added to the certificate was 'miscarriage'.

All of the men in the case lied under oath. William McDonald was as unable to 'rid himself of the habit of telling lies as he was to shed his skin', according to the coroner. He had even gone to the trouble of writing letters to Winnie during the time she was missing, letters designed to establish that he had not seen her since the date of the proposed trip to the Show.

'I only met the girl,' McDonald said, 'in order to learn something about San Francisco.'

'You are like many another man,' the coroner said to him. 'There was no telling what you could do until you were pushed.'

To Sheridan, the coroner said, 'Will you swear that you have not the slightest idea as to what the young lady's purposes were in coming to you?'

'Yes,' answered Sheridan.

'Are you frequently consulted by ladies as to their condition?'

'I think that I ought to refuse to answer that.'

'Why?'

'Oh, I don't know.'

The jury found that Winifred Goater had died of haemorrhage following a miscarriage and that it was induced by unnatural means. They further found that Sheridan had performed such operation on 13 September 1905, and that McDonald had been fully aware of Winnie's intention to have the operation. The coroner therefore brought a charge of wilful murder against Sheridan, and an equally guilty McDonald was also charged and committed for trial. While the jury was out, the coroner had also hit McDonald with a charge of prevarication, and inflicted a fine of £15. After delivering their verdict, the jury commended Mrs Goater and the police on their persistence and ability.

Winnie Goater was re-interred in the cemetery. This time her funeral cortege set out from the morgue; a mourning carriage carried her mother, two uncles, and other relatives. Public sympathy was running high, for there must have been many young women who felt that there but for the grace of God they themselves might lie buried under a false name. Several hundred people turned out for the funeral service, and the coffin was covered with wreaths. Winnie Goater was not returned to the plot into which she had been so hastily and deviously shuffled by Sheridan, Coombe, and Elliot under the name of Mary Elliot, but rests instead in the family burial allotment. The address is Road 1 South, Path 15. Plot 37 is on the eastern side. It is easier to walk down Road 2, and the unmarked site is under the canopy of a sheltering gum on the corner of Path 15.

That December, Sheridan appeared before the Criminal Court, but the murder charge was dropped due to insufficient evidence.

⚜

In the last week of January 1906, twenty-one-year-old Ruby Barrington arrived in a cab at Dr Hynes' Private Hospital in Flinders Street. She was brought there by a woman, Miss Johnstone, who described herself as a friend. Miss Johnstone explained that she had just collected Ruby from the railway station, that Ruby had arrived in Adelaide that night from Gladstone, where her parents ran the Booyoolie Hotel, and that she appeared to be very ill. As soon as the sick girl was admitted, Miss Johnstone left the hospital. She would advise Ruby's parents, she said, but the parents did not appear and Miss Johnstone never returned.

Ruby told Dr Hynes her condition was due to natural causes, but when he advised her that she would not recover she broke down and admitted that 'Dr Sheridan took the baby away last Wednesday at his house'. Sheridan had made her promise not to mention him by name or say what had been done, and the friend who had brought her in the cab was the doctor's wife, Mrs Sheridan.

Ruby's parents were contacted and they arrived in time to speak to their daughter. At first, Ruby would not say much, but eventually she admitted to her mother that it was the young man she had been keeping company with, Naismith, known to the Barringtons as 'Son', who had got her into trouble. Mrs Barrington had last seen her daughter on 15 January when she left to take a holiday in Adelaide. She had no idea anything was wrong, although by Ruby's own admission she could have been as much as five months pregnant. Now, though, Mrs Barrington cast her mind back to Ruby's previous holiday in Adelaide. It had been a year earlier, and she had stayed away for five or six weeks. When she returned she was in good health, but some time afterwards Mrs Barrington came across an account in Ruby's drawer: it was for an amount of £20 for the medical attendance of Dr Sheridan. Later still she found a letter addressed to Ruby. The sender's address was Young Street, Parkside.

Dear Miss Barrington, I shall feel very much obliged if you will forward me the balance of your account viz., £11.5s. by return mail, as we are without any means whatever, owing to the doctor's misfortune, which, no doubt, you have read in the papers. I am sorry to have to ask you but the circumstances compel me to do so, which must be my apology for writing to you. I need hardly tell you that this unfortunate affair has completely upset me. Trusting you will remit by return: I remain, yours respectfully, L.A. Sheridan.

The 'unfortunate affair' to which Lillian Sheridan referred was the death of Winnie Goater. Ruby must have read all about it, for 'The Strange Case of Miss Goater' had filled many column inches in the *Advertiser* and other newspapers. And yet still she entrusted her life to Doctor Sheridan, probably because he had safely relieved her of a previous burden.

With the memory of Winnie Goater still vivid in the public mind, Sheridan had not dared to approach the hospital directly but instead dealt through a chemist. Mr Wastell of King William Street telephoned Dr Hynes on Sheridan's behalf and arranged for Ruby Barrington to be admitted.

On the day before she died, Ruby asked her mother whether the doctor thought she would survive the blood poisoning. Mrs Barrington answered that the doctor was doing all he could, but she must have been sore at heart. In a moment of seeming acceptance of her fate, Ruby asked to be buried at Laura with her two brothers;

she asked her mother to wear her bangle, and to send her ring to her brother Jack. She also sent her love to two girls who worked with her at the hotel, Jessie and Nellie, with instructions they were never to leave her mother – a thinly veiled warning to the pair not to follow in her footsteps.

Sheridan fled after Ruby's death, but he was arrested on the southern railway line near Nairne and brought back to the city. Francis John Sheridan and Lillian Sheridan were charged at the Criminal Court with the wilful murder of Ruby Hartley Louisa Barrington on 25 January 1906. At the conclusion of the Crown's case, Justice Homburg directed the jury to acquit both accused, and this was done.

But Sheridan was incorrigible. In September 1906 the body of a woman known as Addie Ray was discovered on an operating table in his house. Adelaide Ray was a young married woman, and her husband Albert Ray of Hill Street, North Adelaide, identified her body. Sheridan's ongoing absence made newspaper headlines. A warrant was issued, with his arrest described as 'very desirable'.

There are two photographs of Francis Sheridan in the *Police Gazette* of the time. One shows him in profile, and in the other he looks me straight in the eye. I gaze at this image with a degree of wonder, for I am face-to-face with the man who hovered over Winnie Goater as she lay dying; I am looking at what must surely be the last face she saw before she lost consciousness. Sheridan's figure is short and stout. The police description uses the word 'corpulent', but he does not visibly sag with fat; his excess flesh is contained within the smooth shell of his waistcoat, his dark jacket. His pale face, an oval accentuated by a well-trimmed brown beard and moustache, is empty of expression. Although the photograph is in black and white I know his eyes are a cool dark blue. His two missing teeth are not visible, nor his habit of nodding his head and bending his neck forward when he speaks. Sheridan habitually wore a black Beaufort coat, dark vest and grey tweed trousers; a black hard hat completed the image of a respectable medical man. Francis Sheridan would have made a convincing Dr Watson.

After evading the police for several weeks, he was eventually traced to the Hackney Hotel. When constables Garland and Richmond entered his room he was in the act of shaving off his beard.

'Good morning, Sheridan,' said one of the officers.

'I'm not Sheridan,' he replied, deadpan, before realising the game was up. 'Oh, all right,' he said, 'I was going to give myself up.'

For Sheridan, it was a case of 'third time unlucky', for he was finally convicted of the manslaughter of Adelaide Ray and sentenced to ten years hard labour. The *Police Gazette* noted that he was due to be freed from Yatala Labour Prison on 22 July 1912.

⚜

A coda to this story of the girls who died in Young Street, Parkside, at the hands of Francis Sheridan concerns the indefatigable Mrs Goater. In the winter of 1906, after Ruby's death but before Addie's, an article appeared in the *Advertiser* with the headline 'Mrs Goater Breaks Her Umbrella'.

Mrs Goater had gone into town with the intention of meeting a relative who dined at Jackman's Grill Rooms and as he was not there she waited for him in the street. After standing for twenty minutes outside Charles Wells's chemist shop next door, her attention was caught by a man walking along the edge of the pavement. Their eyes met, and she recognised Sheridan. By her account, he came over to her.

'I am very sorry about your daughter,' he said. 'You would not believe me, but I did all I could to try and find you. But your daughter gave me a false name and told me lies. She said she came from the West. If you will come over to my house and have a friendly conversation, I will tell you something very gratifying about your daughter.'

'You had better tell me now,' said Mrs Goater.

'I cannot.'

'What is it you can tell me about my daughter; is it as to the one who wronged her?'

Sheridan said that he did not know the man. 'If you will come to my house and have a talk, I will tell you something.'

'I told him to be off about his business, and not to dare to speak to me again. He moved away a few feet, and then repeated in a sneering tone, "Go off about your business!"'

Sheridan then made a remark about her and her daughter, to which Mrs Goater took the strongest exception.

'I moved towards him and struck him with my umbrella somewhere about the head. I followed him some distance and struck him several more times. My only regret was that my umbrella, which broke, was not much heavier.'

Sheridan hailed a police constable who was near the corner of Grenfell Street, but as the officer had not witnessed the assault he declined to take Mrs Goater into custody.

'Do you think any decent woman could hear a charge against both her poor dead daughter and herself and not use her umbrella?' Mrs Goater demanded. 'I might tell you it was nine months last Wednesday since they buried my daughter unknown to me.'

Naturally, Sheridan's account of this meeting was quite different to Mrs Goater's, although he admitted having said that her daughter was not all she thought she was.

I cannot find a photograph or even a description of the redoubtable Mary Ann Goater, but I picture her as a short woman like her daughter and thin as a hairpin; a woman with a plain scrubbed face and penetrating pale-blue eyes under a no-nonsense hat. In testifying to the court, she revealed that Winnie's three-year-old child had always been strong and healthy. I imagine she raised the boy, John Walter, and that he flourished under the protection of his grandmother's fierce devotion.

⚜

Sheridan had married his wife at Port Augusta in 1899. Sometimes her name appears as Agnes Lillian and at others it is Lillian Agnes, though she seems to have preferred the latter. On 4 October 1906, Lillian gave birth to a boy, Francis Brinsley Gordon Sheridan, at

Miss Best's Private Hospital in Hutt Street. It was she who registered the birth, listing her husband as a medical practitioner, because by then Sheridan was in gaol beginning his ten-year sentence for the manslaughter of Adelaide Ray. The address she gave was Melbourne Street, probably because by then they had lost the house in Parkside. When Sheridan was arrested at the Hackney Hotel the police found in his pockets a number of letters appealing for financial help. In them he explained that he had lost everything – house, land, and furniture – and that all he possessed came to less than £3, which was not enough to get him 'away'.

After his release from prison, the illegal operations swiftly resumed. In 1917, Eva Brokensha, the thirty-three-year-old proprietoress of the Adelaide Fibre Plaster Works, died from blood poisoning, and Sheridan was once again committed for trial. In 1918 it was the death of Minnie Ward Irving – at that time he appeared to be renting rooms with a convenient back entrance at 36 Wakefield Street, where a brass plaque was engraved: *Dr Sheridan*. He had a waiting room, and set consulting times.

In 1924 he was arrested in connection with Helen Kathleen Frape, and again in 1929 he was tried for an attempted abortion on Florence Annie Ellen Ross. He was convicted and sentenced to two years and six months hard labour on that occasion. His age was reported as seventy-five, though it varied from trial to trial. But he was certainly described as 'elderly', and Justice Parsons remarked that it was sad to see 'a graduate of the University of Cambridge in the position in which the accused found himself'. Madeleine Kennedy, a twenty-five-year-old machinist, was charged as his accomplice in the Ross case, and sentenced to six months with hard labour. As late as 1937, the eighty-one-year-old Sheridan was in trouble for using an instrument on a woman by the name of Schebella at Glen Osmond. He ended up with a fine of £40, plus court costs, for a breach of the *Medical Practitioners' Act*.

Sheridan died in March 1939; for all his hard labour behind bars he had reached eighty-seven (give or take a year or two, for his age was constantly shifting). His last address was Robsart Street,

Parkside, close to his old stamping ground. On his death certificate his occupation is given as 'ship's surgeon', and I suppose there is a metaphorical truth at work here in that his was the hand that guided women in trouble, many of whom ended up journeying to 'the other side'. He was buried at Mitcham Cemetery, but the lease appears to have expired and there is no headstone. His wife Lillian lived until 1961 when she was ninety-one. She died at Nairne and was buried in the cemetery there. The inclusion of Brinsley in their son's name floats the possibility of a connection with Richard Brinsley Sheridan, the Irish playwright and poet. Perhaps the infamous 'Dr' Sheridan was the black sheep of that particular family, and if so it is beyond ironic that the best known of Sheridan's plays is *The School for Scandal*.

In a career as an abortionist that spanned at least three decades (and if the whole truth could be known it was probably longer) countless unhappy women passed through Sheridan's hands. It must be assumed that most survived, but if I believed in ghosts I would say that Winnie Goater, Ruby Barrington, and Addie Ray must haunt that old house of his on the corner of Young and George streets, Parkside.

⚜

With the deaths of people who were not affluent there is often not much remaining in the way of a headstone. The first thing to do is establish whether the cemetery records provide an address, and I have learned to do this through West Terrace Cemetery's online archive. This is where every search begins, and it is always gratifying when the name I am interested in is listed. Then, at the curator's cottage at the entrance to the cemetery, a touch screen available for public use allows you to search for names and print out a map. It is useful to do this for any visit, but essential when the grave you are searching for is likely to be unmarked. The maps show the names associated with the surrounding plots, and more often than not it will be possible to pinpoint an unmarked location from the proximity of other monuments.

The women I have visited on this walk were not notable, they were not making history, at least not intentionally. It is because of their unhappy ends that they have become visible, and if it were possible to scroll back through their lives, though doubtless vivid to them, many hours would be filled with quiet and unremarkable moments of ordinary domesticity such as we all experience. They were women whose stories took a sudden turn. There was a moment of inattention, recklessness, or desire, and it changed the direction they were headed. Some were overwhelmed by circumstances and it is safe to say they would have hated the public nature of their endings.

But there must be many other women they stand in for, those who slipped through life unnoticed because, for example, the poison they swallowed, rather than killing them, only made them violently sick, or they survived Bessie Challacombe's or Dr Sheridan's catheters. As for those girls who didn't get away, the ones whose brief lives and the facts surrounding their deaths rendered them less than respectable – their desperation and raw courage is humbling in an era where we have far less risky ways of resolving the same problems.

10

Desperate Men, Desperate Measures

THROUGH MONTHS AND YEARS IN PAIN AND FEAR,
THROUGH TROUBLED PATHS I TROD,
MY SAVIOUR'S VOICE BID ME REJOICE,
AND CALL'D MY SOUL TO GOD.

In his essay 'Night Walks' Charles Dickens passes the Bethlehem Hospital in London, and the sight of its walls and dome shrouded in darkness prompts him to ponder whether at night the sane and the insane might become equal. Dreams thrust all of us into the confused conditions inmates of the asylum experience during the day: events, times, and places become jumbled; we associate with kings and queens, and sometimes even believe that we can fly.

While Dickens's London was no place to get lost in, it seems that people in the new colony occasionally fell into an even deeper darkness. Many who came to South Australia in the hope of a better life grew disillusioned when things did not work out as expected. Finding themselves stranded at the edge of the world, some ended their own lives in lonely, unobserved acts in the bush; others perished surrounded by people, yet utterly alone when it most counted.

As I push deeper into the cemetery and match the inscriptions on headstones with the information held at State Records and in old newspapers, I too begin to wonder at the ways in which people were once judged to be insane, if only for as long as it took them to commit a desperate act.

One such man was Henry Lancaster Beddome, who in March 1890 was found by the coroner's inquest to have died of a gunshot wound, self-inflicted, 'while in a state of Temporary Insanity'. The death of a thirty-seven-year-old man in his city office is not in itself remarkable, but after more than a century the details surrounding Henry Beddome's final moments continue to intrigue.

On the night of Friday 21 March, Henry, a well-known and respected citizen, did not go home to his family. Next morning, at around half-past seven, he appeared at his office on the second floor of Grenfell Chambers. A man was sweeping on the floor above, and Henry enquired whether he planned to come down and sweep on his floor. When the man, a tailor, replied that it was not his responsibility, Henry Beddome closed his office door. It was the last time he was seen alive.

Henry was the son of Police Magistrate Samuel Beddome. Although born in Adelaide, he had spent part of his education at a college in Geneva and after graduating he remained in Switzerland for three or four years; he spoke excellent French. On his return to South Australia he worked as a clerk in the offices of the Marine Insurance Company, and also spent time in the bush with different survey parties. Later he worked in the Survey Department in the city, but at the time of his death he was described as a 'broker'. Those who knew Henry intimately reported that he had complained of heavy losses in connection with forward purchases of Broken Hill and other stocks. Having bought when the market was inflated, he was compelled to take up the shares during a period of depression on the Stock Exchange. This evidence points to financial desperation, yet other details make me wonder whether Henry Beddome's death could have been caused by something else.

At about quarter-to-ten on Saturday morning Henry's heavily pregnant wife Margaretta arrived at Grenfell Chambers. She was understandably alarmed at her husband's absence on the previous night, and even more agitated when she found that the door of his office had been locked from the inside and the key removed. She produced a spare key and let herself in, to be confronted by the awful spectacle of her husband's body.

Henry Beddome was seated with his feet up on the desk. His head was thrown back, and in his right hand he held a revolver, while in the left was a novel – *Infelice* – with the corner of a page turned down. His waistcoat, shirt and necktie were burnt, for he had fired the revolver close to his chest; the wound was on the left side, with a remarkable absence of visible blood. Nothing in the room had been disturbed, but Mr Beddome's cuffs and hat, and the leather holster for the revolver, which appeared to be quite ancient, were set out opposite him on the table. There was also an open letter.

Margaretta's screams brought people running. They included Mr Parr whose office adjoined Henry Beddome's and was separated from it only by a half-glass door. Parr had arrived at Grenfell Chambers at around nine o'clock that morning but had noticed nothing unusual. Neither the girls working on the floor above, nor the tailor, had heard the revolver fired. The dazed and hysterical wife was coaxed from her husband's side into the next room, while Mr Parr ran to the office of the commissioner of police. The coroner's policeman quickly arrived and secured the premises, excluding sightseers who had begun to gather – news of the death had flashed through the city. Doctor Poulton was called in, and after a brief examination of the body gave his opinion that Henry Beddome had been dead for at least three hours. He then attended to Margaretta Beddome, administering 'a restorative'.

Word had been sent to the dead man's father, and Samuel Beddome arrived in company with the police commissioner. The two men went into the room where Henry lay, and the open letter was handed to Samuel Beddome. After reading it he passed it to the commissioner.

⚜

A man reads a passage, or passages, from a novel, then turns down the corner of a page and shoots himself in the heart. 'Mystery breeds misery,' mutters one of the characters in the opening chapter of *Infelice*. Written by American author, Augusta Evans Wilson, and published in 1875, the novel's plot features a secret under-age marriage, deceit, and bigamy.

The handwritten report from the City Watch House to the coroner is brief, merely a statement of Henry Beddome's death; at the point of writing, his body is still in the office and a constable is in charge. Slant-wise across the paper is a note that the inquest will be held at 4 pm at the Imperial Hotel, and for a brief moment I embrace the possibility of a full and satisfying revelation of the contents of Henry's letter, a note, even, of the turned-down page of the novel. I do not yet know that the inquest documents from that year and others have been lost. At State Records the archivist shakes her head; she has heard they were pulped during the First World War. 'Not something we would do today,' she murmurs regretfully.

This loss condemns us to a state of perpetual wonderment, although as I set out in search of Henry Beddome's grave, my novelist's imagination continues to roam. The fact that Henry shot himself in the heart hints at emotional rather than financial distress, and the storyline of a secret under-age marriage sends my thoughts scampering back to Henry's college years in Geneva.

His eldest child Daisy was nine; he and Margaretta had lost a six-month-old infant in 1887, and their surviving son Reginald was five or six at the time of his father's death. Another baby, Doris Violet, would be born on 12 May, a home birth at Angas Street, Kent Town. In a final blow for poor Margaretta, little Doris died three months later.

That romance novel continues to nag at me, as does the fatal wound to the heart, and I am wondering whether there could have been an earlier, clandestine relationship in Switzerland. Could someone from Henry Beddome's past have turned up to haunt him? Where did he spend the night before his death? If the crucial letter remained with the inquest papers it must surely be lost. However, it is possible it was returned to the family, along with the volume of *Infelice*, and that even now one or both of these relics remains with Henry's descendants, or else lies anonymously somewhere, gathering dust.

⚜

After a stretch of scorching March days the weather has broken, and on the morning I visit Henry Beddome's grave the sky is overcast and the air humid; the forecast is for thirty degrees Celsius. It was at this time of year in 1890 that Henry died, and the *Register* reported similar temperatures on the Friday and Saturday in question.

Henry is buried in Section Z, and while it is often difficult to locate addresses here the printed maps are useful. As it happens, this grave will not be hard to find. The walk begins at the main gates, swings left past the curator's cottage and passes along the road lined with tall, tightly clipped, cylindrical shrubs. It turns left at the pepper tree, which, on sunnier days, casts a veil of shade over the turning. At the second path on the left is a handsome memorial to Elizabeth Spicer; topped by an urn, it marks the corner of the path I am looking for. Turning in here, Henry's grave is about six spaces along on the left.

It is surrounded by a modest, still-intact, wrought-iron fence. The gate, I find, still works, and although the little square of iron that acts as a latch is rusted, when I lift it the gate swings inwards with barely a protest. For an early grave it is in good condition, and it strikes me that this might be one of the few suicides marked with a substantial memorial *In Affectionate Remembrance*. The headstone also commemorates Henry and Margaretta's infant son, Percival, who died three years before his father. So it is possible that this was originally the child's grave, perhaps with a less imposing headstone, and then with Henry's death the larger memorial was installed with space to add further names. And as baby Doris was both born and died barely five months after Henry's suicide, his wife would have had to stand here at this graveside and bid farewell to their tiny daughter while her shock and grief for him were still raw. From the inscriptions I learn that Margaretta reached the age of eighty-four and was outlived by her son, Reginald, although only by three years. Her daughter Daisy had married Ernest Esau at Balhannah in 1907. Daisy also outlived her mother, but once again it was not by many years and she was cremated in 1943 at West Terrace Cemetery.

Speckled stones are heaped tidily in a corner. The last burial recorded is that of Reginald's wife Amy in 1981. I remember that year well; it seems like yesterday, even though more than a quarter of a century has elapsed. This site looks as if it will endure for at least that long again, and in all probability it will last much longer. In the middle of the path, as I walk away, a humid breeze stirs the fluffy heads of a patch of low-growing grasses. When my long skirt brushes them, and a couple of the arrow-shaped seed heads cling, I reflect that Henry Beddome's story has worked its way into my imagination because of its small, strange details, and that it will forever remain there, an unresolved and teasing mystery.

⚜

Men do not get much more desperate than young Alfred Lines, who in the winter of 1885 committed a double murder and immediately took his own life. Unlike the case of Henry Beddome, no clouds obscure Alfred Lines's motives, which remain startlingly clear and perhaps shed light on other 'eternal triangle' crimes through history, even though each, when examined, is unique in its details.

The murders occurred on Friday 12 June in Stanley Street, North Adelaide, but the events that led to them had been set in motion much earlier at Burra, where those involved had been living.

Elizabeth Jane Stephens was seventeen in September 1881 when she married Alfred Lines. It appears Lizzie was an illegitimate child, with no father's name listed on her marriage certificate. Alfred was twenty-three when they wed, and by his father Joseph's admission at that time his son was courting another girl. The young couple lived with Alfred's parents, and Joseph Lines claimed that at first the two were happy together but that after the birth of their first child Maud, Alfred had a fall; since he worked as a drover it seems likely that he was thrown from a horse. Joseph Lines insisted that his son injured both his head and heart, and that the fall permanently changed his temper. A second child was born, a boy named Stanley, who was around fourteen months old at the time of the murders.

On 5 June, a Friday morning, while her husband was away droving at Cooper's Creek, Lizzie left the Burra and travelled to Adelaide under her maiden name. With her was a young man called

Maurice O'Connor. Nineteen-year-old Maurice, a farm labourer, had been lodging about a hundred yards from where Lizzie and Alfred lived at Mitchell Flats, at the residence of Thomas Highet, Alfred's brother-in-law. Up to this point all is clear, but then the devil creeps into the details.

On the Thursday before Lizzie and Maurice quit the Burra, Lizzie's sister Amelia gave birth to a child. The letter Lizzie left on the kitchen table for her husband makes it clear that it was this event, and what led to it, that rang the death knell for their marriage.

Good-bye, Alf; you must never trouble after me. All you have got to do is to look after the children. I could never live happy with you any more. It seems you are struck after Amelia, and she is putting all trust in you. She is determined to have you, and the best thing you can do is to go and get her to come and look after the children altogether. Here are your rings. Good-bye for ever.

Alf Lines, although only twenty-six, had already appeared many times before the magistrates at Kooringa, most often on charges of drunkenness and disorderly behaviour. His father admitted he had recently paid a fine because his son had assaulted a police constable. A reporter for the *South Australian Weekly Chronicle* commented that, 'if the veil were only drawn aside it would show the deplorable life he has led'. Alf had openly acknowledged paternity of his sister-in-law's child. The mother, Amelia, was only sixteen.

Notwithstanding his 'improper intimacy' with his wife's young sister, when Alfred Lines read his wife's farewell note his rage was such that he resolved to follow up Lizzie and Maurice and 'deal desperately' with them.

⚜

When Lizzie and Maurice arrived in Adelaide, Maurice got in touch with some of his family in the city. An uncle, John O'Connor, a labourer, was living in Sussex Street, and he had two sisters in domestic service in North Adelaide. He also visited his aunt,

Catherine Ryan, a widow who lived at Glen Osmond. He introduced Lizzie to all of them as his wife, saying they had been married six weeks earlier at Gladstone. This was news to his family; they had not heard he was keeping company with Lizzie Stephens, and they were surprised that Maurice was wed because of his youth. He said he and Lizzie planned to settle in the city, and his sisters were delighted, expressing the hope they would then have a home to go to should they ever strike a period of unemployment. The sisters, Kate and Mary, took a great interest in all Maurice's arrangements and appeared to form an instant attachment to Lizzie.

Catherine Ryan took the couple in. On the first day she noticed that Lizzie wore no rings, but by the second day she had a wedding ring and a keeper, and Mrs Ryan was satisfied they were married. The pair appeared unusually quiet, Mrs Ryan thought, but there was no reason not to believe what her nephew had told her. She let them stay in her house for a week, during which time Maurice shared a room with her son and Lizzie slept in with her. They seemed happy and agreeable, Catherine Ryan said, and for the whole week they did not sleep in the same bedroom. The two would go out early every morning, and return around six in the evening. Maurice was searching for a job and quickly obtained a promise of employment.

On Tuesday, while they were still staying at Glen Osmond, Lizzie and Maurice called on a Mrs Weger and asked to rent an empty cottage in Stanley Street, which was next to the right-of-way. It was available for seven shillings a week, and as the two appeared a well-behaved, respectable couple, Mrs Weger accepted them as tenants. On Thursday, furniture they had ordered was delivered, and Lizzie spent time putting the cottage in order with the help of Maurice's sisters. Early on Friday morning, a week after they had left the Burra, they told Maurice's aunt they had taken a house at North Adelaide and at eight o'clock they left Glen Osmond.

The cottage they had rented was one of a block of low-roofed buildings, each containing three rooms. The yard at the back was open to all the tenants and was a good-sized piece of land that adjoined the gardens of the houses in Sussex Street. It had been arranged that Maurice and Lizzie should finally take possession on Friday 12 June and on that morning, as they travelled down from Glen Osmond, Lizzie must have imagined that a new and happier life was about to open up for her.

She borrowed one or two articles from their neighbour, Mrs Agnes Schutt, and at 1 pm she and Maurice sat down together to eat lunch in their own kitchen for the first time. The room was simply decorated, with its floor covered by strips of coconut matting, and chintz curtains at the windows. It was furnished with a pine table and three chairs they had bought in Rundle Street, and whatever crockery Lizzie and Maurice had gathered to begin their life as a couple. The second room in the cottage contained a double bed. The third was empty, but had they lived it is safe to assume it would soon have been furnished with a child's crib.

※

While Lizzie and Maurice were arranging to rent their cottage and setting it to rights, Alfred Lines had arrived in Adelaide from the Burra. Early on Friday morning, 12 June, he went to gunsmith Frederick Wilson and asked to buy a British bulldog revolver. Wilson showed him some. The price was thirty-five shillings. Lines said he would take one, and fifty cartridges. When Wilson asked what he was going to do with it he replied in a matter of fact way that he was 'going to shoot some enemies'.

'Surely you are not going to shoot anyone,' Wilson exclaimed. 'Do you mean that?'

'Oh yes,' answered Lines.

'"Then I cannot sell you a gun. If you shoot anyone I shall get myself into trouble.'

Lines muttered that he would have to go elsewhere to buy a weapon, and then, with a sudden change of story he said that he only wanted it to shoot kangaroos, as he was leaving for the country.

'You must be a pretty good shot to hit kangaroos with such a weapon, unless in close quarters,' Wilson said.

'I am a good shot,' Lines replied.

Mr Wilson refused to sell the revolver.

'Well, I must get one at another shop then,' Lines said.

Alfred Lines had been waiting outside for the shop to open, but the gunsmith thought him perfectly cool and calm. Wilson was always careful when he sold revolvers, and he had decided not to let Lines have the weapon because he thought he intended to commit suicide.

At ten o'clock, Alfred called at the premises of another gunsmith, William Ekins. Ekins was out, but Alf Lines inspected some guns and told an assistant that he was lodging at the Coffee Palace and would call again later that morning.

By coincidence, Police Constable Molloy, who had been stationed at Burra the previous winter and knew Alfred Lines quite well, was on duty outside Government House. At a quarter-past-nine that Friday morning he saw Alfred on North Terrace, together with Maurice O'Connor and Lizzie Lines.

How Alfred had managed to locate the runaways was never explained. He had returned to the Burra from Cooper's Creek on Tuesday 9 June and set out for Adelaide two days later. What did he do during that interval in Burra? Did he spend the time with Amelia and their newborn child? Did he even visit the girl? For on Thursday 11 June, while Lizzie was waiting for Le Cornu's to deliver her furniture, Alfred was making his way towards the city. Even if he had known where Mrs Ryan lived and guessed that Lizzie and Maurice would stay with her, he could hardly have waited outside her house and followed them that Friday morning, for he was at Wilson's gun shop by 8.45, and only half-an-hour later Molloy saw him outside Government House with his wife and Maurice O'Connor.

Catherine Ryan never saw Alfred Lines, but, improbable as it seems, I have wondered whether he loitered, or even camped the night, outside her house and somehow found out Lizzie's plans. A receipt was later found in his pocket, payment for a dinner and feed for a horse from the Imperial Hotel. Inexplicably, one report dates the receipt as 21 May when Alfred Lines was away from home droving. In trying to understand how he found them so quickly, I remember that in 1885 the city of Adelaide was a smaller place with a smaller population. Perhaps just being about the streets at eight o'clock on a Friday morning was enough to bring about the fateful coincidence of bumping into a furious husband. In any case, Alfred's rage was clearly of the cold and calculating type, and he lost no time in tracking down his wife and carrying out his intention to 'deal desperately' with her.

On North Terrace, Alfred came up to Constable Molloy and, pointing at Lizzie, told him that she was his wife, and that she had run away and was living at North Adelaide with O'Connor. By Molloy's account, Alfred Lines was quite calm. The other two were standing a little apart, but close enough to hear what was being said. When they attempted to move off, Alfred spoke to them.

'Don't you move. If you do I will give you in charge for stealing my money. You had no right to go away only in the clothes you stood in.'

To Molloy, he said, 'I am going up to their house to see them in it.'

As Molloy was on duty, he asked Lines to go away and he left, the three of them going in the direction of North Adelaide. They were talking together, and walking quietly. Later that same morning at around 11.30 am Molloy saw Lines again. This time he was alone.

'I have been down to North Adelaide and seen them in the house together,' he said. 'I have a good mind to shoot her.'

Molloy took it as a casual remark. 'Oh, go on,' 'he replied.

'My wife loved me up till last January,' Lines said. 'It is a bit my own fault. I suppose she noticed me having a lark with the girls.' He added, 'I am going home by this afternoon's train. Have you got any message to send to the Burra?'

Molloy shook hands with him and said goodbye. For the first time Alfred appeared troubled.

'Good God, it is awful,' he said.

Within half-an-hour he had returned to Ekins's shop where he explained that he was going to Cooper's Creek and wanted a pistol to shoot wild dogs. He had learned from his experience with Wilson that it did not do to make dangerous statements when buying a gun. Alfred eventually selected the revolver, and Ekins sold him forty-five cartridges. The revolver cost £3.12s. and the cartridges 3s.6p. When Lines left the shop, the weapon was empty. Ekins remarked that he seemed very calm and a pleasant fellow.

⚜

Events now unfolded quickly. At one o'clock Alfred Lines took a cab from the King William Street stand. The driver, Tom Taylor, said he drove him to the Stanley Street Congregational Church, where Lines paid his fare and got out. During the course of the journey, Alfred Lines told Taylor that his wife had cleared with another man – it is as if he just could not contain this information and that he was working himself up, although he gave the cab driver no indication of his intention to do them an injury.

Alfred Lines was seen walking along Stanley Street; he was looking into the cottages with an anxious, eager stare. Lizzie and Maurice, having finished their lunch, had cleared the table and tidied everything away when, without warning, Alfred ran into the cottage with the British bulldog revolver in his hand. There were no witnesses to what happened next, except of course for those in the kitchen, but it appears Alfred went straight up to Lizzie and before she could do more than utter one piercing scream he shot her just below the breast. When she fell to the floor, Alfred turned the gun towards Maurice, who bolted outside.

Their neighbour, Mrs Schutt, had gone out, but she had left her key in the front door, and Maurice ran inside. Alfred overtook him in Mrs Schutt's kitchen, where he shot him in the heart. A wooden bar, used to close the door of Schutt's sitting room was found on the floor. Perhaps Maurice had pulled it free in a desperate bid to hide from his attacker.

None of this had yet disturbed the neighbours. Agnes Schutt

had been in her mother's house and had returned through the right of way to go shopping. She had reached her own front door when she heard a scream and several shots, one after the other. This she imagined must be O'Connor and his wife amusing themselves by exploding paper bags. But when somebody ran through her yard, Mrs Schutt went to investigate and came face to face with the murderer. He had a look of wild excitement on his face and in his hand he held the smoking gun.

'That woman is my wife,' he said, 'and not the wife of that fellow. I have shot them both and now I'm going to shoot myself.'

Mrs Schutt put her hand up to her face in terror. 'Oh, don't do it before me,' she cried.

She ran out of the right of way into the street, and when the murderer followed she thought he was chasing her. However, when she looked back she saw him stop on the pavement and shoot himself in the breast. He fell down full length upon his back, and after breathing hard for a few moments, died. It was now 1.45 pm, and the whole thing had not taken more than a few minutes.

News spread like a grass fire. Constable Wellington was alerted to the shooting by a boy named William White. He found Alfred Lines lying in front of the passageway that lead to the cottages, saw the face quiver and thought the eyes moved. There was no blood to speak of, but a bullet wound in the centre of his breast. Agnes Schutt then called to him.

'Oh, come to the back, Wellington, there's a woman shot!'

He left Lines's body and ran into the front room of O'Connor's cottage, where he found Lizzie.

'There was a strong smell of powder, and her clothes seemed to be smoking. She appeared to be dead.'

By now, Mrs Schutt had observed that the door of her cottage was open; she went in and cried out again to the constable. 'Oh, there's a man in my kitchen!'

Wellington found Maurice O'Connor lying on his back; the face was twitching and his eyes opened and closed a couple of times. The constable returned to Lines, and at that moment spotted Dr Görger driving past. He waved him down and the doctor put his hand on Alfred's chest and pronounced life extinct. He then examined the other two bodies and expressed the same opinion. Doctors Melville Jay and William Campbell came next and confirmed the verdict. The bodies were carried into the cottage Lizzie and Maurice had so briefly occupied and laid side by side in the bedroom.

⚜

A letter was found in Alfred Lines's pocket.

> *Adelaide*
>
> > *June 12, 1885*
> >
> > *My dear mother and father I have found lisey {Lizzie} and moris {Maurice} and they are living to gether as man and wife, and mother I hope that you will look after my dear children for wen you get this letter I shall be dead, so good By all and god Bless you all but be kind to my loving children, but that as for me to live I kood not not to know that they are living together so I have bought a Revalver and I going to shote the Both of them and then shoute my self and I hope that god will for give me for it and it is all her sisters doings so good By aunt and tom and my dear Brother and father and mother from your son*
> >
> > *alfred lines*
> >
> > *do not fret my mother, I hope to meet all of you in heaven, but I could not live, I ham broken hearted god bless you all.*
> >
> > *but do be kind to my children all of you and tell my Brother good By and I love him and I hope that god will forgive me for what I have done.*
> >
> > *Pleass berry me at the Burra wat ever you do alfred lines – and I got three pounds or about that on me.*

⚜

Lizzie wore a dark-blue serge dress trimmed with braid and lace. Around her neck was a silver locket, and she wore a silver brooch with earrings to match. On her left hand was a wedding band and a keeper, both said to be new. Her face looked troubled. There was a bruise on her right hand and, below her breast, the bullet wound. The gun must have been pressed close to her body, for a two-inch square of cloth was charred and smoking. The bullet had passed right through her and she bled profusely, blood pooling in a great stain on the coconut matting. Lizzie was found to have 18s. 8d. in her dress pocket, and a purse containing the following document, obviously much handled, and frayed where it had been folded:

March 17, 1835.
I hereby give my handwriting stating that I ham no longer the
husband of Elizabeth Lines, she can goe ene were she likes and can
marry who ever she likes.
Alfred Lines. This 17 of March 1885

Also found was a ticket for two boxes left at the Adelaide railway-station, dated 5 June; a key of a box; two eardrops; a piece of crepe; a pocket handkerchief.

When the handwriting on this note was compared with that of the letter in Alfred Line's pocket, it appeared to have been written by the same hand. The most likely explanation for its existence is that Lizzie forced her husband to write it when she discovered he had made her sister pregnant. Back in March, Amelia's condition would have just begun to show and Lizzie must have caught Alfred at a moment when his conscience had got the better of him. Naively, she believed this note had dissolved her marriage and left her free to marry Maurice O'Connor; she believed it would keep her safe.

⚜

Found on Maurice O'Connor: one pocket handkerchief; a box of matches; purse; bill for furniture from P. Le Cornu amounting to £5 12s. 6d., with the words 'Paid on account £3 10s.'.

⚜

The two men were laid out side by side on the bedroom floor. They were both of respectable appearance, with O'Connor looking more mature than his nineteen years. He was about five feet ten inches in height, well built, and with a thin beard covering his chin and the sides of his face; he wore a tweed suit, and his soft felt hat was at his side. In a strange reversal, the murderer looked younger than his twenty-six years. Shorter than Maurice, at around five feet eight inches, he was of heavy build with a light complexion and slight moustache. Maurice O'Connor was shot near the heart and Lines below the right breast. In death, their faces, like Lizzie's, wore troubled expressions.

Lizzie was carried in and laid beside them. The revolver that had ended three young lives so efficiently was on the kitchen table, its barrel empty. Nothing in the house had been disturbed; nothing was out of place when Kate O'Connor arrived. She was brought to the room where the bodies lay, but could not bring herself to cross the threshold. The room with the three corpses lying side by side was described as resembling 'a grim chamber of death'. About half an hour later, having gathered her courage, Kate returned and identified the body of her brother, that of Alfred Lines, and the woman she referred to as 'poor Lizzie'.

⚜

The coroner's jury was sworn in over the bodies. They were Messrs Thomas Hills, Joseph Tilbrook, John Hutton, Philip Brideock, William James Bailey, Thomas Rawson, Charles Irvin, Henry Smith, William Albert Nicholls, William Edward Allen, John Hillier, Edwin Botten, and William H. Graham. Mr Bailey was elected foreman. Each corpse was carefully examined. Dr Jay, who showed the wounds, commenced with the body of Lines, tracing the bullet's course through the outer clothing and unfastening the flannel guernsey. He exposed the wound, and then probed for the bullet. Some of the jurors found this 'a sickening sight' and no doubt there was a general feeling of relief when a move was made from the cottage to the Lord Melbourne Hotel.

Police constables Wellington and O'Connor searched two boxes belonging to Maurice O'Connor at the Adelaide Railway Station on Saturday 13 June. In one box they found trousers, coats, vests, etc., which had been recently washed, while in the other were a few items of ladies' clothing and linen.

✤

Lizzie Lines was shot twice at very close range, with a bullet in her chest and another under her armpit, which had set fire to the sleeve of her dress. O'Connor had also been shot twice. The first bullet struck him when he was in the kitchen and lodged in the doorframe to the bedroom. Wounded, he spun away and bolted into Mrs Schutt's cottage, where he was felled by the second bullet. Five bullets were used from the box of forty-five Alfred Lines had bought from Ekins.

When the coroner released the bodies for burial, Joseph Lines declared he could not afford to bury his son. Had it not been for the kindness of a gentleman in Burra, who had loaned him thirty shillings, he said, he would not have been able to come to Adelaide. Lizzie had no father, and no other relative came forward to claim her body and arrange her funeral. Joseph Lines resolutely refused to have anything to do with burying Lizzie.

'She is nothing to me,' he said. 'If I had my way I would have her thrown down a hole or into a brick kiln.'

The Government had to bear the expense of the funerals of both Alfred and Lizzie, though the coroner said he would apply to the Oddfellows Lodge, of which Lines was a member, to recoup the cost. They would not return Alfred's body to Burra, despite his last request. Mr O'Connor attended to the interment of his son. It was reported the bodies were buried on Monday afternoon. I have not been able to discover where Maurice O'Connor lies, but Alfred and Lizzie were buried in the one grave.

✤

Although this story is furnished with enough precise details to entertain the curious – even down to the contents of their pockets – there is still so much that remains unknown. Even at the time there were crucial pieces missing, because we hear what people say, we see what they do, we even read their suicide notes, yet the dark thoughts that rattle inside their heads, the emotions that wrack their hearts, are destined always to remain mysterious.

What shocks me about this case is that a man who after four years of marriage could not spell his own wife's name was able to carry off such a crime to its terrible conclusion. I am shocked at Joseph Lines's statement that if he had his way Lizzie would be thrown down a hole, or into a brick kiln – Alfred had impregnated his wife's sixteen-year-old sister, yet Joseph Lines had little to say about how that must have humiliated and shamed Lizzie in a small country town. I am also shocked by the sense that what drove Alfred was not love for his wife but the thought of her living with another man. His letter to his parents makes it clear that not even his children mattered more to him than establishing his owner-ship of a woman who he had repeatedly wronged. Indeed, whenever Alfred speaks, unless it is to buy a gun, it is to tell whoever will listen to him that Lizzie is *his* wife not Maurice O'Connor's. It is the last thing he says to Agnes Schutt before he shoots himself in the heart. But what shocks me most of all is that the murderer and his victim were buried together, lumped into the one grave for all eternity. Did they even have a coffin?

⚜

I suspect that there will be no monument to mark the place where Elizabeth Lines lies buried. Still, I decide to pay her a visit, if only because she seemed so alone throughout her short life and her violent death. To find the place, I walk right to the bottom of Road 3, take the bend and follow the road around, keeping the oleander bushes on the right. I am looking for Path 37, and I have a map listing all the surrounding names in case I need to identify the site by its relationship to them.

There are gravestones here dating back to the 1890s but, frustratingly, none match those on the map. Close by are a number of modern Greek and Italian tombs, but I do not think any of them cover Lizzie's grave. Finally I locate a marker: Marion Deacon's name is on the map and I have found her headstone. A tree spreads its thick canopy over this corner, and in the empty space behind Marion Deacon's headstone, and a little to the left, is the bare patch of earth where Lizzie and Alfred Lines lie together. There are worse places, but I cannot help thinking that Lizzie was intent on escaping her marriage and that she would rather have been buried with Maurice O'Connor.

⚜

While a murder and suicide like that of Lizzie and Alfred Lines might shock us, we do not find it difficult to understand. But our communal history is irregularly dotted with episodes of ferocious violence that arrive like dust devils out of a clear blue sky and remain as impossible to pin down as dust devils. The men who perpetrate them, and it usually is a man, are not only desperate but secretive. Their heads must be seething bogs of distress, abysses of inconsolable misery, yet they go about their everyday business as if all is more or less right with the world – until they strike. Certainly they give no signal that they are about to destroy their family.

Such was Henry Oxley, known as Harry, who in the early hours of Christmas Day, 1893, took a tomahawk to the heads of his wife and three children while they slept, and ended by fatally cutting his own throat. Another was George Burgess who on the morning after a family celebration for his wife's birthday in 1899 killed both her and their two youngest children with a butcher's cleaver.

'Harry' Oxley had lived for many years at Naracoorte, where he worked on Thomas Magarey's sheep station. He had recently moved the family to Adelaide, and the reason given was so his children would have better opportunities. He bought a greengrocer's shop at the corner of Sturt Street and Hobson's Place from Mr F.B. White, and had only been in possession for about a week.

133

Harry Oxley was said to have much to make life attractive. At thirty-one he was still young; he had a loving and frugal wife, a bright boy and two pretty and intelligent girls, and he was not in financial difficulties – there was a bank deposit of £1300, and he received regular remittances from England. And yet there is no doubt that after only a week in business he had got it into his head that he had somehow been swindled over the greengrocer's shop. The takings were not as high as he had been led to suppose by White, and he had worked himself into such a stew about it that he wanted to sell it back. There was some evidence that he and White discussed this and came to terms at a price that would represent a loss for Oxley, though not one that would have left him impoverished.

The alarm was raised by William Stanley, a fruiterer of Angas Street. Oxley had employed him to help in the business, and on Christmas morning he had arrived and gone to the stable to tend to the horses. Afterwards he went to the back door to get the key to the storeroom from Oxley. No one was stirring, and Stanley called out.

'Are you not going to get up today?'

When he had called twice, Stanley went to the kitchen door, from where he could get a view of the young boy on the sofa. There was blood, and Stanley saw at once that he was dead. From there he ventured to the bedroom, where the terrible sight of Harry and Emma Oxley and their two young daughters lying in pools of blood sent him stumbling from the house.

Dr Robert Robertson was summoned and found that the two young girls, Ethel and Grace, though mortally injured, were still alive. He sent them to the hospital, where they later died. Shortly after half-past-four on Christmas Day, the city coroner, Dr Whittell, visited the premises along with six jurymen. They viewed the bodies of Harry Oxley, his wife Emma, and their nine-year-old son, Harry Walter.

In part, it is the Christmas setting of the Oxley murders that makes them so poignant. It was the season of peace and goodwill; there was a Bible in the sitting room with all their names written in it; one of Oxley's horses had been hired out to a group of carol singers. It was Christmas Day and yet for this family it was their darkest hour. Christmas can be a time when families crack under the pressure of social expectations and financial obligations, but what is noticeable about that Christmas Day in 1893 is that it was almost a day like any other – William Stanley turned up early to feed the horses; he was looking for the key to the storeroom; in other words, he had got up and gone to work.

The unwavering affection between Harry Oxley and his wife was stressed. The family was said to be a happy one, almost perfect. Yet in the light of the emotions that drove Alfred Lines to hunt down and kill his wife Lizzie and Maurice O'Connor, it is tempting to question whether there was more going on between Harry and Emma Oxley than people knew. Why had they suddenly left the country property where they had lived and worked for almost their entire marriage? Did something happen there that they wanted to put behind them? Was it not for the sake of the children but rather a fresh start for themselves? There may once have been people in the Naracoorte area who had private opinions about the Oxleys, but the coroner's jury, who could only weigh what people had seen and heard, and with only the mutilated remains to go on, concluded that Harry Oxley had committed the acts during a fit of insanity.

⚜

From the Oxley family's house in Sturt Street it was a straight run to West Terrace Cemetery. Standing at the intersection of Sturt and West Terrace, the entrance gates are directly ahead. Their address now is in the area known as Plan 3, Path 22, Plots 148 and 149.

Plan 3 flows on from Plan Z where Henry Beddome is buried. I follow the road south towards the maintenance buildings and Path 22 is easy to spot.

The Oxleys' gravesite is marked by a broken column, and includes a cross and a wreath. From the map, it appears that Ethel and Grace Oxley may have been buried in one plot and the rest of the family beside them.

In Loving Memory of Harry Oxley, His Wife, and their three little lambs.
Died 25th December, 1893.

There is nothing to mark this as the grave of four murder victims and a suicide. The children's names are not listed; they are only 'lambs'. And as I leave this spot, which became the final destination of madness, sadness, and who knows what strange dark passions, I wonder if this inscription is written in the secret language of the Victorians, a subtle method of ensuring that all who read it are warned that even a fit of madness is no defence for the slaughter of sleeping children.

He is with thee in thy dwelling
Shielding thee from fear of ill;
All thy burdens kindly bearing;
For thy dear ones gently caring;
Guarding, keeping, blessing, still.

Sometimes a background detail of one of these terrible events is almost too painful. The verse above was the motto that hung over the cot of a child murdered in an attack strikingly similar to the Oxley murders. Indeed, the Oxley murders were still remembered throughout South Australia, and beyond, when in March 1899 George Burgess, a baker and general storekeeper with a thriving business on the Port Road at York, killed his wife and his two youngest children in another inexplicable fit of insanity.

Burgess and his family had lived in the house at York for about twelve years. Once again there were many testaments to familial happiness and affection; by all accounts George was a model husband and father, until he wasn't. But the evidence is that he was a hardworking, steady, and sober man. He employed four men in his flourishing bakery business and was financially secure. Bakers generally keep unsociable hours, but George had worked his business up to the point where there was no need for him to rise from his bed at four in the morning to bake. He often did rise at that time – perhaps the habit of a lifetime was difficult to break – but once he had checked on the bakehouse he went back to bed. He and his wife, Alice Emily, were members of the York Christian Church, which was only about 200 yards from their house.

On the evening before the murders, there had been a small gathering to celebrate Alice Burgess's thirty-fifth birthday. Mr and Mrs William Brooker were present, along with Alice's mother Mrs Bruer and a few other friends. After tea, the Brookers and Alice Burgess attended a church service. George stayed behind to mind the children. He appeared in good spirits, both before and after the birthday tea. Mrs Bruer told how George put his small son Stanley to bed that evening with great affection. She herself undressed little Dora and got her ready for bed, and then her father carried her into the bedroom.

It was Wednesday 29 March 1899 when Edgar Mossop arrived at 4 am for work at the bakehouse. At a little after five o'clock Burgess came out of the house and crossed the yard to an outside bedroom where his nephew, William Jones, was sleeping. William was living with the family to learn the bakery trade, and it seems like a stroke of the worst possible luck that while delivering bread two months previously he had found a butcher's meat cleaver on the Findon Road. Not only that, but he had showed it to his uncle and told him it was in good condition, and very sharp. William kept the cleaver under his bed, and on Wednesday morning he was roused by someone groping about the room. He sat up in bed and saw his uncle.

'It's all right,' Burgess said. 'I only want that cleaver. I want to chop off a fowl's head.'

'Well mind your fingers, Uncle,' William said. 'It is very sharp.' He then went back to sleep.

Freda, the Burgess's fifteen-year-old daughter, rose at seven o'clock and went to practise the piano for an hour before breakfast. She had almost finished when a servant girl, Hettie Aird, came in and asked her to go and call her father. Freda's grandmother Elizabeth Bruer had already tapped at George and Alice's bedroom door. She did not yet consciously realise it but she was uneasy: the two young children who slept in the room with their parents, Dora Alice and Stanley George, were always awake long before breakfast, and Elizabeth Bruer had not heard them make a sound.

Freda left the piano, and as she walked towards her parents' bedroom her five-year-old sister Edna came up the passage and opened the bedroom door. She had to look around it to see the bed where her father was lying, when Freda, noticing a pool of blood by the door, drew her sister away and ran to call her grandmother.

Edgar Mossop came in from the bakery and went into the room. It was a gruesome sight. Alice Burgess's injures made her unrecognisable, but in her arms she held the little boy, Stanley. He had died there, most probably while asleep. It took some time for the distressed onlookers to discover the small body of the child Dora, for George Burgess, having cut his throat with a horn-handled kitchen knife, had fallen back and covered her. Burgess was mortally injured, though not yet dead. The bed was saturated with blood. On the floor was the cleaver, along with the knife.

⚜

George Burgess was born in Bradford-on-Avon, England, and had lived there until he was eighteen years old. He had travelled to South Australia aboard the *John Elder*. His future wife Alice Bruer had arrived in the same year. From a drawing that appeared in the newspaper, George was a presentable man with dark hair, regular features, and an impressive dark moustache. A sketch of Alice shows an oval face with dark hair drawn back, a pair of strong dark brows, and serene expression. It is likely that the drawings were made by Alice's brother, Jeffery Bruer, an engraver who had just that week offered his services to the newspapers.

At the hospital, Dr Morrison wrote a question on a piece of card and showed it to Burgess. *Who did this? Did you do it yourself?* Burgess nodded, indicating that he had. The doctor was of the opinion that, though dying, Burgess was aware of all that went on around him. But his windpipe had been severed and he was unable to speak.

I cannot rid my mind of the thought that in the early hours of that morning, the mortally injured George Burgess, soaked in the blood of his wife and children and struggling for breath, must have listened to Freda playing the piano. What passed through his mind as he lay there, or was it blank with shock and pain? There was evidence that he had suffered some kind of stroke two years previously. For a time it affected his speech, but he had seemed to recover. In the weeks before his wife's birthday, however, there were reports of dizziness, and headaches. It must be supposed that there was a physical reason, some terrible growth that pressed upon his brain and filled him with homicidal delusions. Perhaps this tells us something about Henry Oxley. Perhaps, as the inquest concluded, it really was a fit of insanity in both cases. Or, as with the Lines murder and suicide, were there other emotions at play? Why did Burgess kill only the youngest children? He would have had to murder his mother-in-law alongside the older girls, but it is hard to believe that her presence would have deterred him if he had determined to end their lives.

⚜

The little town of York shut down in mourning. Alice Burgess's sister, Mrs White, was said to have suffered a breakdown. The Burgess family was not buried at West Terrace but at Cheltenham Cemetery at Woodville. It was described as one of the saddest funerals ever witnessed. Alice and little Stanley were buried together in the same coffin, and in a gesture of compassion for his illness, George Burgess was buried with Dora. The hymn 'We Shall Gather at the River' was sung.

Another detail that troubles me is that the funeral director was F.T. Elliot of Bowden, the Frederick Elliot who, a few years hence, would play such an infamous part in the burial of Winnie Goater.

A postscript to this sad tale is that the younger of the daughters who survived that awful morning, Edna Marianne Burgess, died on 28 March 1917. The date looks suspiciously close to an anniversary of the family's triple murder and suicide. She died at Main Road,

York, perhaps even in the family home. The newspaper notes her death as *the beloved second daughter of the late George and Alice Burgess, aged 25 years. At Rest.*

There is a heaviness that hovers over those final words, a hint that a long suffering had come to an end. It makes me wonder how Freda and Edna managed to live with the horror of what they had seen in their parents' bedroom. It can only be hoped that their grandmother was a strong enough woman to sustain them. But for little Edna, so young at the time and the first to open the bedroom door, the murders must have dominated the whole of her too-short life.

⚜

In the early days of the colony, many throats were cut. Like Lysol, and Phenyle, a razor was easy to lay hands on in most households. Agnes Schutt, in whose cottage Maurice O'Connor expired, claimed that she was no stranger to tragedy as she had witnessed a man cut his throat. It was, literally, a cut-throat world, and often a lonely one.

In Adelaide, as elsewhere, a culture of lodging houses had sprung up in response to need. Almost at once there was evidence of overcrowding, and the insanitary conditions migrants had thought to leave behind in England. In 1876 the plight of lodging house inmates was briefly brought to public attention by the death of William Hooper Maidment who, at the height of summer, had shared a tiny attic room with two other men. At the inquest into his death the space was described as miserably inadequate for more than one person. In the stifling, unventilated room, William Maidment lay down to sleep at ten o'clock on a Sunday morning and by six that evening he was dead. It was reported that he was fit to work, although his health had suffered from exposure to the weather during the week and a 'system deranged by intemperance' at other times. Maidment's death was described as 'nothing more or less than suffocation', which likely would not have happened had he occupied a larger room.

A report from the City Watch House dated 26 July 1916

records desperation of a different stripe, and with it comes the suspicion that it might have been more common at the time than most people imagined. It concerns the death of Patrick Flaherty, a thirty-two-year-old returned soldier. Flaherty was living at the boarding house of Mrs Meires at 135 Hindley Street. He had been living there for some months, drinking heavily, according to the landlady.

At ten o'clock one morning he was seen by a man called Cooper and appeared all right, but an hour later, when the landlady went upstairs to make her bed she looked through the doorway into his room and saw him sitting on a chair with his head hanging down. There was blood on the floor, and she called for another returned soldier, John Retallack, who lived a few doors away. Retallack came and saw the blood; on the bed he found a bloodstained razor.

'John, go for the police,' said Patrick Flaherty.

John went for the police with all speed, and when he returned he said, 'You have cut your throat, Paddy.'

Patrick Flaherty replied, 'I couldn't breathe. I had to.'

He was taken in a cab to the Royal Adelaide Hospital and died four days later from pneumonia caused by the cut throat.

As far as I can tell, Flaherty, whose first name may have been William, is buried in the Catholic Old Area of West Terrace Cemetery. His grave is unmarked; its location unknown. Just what made Flaherty feel he could not breathe will also never be known, but his return after two years from a war in which poison gas was used against the Allied troops and eventually by the British cannot be discounted.

Early gas masks were crude and not always effective; if caught in the open without a mask it was possible for a soldier to improvise with a cloth soaked in his own urine. A gassed soldier might suffer in agony for days or even weeks before he finally died; phosgene gas was especially feared, as its effect was not felt until hours after it had been inhaled, by which time it had penetrated the lung tissue and little could be done. Aside from gas there was the horror of the trenches, and if soldiers survived to return to civilian life they were expected not to dwell on what they had seen.

Most of us have family stories handed down from the First World War. My maternal grandfather survived his time in France but on the ship coming home his best friend jumped overboard, to his death. It was a less messy end than poor Paddy Flaherty's, but no less desperate. There exists an ocean of stories of the young men who remained traumatised long after the war was over. It was out of concern for them that The Returned Sailors and Soldiers Imperial League of Australia was formed. Only a few years later, Australia's oldest military cemetery would be established here at West Terrace, although it was too late for the likes of poor Paddy Flaherty.

11

Ghost Walk

The sky is overcast on this morning in late March. Stones gleam in the diffused light while trees subside into their own soft shadows. The angels on their plinths are luminous. Leaves silkily stir the hush, and there is the tingle of approaching rain. In short, it is the perfect moment for a ghost walk.

I do not think that I believe in ghosts, but just for this morning, just for the time it will take to ramble through this quiet city under clouds the colour of tin, or of pigeon's wings, I am going to believe in them. South Australia is much haunted. The Old Adelaide Gaol is famous for it, although I wonder that the banks of the Torrens do not teem with ghosts because of the numbers who have perished in the river, especially children. The parklands, too, must have their sad spirits, Aboriginal men who were hung there for suspected crimes, and people without hope who contrived their own hangings. But this morning it is the ghosts of the Adelaide Arcade I plan to visit, and what an interesting crowd they are: Francis Cluney, the arcade's beadle; baby Sidney Byron, and 'Madame Kennedy', palmist and clairvoyant; Florence Horton, young estranged wife of 'Anglo the Juggler'. Reeling off their names I feel a ping of pride to inhabit a city strange enough to have been populated by such characters.

The Adelaide Arcade was officially opened on 12 December 1885. Mr Gay's Furniture Warehouse and Barker Brothers Horse Bazaar had previously occupied the site. Mr Gay's name has endured in the lovely arcade that opens off the eastern side. An orchestra played the 'Adelaide Arcade Grand Polka' at the opening ceremony. It had been composed by the Italian violinist Raphael Squarise; a newspaper cutting on display in the arcade's museum shows a rather intense-looking young man with thick dark hair and shining eyes. He had studied at Turin and came to Australia as leader of the Cagli and Paoli Opera Company; when the company dissolved in Melbourne, Squarise came to Adelaide, where he led the orchestra at the Academy of Music, and the Theatre Royal.

The arcade was one of the first establishments to install electricity, still a novelty in 1885. The electricity plant was housed in a narrow room on the eastern side of the arcade. In it was an Otto Crossley horizontal gas engine, with two heavy flywheels each weighing a ton; the engine supplied the power for two dynamos, spaced about ten feet apart and connected by bands. The plant, once started up, was automatic, feeding itself with oil and requiring no particular attention.

Francis Cluney, the arcade's beadle, was the equivalent of today's security guard, and although the position was humble, Cluney was a well-known, almost public figure. He had been a sergeant major in one of the British regiments and had served in the Crimea, where he distinguished himself and won several medals. In his role as beadle, Cluney liked to dress in his old military uniform.

Henry Harcourt was the electrical engineer to the Arcade Company. On the night of Tuesday 21 June 1887 he left the machine room to install a number of electric lamps at the Adelaide Jubilee Exhibition. He put the beadle in charge, with instructions to see that the machinery was going on all right but not to touch anything, although Cluney was to shut it down if anything went wrong. He had often helped Harcourt start the engine. On this Tuesday in early winter, the lights were lit at 5.15 pm, and Harcourt left the arcade just after eight o'clock. He had hardly departed, when all the electric lights went out and Charles Horne, an employee of Wendt's jewellery shop, went to the machine room to see what was wrong. At the horrible sight of a pair of legs protruding from the workings, and clouds of gas escaping, Horne ran outside shouting that a man had been killed. Constable Pawson and the manager of the machine room at the *Advertiser*, Mr Simms, arrived together, and having turned off the gas saw that Francis Cluney had suffered a catastrophic accident.

About fifteen minutes before the lights went out – which must have been the moment Cluney fell into the machine – William Tuttle, a photographer, had needed the beadle's help to deal with larrikins who had broken one of Tuttle's frames in the arcade. The beadle helped him catch the offender and made him pay for the damage. If the larrikins went on like that, Cluney said, he would do what he had done the night before and put the lights out. Cluney's body was found jammed between the engine and the flywheel. The injuries he sustained were terrible.

On the following day a coroner's inquest was held at the Sir John Barleycorn Hotel. Edwin Burnett, a stationer's assistant, testified that Francis Cluney was his father-in-law. Cluney had left a wife and seven children, the youngest only seven. He was not insured, nor was he a member of any benevolent society; he left nothing for his wife and children.

Rundle Street was not a pedestrian mall then, and newspapers of the time report that the street and arcade were busy. Why else would the man run from Wendt's to see why the lights had gone out? Would a jeweller's shop even be open now in Rundle Mall on a Tuesday night, especially a cold night in June?

⚜

Francis Frederick Cluney's address is Road 1 North, Path 43, Plot 7. I walk from the main entrance down Road 1, and the path is on the right at the bottom just before the road swings left. I have come, expecting to find a memorial, something solid and respectful erected by the Arcade Company, or even a modest headstone got up by a subscription among the traders. What I find instead is a large number of unmarked graves; the soil is stony here, and it looks less kempt than other places. One or two of the plots, though bare, are touching in their detail: the spot beside the place where Cluney lies lacks a headstone but is carefully outlined with small white pebbles; there are artificial flowers in a vase, and terracotta edging tiles laid out flat at the foot of the grave. On Cluney's other side the plot has also been outlined with stones; these have not been as carefully chosen and not all remain in place. In its centre a small heap of broken tiles and the remains of flowers poke from the reddish soil, the vestiges, perhaps, of something damaged and swept away.

Francis Cluney's plot is bare but for a scattering of white pebbles. The only way I can tell that this is his last resting place is that on the map the graves of Thomas Tregoweth and Matilda Jane Abbott stand slightly behind his, and their headstones, especially Tregoweth's, remain intact.

Standing at the spot where the beadle was laid to rest it occurs to me that if Francis Cluney haunts the Adelaide Arcade it could be for a number of reasons. The first is that the word 'beadle' has vanished from the working vocabulary. Next, and more compelling, is that the Arcade Company did not fund a monument to mark his grave even though he died while on duty. Third, and much more serious, is that the larrikin he forced to pay for the broken frame did not leave the arcade, but followed him into the machine room for a bout of push and shove. This is, of course, speculation. But as for the rest, I am sure that if I had been Francis Cluney, a man who still wore his old soldier's uniform and medals with pride, I would have bitterly resented the lack of official recognition and I might have resolved, if it were possible, to return from time to time and express my displeasure.

I am about to move on, when the name Tregoweth again catches my eye, stirring a memory of a story about a different ghost. Constable Thomas Alfred John Tregoweth, whose family grave here includes a separate headstone for him, is said to haunt an area of Waterfall Gully close to the chalet that was once a kiosk and tearooms. In the hot December of 1929, a fire broke out in the gully and a carload of police arrived to lend a hand. Constable Tregoweth and a colleague were on the steep hillside above the chalet beating out flames in the long grass. When the fire crept up behind them,

Tregoweth lost his footing and tumbled down the sheer slope, sustaining injuries and fatal burns.

Thomas Tregowth had survived service in the First World War in France; survived, too, being captured by the Germans and his twenty months as a prisoner of war. On his return from Europe he had joined the police force, only to lose his life in the Adelaide Hills. He left a wife and infant son.

Over the years there have been many sightings in Waterfall Gully of a young man dressed in the blue police uniform of the era. Almost all the reported encounters specify the colour blue, and he is thought to be a helpful ghost. Tom Tregoweth died, like Francis Cluney, in the line of duty, and here they lie not ten yards apart. In life the two were very different men, though both had been soldiers; in death it seems their spirits share the same restlessness.

⚜

Before the upper gallery was added to the Adelaide Arcade, each of the ground-floor shops had a staircase that led to the rooms above. Some of the rooms were used as workshops; others were apartments for the proprietors. Bridget Lauretta Byron Kennedy, known as the clairvoyant 'Madame Kennedy', lived and worked at Shop 11 with her husband, 'Professor' Kennedy. The pair advertised as 'intuitive palmists, phrenologists and clairvoyants'. The story of the mother and child who are said to haunt the arcade probably begins at the moment when the Professor left his wife and went off with a woman named Ada Brown, otherwise known as 'Madame Cleira', a practitioner of the arts of both palmistry and abortion.

'The palmistry was only a blind for the other,' Madame Kennedy bitterly insisted.

When her husband left he took with him their only child, Sidney, a bright and robust little boy of about three. Madame Kennedy pined for Siddy and paid a detective to find out where he had gone. She placed advertisements in interstate newspapers, until at last it was established that the father and son were in

Tasmania. Just before the Christmas of 1901 Bridget Kennedy travelled to Tasmania, found her child and brought him back with her to Adelaide. Unfortunately her troubles brought on bouts of insomnia, which led to the use of drink and drugs. By January of 1902, Madame Kennedy was in a state of depression.

On the evening of Friday 10 January she asked Jeannie Barrett, a girl of thirteen who worked as Sidney's nursemaid, to copy out something she had written onto a fresh sheet of writing paper. Jeannie first of all copied what Bridget Kennedy had written onto a piece of cardboard, and then onto the notepaper. What she wrote looked suspiciously like a suicide note.

Tired of life; heart broken; husband in Tasmania, with long Ada Brown, called Madame Cleria, aboichest, by trade. Let my baby and myself go to the students to the hospital. Has been connected with Mrs. Brown for about two years. Anything I have left will go to my friend Mrs. William Clarke, Mirtna, Charters Tower, insurance money, or any money I have left.

Jeannie did not understand the word 'aboichest' and asked Bridget Kennedy what it meant. Later she would report that Mrs Kennedy had said it meant abortionist. That night, with baby Sidney asleep on the dining-room floor, Bridget sent Jeannie out to buy a bottle of champagne. Then she asked the girl to bring pillows and blankets and make up a bed for her beside the baby. Jeannie did all of this, and when she left she took the piece of cardboard with her and gave it to her mother.

On Saturday morning at a few minutes before seven o'clock, Elizabeth Marshall who had worked off and on as a cleaner for Bridget, arrived at the arcade and let herself into the apartment. She at once noticed an overpowering smell of gas, and after rousing Bridget from sleep, asked if she could open the windows. Bridget agreed, and asked Elizabeth if she would turn off the gas jet on the wall, which was 'on just a glimmer'. Afterwards Elizabeth helped Bridget to her room, and then she went downstairs to the shop, where she scrubbed out two rooms. In need of a duster, Elizabeth

Marshall returned to the dining room where she had seen one covering the birdcage. On removing the cloth she found that the bird was hanging on the side of its water bowl, dead. She took the birdcage to Bridget Kennedy, who showed little reaction. A few minutes later Jeannie Barrett arrived, and Elizabeth heard the girl cry out that she could not wake Siddie, that he was not breathing.

'Don't say that!' Mrs Marshall exclaimed. But the panic in Jeannie's voice sent her running back into the dining room, where she turned the sleeping child over and found that his little hands were cold.

'Madame, your child is dead,' she told Bridget.

'Is he?' Bridget answered quietly.

Dr Hines was called. Although Bridget smelled strongly of gas, he noticed a telltale odour of alcohol and chlorodyne on her breath. Bridget Kennedy was in a state of collapse. It would be reported in the newspaper that she was dazed by drugs and gas, and the coroner, William Ramsay Smith, would take a dim view, claiming that nobody had forced the drugs down her throat and that it did not prevent her being responsible for her son's death. Bridget told the doctor she did not know how her boy had died; she did not know what was done the previous night. She added that she had taken half a bottle of chlorodyne, though the normal dose was from ten to thirty drops. Doctor Hines gave his opinion that Sidney Kennedy Byron met his death by coal gas poisoning. Bridget Kennedy was taken to the City Watch House 'for her own safety'.

⚜

In Victorian and Edwardian England, spiritualism, clairvoyance, palmistry and other esoteric arts reached a peak. From tarot cards to table-rapping, people were avid to be in touch with loved ones who had died. With emigration itself a kind of death, in South Australia, and far flung places like it, where communications were agonisingly slow (Mary Thomas, for instance, wrote many letters from Adelaide to her brother George, and it was only when a prolonged silence ensued from his side that she began to suspect he had died) people yearned for one last word with those who had expired in their absence.

Séances were also an opportunity for women to achieve a degree of power and influence that rarely came their way in the normal course of life, for although powerless in most other respects, they were reckoned to be more spiritual than men and were therefore in greater demand as mediums. For a woman without means, the role of the medium was one of the few jobs she could take up, and it was a job for life. Those with a talent for sensing what people wanted to hear could make a comfortable living – if a clairvoyant like Madame Kennedy could afford a charwoman and a nursemaid and premises in the Adelaide Arcade, I am surprised that Caroline Carleton didn't think of it; it would probably have brought in more than school-teaching and certainly more than selling her book of poems.

Queen Victoria and Prince Albert took part in spiritualist séances, and in 1846 the clairvoyant Georgiana Eagle performed before the Queen at Osborne House on the Isle of Wight. As the daughter of a renowned magician ('The Wizard of the South') Georgiana had learned magic from her father then mixed in hypnotism and her own brand of spiritualism. She performed mind-reading tricks and promoted herself as clairvoyant. Around the time Georgiana demonstrated her powers before Queen Victoria, she was performing as 'The Mysterious Lady' and 'The Celebrated Enchantress'. She must have read the Royal mind to the Queen's satisfaction, because she was presented with a gold watch to commemorate the Royal pleasure. *Presented by Her Majesty to Miss Georgiana Eagle for her Meritorious and Extraordinary Clairvoyance Produced at Osborn House, Isle of Wight, July 17, 1846.*

Ghosts and the spirit world became part and parcel of the Victorian experience of death. No contradiction existed between their belief in ghosts and their religious beliefs. In an era when mysterious advances in photography, telegraph, and telephone communications worked by unseen means, contact with those beyond the grave could seem like just another scientific endeavour.

Sir Arthur Conan Doyle was an influential advocate, writing two volumes on the subject, including a history of spiritualism. More pragmatic literary figures, like Robert Browning and George Eliot, took against the spiritualist movement, with Eliot declaring it the most 'painful form of the lowest charlatanrie'. But popular demand for ghost stories was strong, and clairvoyants, if they were not caught out as frauds, continued to flourish.

In her role as 'Madame Kennedy' Bridget Kennedy practised palmistry, or cheiromancy, a predictive art with roots that reach back a long way. Antique palm-reading charts show lines for every conceivable condition, from injury in a duel, to incest, and death through melancholy.

Perhaps the most famous palmist who carried the art forward into the twentieth century was a man born outside Dublin and baptised William John Warner. Having reinvented himself as Count Louis Hamon, Warner is said to have travelled to India where a Brahmin guru allowed him to study an ancient book on hands, a book with pages made of human skin. After two years he returned to London and launched a career as 'Cheiro the Palmist'.

He read the hands of the rich and famous, people like Mark Twain, Mata Hari and Oscar Wilde. Later he moved to America, where his final years were spent in Hollywood seeing as many as twenty clients a day. He even did some screenwriting. When he died in 1936 his widow the Countess Lena Hamon said her husband had predicted his own death to the hour. *Time* magazine reported that Cheiro had amassed $250,000 from rich female clients, and that on the night he died the clock outside his room struck the hour of one, 'thrice'. Another admittedly unsubstantiated report mentions a charge of mishandling a client's money and a subsequent term in jail. On his release, both money and friends deserted him.

I am inclined to side with George Eliot but, then again, which of us hasn't swirled our tea leaves in a cup and studied the pattern, or turned the pages of a magazine to find our horoscope? Years ago a friend encouraged me to visit a palm reader by the name of Mary Love, who told me that I would have great success as a writer if only

I would change my name to one beginning with the letter A. She showed me that I had a perfect letter A in the palm of each hand. So one afternoon I went with my mother, who was not against the change, to West Brighton Cemetery to choose a suitable name. Annie, we found on every second or third tombstone, and as it could legitimately be made out of my middle name I began to brace myself for the tedious business of changing every last deed and document, every plastic card: I would be Annie Lefevre. And then it was pointed out by someone with a clearer eye that almost everyone can find the letter 'A' in the lines of their hands. I inspected palms, even asked strangers if I could look. It was a disappointment, for I had begun to quite hanker after Annie. But even if I could have got over being duped, in the end I could not be bothered with the paperwork.

⚜

When Bridget Kennedy appeared in the Adelaide Police Court the gallery was packed with spectators. The charge was read, words to the effect that on or about 11 January 1902 she 'did feloniously, willfully, and of malice afore thought, kill and murder one Sidney Kennedy Byron'. Madame Kennedy was exceedingly pale, though 'daintily attired in light jacket, white gem hat, and dark veil'. The Professor had arrived from Melbourne and visited her in the Adelaide Gaol; he sat in the front row of the court and paid close attention. The details of the case were combed through, but in the end the case against Madame Kennedy was dismissed since it could not be proved that she rather than the child had turned on the gas.

That August a woman was found dead in the West Parklands, and the Professor identified the body as that of Bridget. Bottles of caustic potash and prussic acid were found in her belongings, and poisoning by one or both of these substances was recorded as the cause of death.

The Professor continued to operate a business at Shop 11 in the Adelaide Arcade. I do not know whether Ada Brown came with him and continued to ply her trades.

Scarves of light press through the cloud as I cut north-east across the cemetery towards the Smyth Chapel; the Catholic Eastern Ground is just inside the gates that open onto Wylde Road. I am looking for Path 34, and it is marked by a tree with a sheltering canopy and a sturdy trunk. As I turn into it I see with resignation that there are many unmarked graves in this area. The ground is covered with dried leaves and seed pods. I make a rough count of the plots, expecting that once again I will have to consult the names on the map to pinpoint the spot. But then, there it is along on the left, a simple headstone, child-sized. There was once a low iron railing around the narrow plot, and the rails are still in place, though one has come loose from its posts.

In Loving Memory of Sydney Kennedy Byron, who died 10th of January 1902, aged 3 years.

It is the first time I have seen the child's name spelled with a y. I wonder which of his parents arranged for the headstone, and note that no trouble was taken to add Bridget's name even though it is obvious that space was left for it and the records show she was buried here seven months after her 'Siddy' died. Russet leaves cover them in a thick blanket. Close to the headstone, a single white artificial lily head has been planted in the earth; it has probably been blown here from somewhere else, but the simplicity of it suits the spot, and I like to imagine that someone read this little ghost's story and chose to leave it for him.

The sky is breaking up as I walk back along the path. Clouds like old men's bearded faces gather, and the outermost leaves of the trees flash like tiny mirrors in the strange pale light.

⚜

The last of the trio of ghosts who haunt the Adelaide Arcade is a young woman who both in age and the nature of her demise reminds me of Lizzie Lines. Florence Lovell and Thomas Horton were married on 5 November 1903. Thomas had three children from a previous marriage, his wife having died, and Florence had an illegitimate daughter. Thomas was said to be madly jealous of the father of Florence's child, believing that she and he were still on 'affectionate terms'. There seems to be no record of the child's father, or any mention of why he and Florence did not marry: the most likely scenario is that the man already had a wife.

The Hortons lived in McLaren Street, Adelaide, but after only four months Florence returned to her mother in Rundle Street, Kent Town. Thomas also went to live with his mother in Brompton, and it must be assumed it was so that she could take care of his children.

Thomas Horton was a bootmaker by trade although he was better known as 'Anglo the Juggler and Equilibrist', a role he had performed at the Tivoli Theatre. His background was a tough one; his father had died at the Parkside Lunatic Asylum and his mother been detained there. None of which excuses his treatment of Florence, but perhaps puts it into the context of his upbringing and experience.

On Saturday evenings in Adelaide, Rundle Street was the place where young men and women went for a night out. They would parade up and down for a couple of hours, meeting friends, indulging in gossip, flirting and courting. On the night of 27 February 1904, the first bout of excitement occurred when a fire broke out at the rear of the Bijou Hotel. The brigade was called and a crowd soon gathered to watch them put it out. Almost at once, three shots rang out in quick succession from the vicinity of the Adelaide Arcade and the crowd immediately hurried in that direction. Word flew quickly from mouth to mouth, that a man had shot his wife.

※

At around eight o'clock on that Saturday night, Florence Horton, with her friends Bella Smith and Nellie Linnett, came into the city and walked up and down Rundle Street. Thomas Horton approached the trio a number of times, and William Sellick, who knew the girls well, beckoned to them to come away. It was reported in the *Advertiser* that Sellick had noticed a gun in Horton's pocket and seen his hand on it. If this were true it would seem culpable not to have warned the girls, or at least called the police, for it was also reported that William Sellick was aware that Horton had threatened his wife. Although scenting trouble, he left to meet some friends at the railway station, and when later informed of the murder Sellick said he was not surprised. If this is indeed what happened, the only explanation I can think of is that Sellick was himself afraid of Horton, and when he saw the gun he quit Rundle Street as fast as he could.

Horton had bought the revolver earlier the same evening from Alexander Bernstein, manager of the Australian Hardware Combine in Hindley Street. It is hard to believe that a man could go out on a Saturday night and buy a gun and a hundred cartridges, but that is what Horton did. Bernstein thought afterwards that he had wrapped up the cartridges; he had never seen Horton before he came to the shop.

In the street, Thomas asked his wife to go with him up the little dark lane beside the arcade. First of all he said he had a present for her. Then he told her he wanted to 'settle the business of parting altogether'. When Florence declined to accompany him, and the girls turned away towards King William Street, Horton appealed to one of her friends.

'Nellie, coax her, won't you?'

He was about a yard behind them when he fired three times at Florence's back. Nellie Linnett, hearing the shots, cried out. 'Thomas Horton has done it!'

Sergeant Robert Hill was near the end of the arcade that night and heard the shots and saw the smoke. He rushed across as Florence walked to the footpath, and she collapsed into his arms. He asked Bella Smith what the matter was, and she told him Horton had shot his wife. Hill laid Florence on the pavement, blew his whistle, and sent a constable to fetch Dr Verco.

Meanwhile, Thomas Horton had run away up Charles Street, and although a few people set off in pursuit, who could blame them if their legs did not carry them as fast as they might have, for Thomas Horton still had the gun.

Florence Horton was carried into Mr Solomon's tobacconist's shop in the Adelaide Arcade, where she died. Doctor J.C. Verco arrived and pronounced life extinct. The murdered woman had often complained to her friends of Thomas's treatment of her. She said that he had previously threatened to shoot her, to blind her, and to throw her into the Torrens. So convinced was she that she would be murdered by her husband, that Florence had gone so far as to write a letter and place it in the care of Nellie Linnett.

{Horton} has threatened me to my face, and my sister, my several friends, who if necessary will gladly appear if anything happens to me. This letter is for the protection of myself and others, who he said he would blame for {my death}. It will be by no other than Mr. Thomas Horton, false name Anglo, the juggler, Chief-street, Brompton, late McLaren-street off Regent Street, Adelaide. This letter will be produced on sudden death. Others will not suffer for him . . . He held me down with a knife, but I got away from him. Then he said he would give me an overdose of ether, and go for the police, and swear he found me like it. I hope if anything does happen, and you read this letter, that you won't bring it in that I am in an unsound mind. Everything I have written is true, and I know what I am doing. I am getting two witnesses to sign this letter as soon as I have written it, and will leave it in the possession of Miss Nellie Linnert, O'Halloran-street off Gilbert-street, Adelaide. The murderer will be Mr. Thomas Horton, juggler, at present living in McLaren, otherwise Mr. Anglo, off Regent-street, Adelaide. Witnesses – I am, believe me, Mrs. T.F. Horton. In sound mind. 2/2/1904

On 29 February, Mounted Constable Henry Schumann arrested Horton between Bridgewater and Ambleside. He was still armed, with five bullets in the chambers of the revolver and ninety-two spares: the three bullets he had fired at Florence made up the 100 he had bought from Bernstein.

The inquest into Florence's death was held at the Elephant and Castle Hotel. Dr William Ramsay Smith presided. In summing up, Smith said the jury's task was a hard one, as they had to decide between murder and manslaughter. Allowing that Horton was jealous of his wife, of which there was ample evidence, how far did the law excuse a man for an act arising out of that jealousy? After a short retirement the jury returned the verdict that Florence Horton had met her death by a pistol shot wilfully inflicted by her husband Thomas Horton. As Ramsay Smith said, it was, in legal language, a finding of wilful murder.

Horton was tried and sentenced to death. He was hung at nine o'clock on the morning of 12 May 1904. He was said to be pale, and who would not be, yet he walked to the gallows inside the New Building with remarkable steadiness, never glancing round, keeping his face turned towards the opposite window 'which opened into a sun-bathed world'.

Thomas Horton is buried between the walls at the Old Adelaide Gaol. The site of his grave is marked with the number 14, as he was the fourteenth person to be hung after graves began to be marked, and the first to be hung after Federation. *T.H.* and his date of death are painted in plain black letters on the red-brick wall.

Florence Horton was an unhappy woman, and Thomas Horton was a desperate man who carried out a desperate deed. They have been included on this walk because of Florence's reputed restlessness, which is said to include appearances in the Adelaide Arcade. But it is obvious that Thomas, too, was a tortured soul whose only glimpse of a sunbathed world came at the last when it was far too late. So it would not surprise me, if I believed in ghosts, to hear that he haunts the desolate strip of turf at Old Adelaide Gaol where, beneath a ribbon of sky, the bones of murderers are held captive between the walls.

Florence Eugenia Horton's address is Road 1 South, Path 19. The map shows that she was buried in Plot 17 on the western side. There is no marker on her grave – perhaps there never was one, and this is why she remains a restless spirit.

12

Nature Walk
No. 2

The affinity between medicine and botany has existed since ancient times, and many notable physicians have been avid naturalists. Dioscorides, the Greek author of the five-volume pharmacopeia *De Materia Medica*, was a physician, pharmacologist, and botanist whose work was widely read for more than 1500 years. In England there was the botanist, herbalist, astrologer, and physician, Nicholas Culpeper, and in the early days of the colony of South Australia quite a number of men actively pursued these dual interests.

William Wyatt had trained in Plymouth as a surgeon. Hindmarsh had appointed him first colonial naturalist in 1837, and he'd had ambitions to become keeper of the gardens, but somehow subsequent governors passed over him for the position and instead he became Inspector of Schools. However, the breadth of Wyatt's activities ensured that he kept many irons in the fire. By the mid-nineteenth century, William Wyatt was a prominent member of a great number of committees: in 1864, along with George Mayo, Thomas Elder and others, he was appointed to look into the state of the Lunatic Asylum; in 1867 he was on the board of the Adelaide Hospital. Eventually, through the Agricultural and Horticultural Society, he would become a governor of the Botanic Garden. He also established a significant garden of his own at the property he named Kurralta.

Whenever he was not at a meeting he would have been at the Adelaide Club, the insignia of which is thought to have been designed by his son, Willie. All this activity must have kept him much from home, and in photographs his wife Julia appears some-what pensive, even surly. Homesickness and loneliness must have played their part, and like so many women of her time Julia suffered the deaths of her infant children.

Julia had been at school in France and as a result was bilingual. She wrote melancholic poetry, and published *The Souvenir*, a book of essays, poetry, and translations, though how these activities fitted with life in the young, struggling colony is difficult to judge. A comment from one of her contemporaries suggests that she was not the greatest housekeeper, and there are strong hints that the Wyatts' marriage was not happy. But as a couple their greatest grief concerned their children. They lost a son while still in England, and then infant twins; in 1849 their seven-year-old son, Charles, died, and only Willie, born in 1838, survived to reach adulthood. Willie seems to have shared his mother's talent for art and languages, and some of his sketches, paintings and etchings still survive. He was a member of George Goyder's survey expedition of 1870, but although he held a government position for a time he later spent many years without settled employment, which surely displeased his industrious father.

On 28 December 1872, Willie went to a cottage in the grounds of Kurralta, ostensibly to speak to James Slape who gardened for his father. Slape's wife, Catherine, was there and warned Willie that her husband had been drinking; she later testified that she begged him to leave. Slape appeared and ordered Willie Wyatt out of the cottage. When he refused to go, Slape left the room and returned with a mattock. Catherine Slape saw her husband raise the weapon above Wyatt's head. She did not stay to watch it descend, but ran to a neighbour. On their return, Willie was found lying dead in a pool of his own blood.

Frederick George Waterhouse was living close by. At the inquest, he testified that he went with James Young to Slape's cottage and saw Willie Wyatt lying on the floor with his head in a pool of blood.

'Good God, Slape, what have you done?' said Waterhouse.

Slape was standing at the dead man's feet and seemed unmoved; Waterhouse said he looked sober at the time, and that he 'exclaimed in an idiotic tone: "I am afraid I hit him too hard."'

When arrested and charged with wilful murder, Slape said he had not meant to harm Wyatt.

'But he is as bad as I am. He should not have lost his self-respect.'

⚜

Bulbs push up in the pathways, escaped, over time, from the old graves. There are scented jonquils and hyacinths, and the drought-resistant *Scilla peruviana* with its strappy leaves and heads of starry blue or white flowers. Birds, too, are everywhere. Down in the Jewish Section crows glide from the treetops to stalk about on the lush grass. They have laid claim to this area between the old Jewish graves and the Linger memorial – at the height of summer they are the dusty black of old top hats, but in winter their blue-black feathers are burnished to a wicked sheen. Elsewhere there are parrots, and cockatoos circle noisily against the clear cobalt Adelaide sky. I am told that there are foxes here with lairs that radiate out into the adjacent suburbs, and I imagine them as the night-watch patrol of these paths, their cubs learning to hunt among the headstones.

What provoked James Slape's murderous rage was never spelled out, but it is impossible not to suspect Slape's wife and Willie of some form of entanglement. The scene in the cottage when Frederick Waterhouse arrived would have been gruesome in its brutality, although, as it turned out, he was the kind of stoic character who could take it in his stride.

Frederick George Waterhouse, though not a physician, was one of South Australia's foremost naturalists. He had worked at the British Museum with his elder brother George, an eminent entomologist and zoologist, when in July 1852 he married Fanny Shepherd Abbott and sailed for South Australia. After an unsuccessful stint on the Victorian goldfields, Waterhouse took employment with C.T. Hargrave surveying the Mount Lofty Ranges.

He was ordered by the government to accompany John McDouall Stuart on his 1861–1862 expedition from Adelaide to the north coast, and he returned from this gruelling trip with many bird, mammal, insect, and plant specimens, including the rare Princess Alexandra Parrot, *Polytelis alexandrae*. It was a punishing journey for both humans and animals. Many of the party's horses had to be abandoned on the return leg, and Stuart, suffering with scurvy and nearly blind, was carried on a stretcher, though he recovered sufficiently to ride the last few miles. Somehow Waterhouse came through all of this unscathed, though one wonders how Fanny felt about his year-long absence.

As curator of the South Australian Museum, Frederick George Waterhouse is credited with building up its early collections. He died on 7 September 1898 at the age of eighty-three, and was buried at St George's cemetery in Magill. But Fanny had died in 1875, and she is buried here with two of their sons, Frederick Edward, and Edward George.

Fanny Waterhouse's address is Road 3, Path 15; Plot 27 is on the eastern side of the path. After turning in, I pass the obelisk that marks the grave of the explorer William Patrick Auld, with its verse adapted from Isaiah 33:17: *Thine eyes shall behold the land that is very far off.* Auld had been a member of the John McDouall Stuart cross-continental expedition with Waterhouse; Stuart and Waterhouse were the same age, but Auld was twenty-five years younger and lived on into the twentieth century. His memorial here was erected by the Royal Geographical Society of Australasia 'in admiration of his pluck, endurance and loyalty to John McDouall Stuart'. Pondering the fact that 'pluck' is a word rarely used these days, I navigate past a large tomb that straddles the path, and Fanny Waterhouse is a little further along on the left. The simple headstone is intact and readable; the plot surrounded by a low iron fence. Fanny rests here with none of the fanfare accorded to Auld, for of course her part in that memorable expedition was only to sit at home and wait.

A palm trunk throws a finger of shade across the path like the blade of shadow on a giant sundial. But hours pass like minutes as I dawdle along, reading names, taking notes, gathering clues to stories. There is a sense that time, if not actually suspended, stretches out in certain places under certain conditions, and it stretches out here.

Joseph Cooke Verco, physician and naturalist, was born at Fullarton in 1851, the sixth child of James Crabb Verco and his wife Anne, both from Cornwall. Joseph became one of Adelaide's leading physicians, and in 1885 with Edward Stirling he founded the University of Adelaide's Medical School. Along the way he acquired the nickname 'Holy Joe' for his devotion to the Church of Christ and possibly for the hymns and religious poetry he had a fondness for writing.

As a child, Joseph Verco had built a museum of shells in his back garden. As an adult, dredging in the Great Australian Bight yielded valuable marine specimens, and his extensive collection of shells was eventually presented to the South Australian Museum. After his retirement, Verco spent much time at the museum as honorary conchologist.

His address is Road 3, Path 10; Plot 4 is on the eastern side. I would have liked it to be decorated with a carved stone shell, but the headstone – now laid flat on the ground – marks a family grave that includes Verco's parents, and it is remarkably plain.

⚜

Richard Sanders Rogers was another medical man who became an important figure in the field of natural history. After winning a scholarship to the University of Adelaide he qualified in medicine, botany, and history, and around 1893 developed an interest in hypnotism. Described as having 'fine brown piercing eyes and a hypnotist's gentle voice', in a medical first for South Australia he performed an operation as both surgeon and hypnotist, removing a cyst from the breast of a young women while she remained awake; the patient is said to have survived into old age.

By 1905, Rogers had begun to study orchids, and he soon became passionately engrossed. There were field trips to New Zealand, Tasmania, Papua New Guinea, Western Australia, and Kangaroo Island, and his wife Jean Scott Rogers accompanied him on many of these orchid-hunting expeditions. *Pterostylis rogersii* E. Coleman and *Prasophyllum rogersii* are named after him.

A modest and companionable man, Richard Sanders Rogers' advice to enthusiasts was to 'study orchids carefully and you will soon acquire the orchid eye. Once that has happened the orchid fever follows, which is the least painful of all known fevers'.

For three decades, Rogers collaborated with Rosa Catherine Fiveash. Rosa was said to be so meticulous that she would wait weeks for one of his rare orchid buds to open. His address is Road 1 South, Path 26; Plot 46, humble in scale for a man with such an illustrious career, is on the eastern side.

⚜

The postscript to Willie Wyatt's story is that on James Slape's removal to Adelaide Gaol he took his own life by unpicking the rope from his canvas camp bed and using it to hang himself, thus saving the gaol's hangman Benjamin Ellis the task. This meant that he was not buried at the gaol, and his address is Road 1 North, Path 33; Plot 22B1 is on the eastern side of the path, but no headstone marks Slape's last resting place.

By contrast, William, Julia, and Willie Wyatt have an impressive white marble tomb on Road 2 South, Path 21; Plot 12 is on the eastern side, but it straddles the path and is clearly visible from the roadway. Young Charles Wyatt is also buried here.

Julia Wyatt always referred to her son's murder as 'Willie's accident', but her sorrow remained sharp. William at least had his work and other interests, and with no heirs for his considerable fortune he made himself busy setting up a philanthropic trust, which still operates today. Julia was close to at least two of Boyle Travers Finniss's children – their third child, Julia Howard Finniss, was her goddaughter and may have been named for her. In 1880 she gave Willie's desk to Finniss's fourth child, William Charles Maxwell Finniss, saying she was unable to bear looking over its contents. William Finniss became the executor of Julia's will, and at her death she left £500 each to him and his sister.

⚜

There is another grave at West Terrace Cemetery with a strong link to Julia Wyatt. It belongs to George Hamilton, a man of many interests and talents who published several self-illustrated books. One of them, *Experiences of a colonist forty years ago: a journey from Port Phillip to South Australia in 1839, and a voyage from Port Phillip to Adelaide in 1846 by an old hand*, contains a thrilling account of Hamilton's stormy passage to Adelaide aboard a ship without anchors. At different times he was a clerk in the Treasury, and South Australia's commissioner of police. As adviser to a parliamentary committee on sparrows, which farmers saw as a curse, he advocated a bounty on the birds and their eggs. As well as reducing their numbers, he believed that sparrow hunting would be a useful outlet for the 'larrikin instinct' of boys. From his writings it is clear that Hamilton was a congenial companion, and his frequent visits to Kurralta led to rumours that Willie Wyatt closely resembled him in looks and mannerisms. Whatever the truth, there is no doubt that George Hamilton and Julia were close and shared many interests and that towards the end of the winter of 1883 he died at Kurralta. His estate, valued at £6500, was left to Julia Wyatt.

Almost a year later, with her husband still alive, Julia wrote to William Finniss and asked him to make arrangements about a grave. From her description of the granite monument, it is almost certainly that of her friend, George Hamilton.

His address is Road 4, Path 29; Plot 31 is on the eastern side. Within its broken iron railings, the imposing grey granite obelisk is discreetly decorated with delicate inlay, and simply inscribed with Hamilton's name and his dates of birth and death. But there is a stature to it, and a loving attention to detail that is, perhaps, not quite what one would expect to find on the grave of a bachelor, ex-police commissioner.

⚜

I leave George Hamilton and walk as far as the western boundary where pepper trees screen the trains. Looking back across a landscape dominated by tall thin palms, the living city almost disappears. When the wind blows down here it sets off the dry, rasping voices of the palm fronds. There are olive trees, too, and the cemetery harvests them and produces a small quantity of olive oil. Around the baby memorial, where the ground is lumpy with unmarked graves, the wind sighs sweetly through the tamarisk trees with the soft, lulling sound of the sea.

13

Above the World so High

In
AUGU
MY
Bo
D

I would I were in cloud-land
Borne on some feath'ry wreath,
Illimitable space above,
And the dancing wave beneath
'Summer Evening Reveries'
— Caroline Carleton, 1860

On Tuesday 5 December 1871, Thomas Gale, aeronaut, appeared in the Adelaide Police Court before Police Magistrate Samuel Beddome; he was charged with being in unlawful possession of a balloon. Among cases of disorderly behaviour, insult and idleness, the unique nature of the offence must have lightened Mr Beddome's morning.

Gale, an American, had arrived earlier that year from Melbourne, and his ballooning exploits had captured public attention. His first South Australian ascent in a hot air balloon was to take place from the Exhibition Building grounds, north parklands. A crowd of up to 20,000 turned out to watch, but disappointingly the event was postponed due to difficulties with inflating the balloon. The next attempt on 24 June was successful. The balloon was inflated in the cattle yards, North Terrace, and once again many thousands of spectators turned out. Gale took one passenger with him, who left a delightful bird's-eye-view account of the city of Adelaide.

They had to heave out their last bags of ballast in order to clear the cattle pens, but as soon as that was done the balloon rapidly ascended, the cheers of the crowd growing fainter as they floated away. Once the rather thick and reddish clouds cleared, he and his passenger were able to look about:

. . . *the whole country lay beneath us like a map, and Adelaide looked a perfect square, or like a well-laid-out kitchen garden. The buildings everywhere appeared to resemble dolls' houses.*

The Post-Office and the Town Hall did not seem to be six feet high.
We could see the train running, but it was more like a child's toy.

This writer's first account of flying expresses his wonder and pleasure, and it reminds us – jaded veterans of intercontinental air travel – that the experience of looking down upon a familiar place was once a novelty worth risking life and limb for. Speaking for myself, the pleasure of seeing trains reduced to playthings and buildings to dolls' houses, or even better, the patterns and colours of the landscape, has never really diminished.

On that flight, Thomas Gale's balloon was swept towards the Hills, which were covered in thick rain clouds. Gale's passenger was busy noticing the landmarks:

We saw the different houses and gardens and roads, and standing out conspicuously amongst them all we could see the Magill Orphanage and Mr. Skelton's residence.

They did not know how high they were or whether they had enough altitude to clear the ranges. With the timbered slopes and gullies a hazard, Thomas Gale made the decision to take the balloon down, and as soon as he opened the valve it quickly began to descend. 'You must obey orders, and do exactly what I tell you,' he shouted to his passenger. 'When we approach the land you must hang on to the hoop of the balloon, not catch hold of the ropes.' Advice his passenger appreciated, writing:

the object and value of this advice became very apparent when we got down. We should probably have been greatly injured if not smashed to pieces if we had held on any other way.

They shaved a large gum tree, but came to rest unhurt. Mr Alford of the Glynde Hotel drove out and picked them up. They had taken with them three aneroid barometers, three thermometers, and one azimuth compass, all of which were lent by Mr Sawtell, of Rundle Street. The readings had changed almost as fast as they could write them down, but the instruments showed that they had ascended to around 4600 feet above sea level, or as high again as Mount Lofty.

Gale's second ascent was made on Saturday 8 July, and as before several thousand people came to watch and cheer. The tethered balloon gave a lift to some of the spectators, taking one or two up at a time to a height as far as the 200-foot tether would allow. One of those brave enough to go 'up above the world so high' was a young woman, Lavinia Balfort of Parkside. As well as earning the honour of being the first woman in South Australia to ascend in a balloon, on 23 December 1871, at St Augustine's Church in Unley, Lavinia would also become Thomas Gale's wife.

⚜

Accounts of Gale's life list varying middle names; in the newspapers he was Thomas Friend Gale, but Freen is the name engraved on his headstone. His adventures were often hair-raising and there were many narrow escapes. Up until he died Gale was said to be always working out a scheme for a new balloon ascent. He was, by all accounts, a passionate aeronaut. Thomas Gale died at his home in Arthur Street, Parkside, at the age of forty-six.

His address is now Road 5, Path 1A. Turning left at the curator's cottage, I walk towards the maintenance sheds where Road 5 begins close to the small Islamic section. On Path 1A, Plot 13 is on the western side.

A second stone has been laid on the site by Gale's grandson, John Loader. It features a balloon and a pony, and tells how Thomas Gale, with his pony on board, ascended over Sydney Heads, and that he later died from injuries sustained during the flight. It makes no mention of the pony's fate.

As for the case of unlawful possession of a balloon, the complaint was brought by Mr Aldridge, proprietor of the Prince Alfred Hotel. There had been complications concerning the sale and repair of the balloon. When arrested, Gale insisted Aldridge was a swindler, that the balloon was his and he would keep it; he spent a night in the lock up. After listening through the ins and outs of the case, the police magistrate dismissed the charges.

14

Night Walk

With what a tender, loving light
The parting sunbeams greet the graves!
While quiv'ring in the breath of eve
The silver wattle gently waves.
'Fragmentary Lines Written in the Cemetery'
– Caroline Carleton, 1860

Twilight gathers up the day in a process as fleeting as it is mysterious. Caroline Carleton knew it well, and although her years here were shadowed by difficulties, the part of her that belonged to poetry found solace in these elusive yet definite stages between daylight and dark. Back then the grounds were wilder and there were fewer trees and headstones – beauty of a different order, yet the same bewitching transition.

As the sun slips from view the treetops thicken; the day's last light gathers below the horizon and floods the western sky. With its stirabout of clouds, the sky is now at its most brilliant, but while it rapidly fades, the broad field of headstones continues to hold the light even when there is almost no light left to hold. The pale statuary and its persistence puts me in mind of a white garden, the way white flowers grow more luminous on the cusp of night.

I have come to walk here on one of the evenings in the year when the cemetery gates are open to the public after sundown. As night draws in the birds fall silent, but for the first time I hear crickets creaking out their songs from hidey-holes among the gravestones. The traffic noise is more intrusive than during the day, as if the sound has somehow been turned up as the picture dims. It is Friday night, and some people will be going out to play, while others head for home, and here, in the company of those with no choice but to bide, the freedom to come and go, the ordinariness of it, strikes me as something not to be taken for granted.

By six o'clock the pockets of darkness beneath the trees have deepened; over all there is an immense stillness. As the landscape gradually subsides into dusk I have the strangest sensation that what light remains is clouded by fine sediment, and that it is settling around the bases of the headstones, around me. I am filled with a wistful desire to see Adelaide as it was when it was first settled – before streetlights or running water, before cars, before poker machines and video games, before the Internet. Along the western boundary, lights from the living world gleam between the pepper trees. A siren starts up close by, its wail raw and urgent, but the alarm it signals, the need to rush towards a crisis, has no meaning within these boundary walls.

More than ever the cemetery resembles a giant white garden, with its flower-like statuary hugging the light while all else sinks from view. Stars appear and the city spills its light upwards. Wormwood releases a dusty pungent odour. A red traffic arrow burns near the entrance, while headlights from the cars queuing at the Sturt Street intersection, their left-turn blinkers, rudely flash against the headstone of Horatio Thomas Whittell and his wife Caroline.

⚜

Tonight I will visit people whose life stories collided with the darker side of Adelaide's history. There are many to choose from, but since the cemetery has had a long and close connection with the Old Adelaide Gaol, I am going to start with the gaol's first governor, William Baker Ashton. Then there is the man who had the worst job in the colony, the hangman, Benjamin Ellis.

In the uneasy relationship between cemetery and gaol, the cemetery has buried the victims of crime, while the gaol has dealt with the perpetrators. In reading of the deprivation and cruelty of prison life in the nineteenth century, I conclude that it must have felt like a living death and that actual death would have been preferable.

Utopia should have no need of a gaol, and at first there were no plans to build one. But early in the colony's history the need for a lock-up became almost as pressing as the need for a burial ground, with HMS *Buffalo* doing duty as a temporary prison. In 1837 the colonial secretary, Robert Gouger, ordered an Aboriginal man Black Aleck to be imprisoned on a barque belonging to the South Australian Company. David McLaren, the manager, complained in a letter that the company's ships were not suitable as gaols, the responsibility being too much for the officers and crew, as well as dangerous. He enclosed an invoice for Black Aleck's keep over 104 days, which came to a total of £26 14/ and included the costs of eighty yards of canvas damaged by the prisoner at 1/6 a yard, and of four broken padlocks.

When the *Buffalo* left South Australia, various temporary gaols were tried, including a tent in which prisoners had to be chained to logs. Later, there was a wooden hut known as the Stone Jug. As the winter of 1838 approached there was a shortage of blankets, and prisoners were supplied with horse rugs. Those sentenced to hard labour at that time were, for once, in luck, since there were no tools for them to labour with. Work on the gaol eventually got underway to George Strickland Kingston's design, which was based on England's Pentonville Prison. But costs soon overran the estimate, and with the colony almost bankrupt, Governor Gawler was recalled to England to give an accounting.

William Baker Ashton was appointed governor even before the gaol was built, with his early days spent presiding over the Stone Jug. An early portrait of Ashton shows a young man in the mould of Ned Kelly: his pale face is partially covered by a fierce black beard, a handlebar moustache, and framed by locks of thick dark hair. Later portraits present an almost cartoon-like character, with piggy eyes beneath a broad-brimmed squatter's hat, and a massively spreading stomach. The gaol, colloquially known as Ashton's Hotel, was still incomplete in 1841 when it took in its first prisoners.

Descriptions of prison life and Ashton's role in it veer from a punishing regime in which the governor complains about prisoners singing in the prison chapel, to his generosity in standing drinks and a meal to condemned men on the night before they were hanged. Whether of good or bad character, there is no doubt that Ashton was colourful, and he ended his reign in typically unpredictable style. When he was discovered after dying suddenly in his office on the top floor, rigor mortis made it impossible for his sizeable body to pass down the narrow stairs, so he was unceremoniously lowered through the window. Some say that this undignified exit is the reason he continues to haunt the gaol.

Ashton's wife Charlotte worked alongside him as matron, a position that was initially unpaid. She gave birth to at least three children during her time there, and one of their sons, Albert Gawler Ashton, who was born in the gaol in February 1841, lived to be more than a hundred years old.

I walk west down Road 1 to where the big three-trunked pine stands like a giant candelabra. There are the silhouettes of urns and obelisks and angels, and patterns of ironwork are projected by the Sturt Street traffic in a flickering and continuous shadow show. The mighty obelisk of Julius Carl Habich – once the proprietor of a bakery business in Flinders Street – and Annie, *wife of the above*, is lit. Aeroplane lights pass overhead, and cars crossing in front of other cars set up a disco-like flicker. Treetops mass into the shapes of whales, and whaling boats; the slender cypresses stand like watchtowers.

William Baker Ashton's address is Road 1 South, Path 25; Plot 11 is on the eastern side. The grave is covered with a slab of black marble bearing his name, and the dates 1803–1854.

⚜

Benjamin Ellis was born in London in about 1813 and by 1853 he was marrying Rebecca Edwards at Adelaide's Trinity Church; at that time his occupation was given as 'bookkeeper'. Later he became a park ranger and conservator of the River Torrens, employed by the Adelaide City Council. That job came with a cottage in the parklands. By 1868, Ellis was a dog catcher, his mission to round up and destroy any stray and unlicensed mutts. Ellis took to disposing of the animals under the footbridge to Botanic Park;

for a time this spot was known as Dead Dog Bridge. The smell alone must have drawn attention to his methods, and sure enough, visitors to the Botanic Garden complained and Ellis was asked to remove and bury the decomposing bodies. To add to his aggravation, the City Council refused to pay him for destroying dogs unless certification was provided that they had been dealt with according to regulations.

Ellis served a month in the Adelaide Gaol, perhaps his first contact with it. A report of the case appeared in the newspaper:

> *Benjamin Ellis, labourer, was charged by Caroline, wife of Thomas Gray of Palmerston, with imposing upon her on October 24, 1872 by representing that he was sent by the Corporation to register dogs, by which he obtained 5s. from the informant, defendant therefore deemed to be a rogue and vagabond. Defendant pleaded guilty, and was sentenced to one calendar month's imprisonment with hard labour.*

In the early 1870s Ellis applied for the job of hangman at the gaol. This gave him somewhere to live, and he had a room under the women's dormitory.

⚜

Ellis was the man who hanged Elisabeth Woolcock, the only woman to be hanged at the Adelaide Gaol. Woolcock died on 30 December 1873 on a portable gallows erected between the walls. It is said that when she walked to the scaffold wearing a white dress and carrying a posy of flowers, Ellis questioned, for the first time, whether he could carry out his hangman's duty.

Elisabeth's story is a shocking one, from its brutal beginning to its terrifying end. Although documented in old newspapers and other places, the best way to hear it is in Elisabeth's own words as she wrote them in her gaol cell for the Reverend Bickford.

> *Adelaide Jail, December 10, 1873. – The last Statement and Confession of Elisabeth Woolcock to Mr. Bickford. Sir i was born*

in the Burra mine in Provence of South Australia in the year
1847 my parents names were John and Elizabeth Oliver they
were Cornish they came to the Couloney in 1842 but they went
to Victoria in 1851 I was left without the care of a Mother at
the Age of 4 years and i never saw her again until i was 18 my
father died when i was nine years old and i had to get my living
until i was 18 and then i heard that my Mother was alive and
Residing at moonta mine she wrote me a letter asking me to come to
her as she had been very unhappy about me and she was very sorry
for what she had done I thought i should like to see my mother
and have a home like other young girls so I gave up my Situation
and came to Adelaide my mother and my stepfather received me
very kindly and i had a good home for 2 years my mother and my
stepfather were members of the Wesleyan Church and i became a
Teacher in the Sunday school for 2 years at the End of that time i
first saw my late husband Thomas Woolcock i believe my stepfather
was a good man but he was very passionate and determined my
late husband was a widower with two Children his Wife had been
dead about 8 months when i went to keep house for him against
stepfathers wishes i kept house for him for 5 weeks when some one
told my stepfather that i was keeping Company with Thomas
Woolcock he asked me if it was true and i told him it was not but
he would not believe me but called me a liar and told me he would
Crippel me if i went with him any more and i being very selfwilled
i told him that i had not ben with the man but i would go with
him now if he asked me if the Divel said i should not this took
place on the Thursday morning i saw my husband in the evening
and he asked me what was the matter and I told him what had
taken place the following Sunday he asked me to go with him for a
walk instead of goin to Chapl i went and my stepfather missed me
from the Chappel and came to look for me and met us both together
so i was afraid to go home for he had said he would break both
of my legs i was afraid he would keep his word as i never knew
him to tell a wilful lie so i went to a cousins of my husbands and
stoped and my husband asked me if i would marry him and for

*my words sake i did we were marride the next sunday morning by
lience after the acquaintance of 7 weeks i was not married long
before i fownd out what sort of man i had got and that my poor
stepfather had advised me for my good but was to late then so i
had to make the best of it i tried to do my duty to him and the
children, but the more i tried the worse he got he was fond of drink
but did not like to part with the money for anything else and
god onley knows how he illtreated me i put up with it for 3 years
during that time, my parents went to melbourne and then he was
worse than ever i thought i would rather die than live so i tried to
put an end to my self in several different ways but thank the Lord
i did not succied in doin so so as he did not treat me any better and
i could not live like that i thought i would leave him and get my
own liven so i left him but he would not leave me alone he came
and feched me home and then i stopped with him twelve months
and i left him again with the intention of going to my Mother i
only took 6 pounds with me i came doun to Adelaide and i stopped
with my sister I was hear in Adelaide 6 weeks when he came and
fetshed me back again but he did not behave no better to me i tried
my best to please him but I could not there is no foundation at all
for the story about the young man called Pascoe, he was nothing
to me nor i did not give the poor dog any poison for i knew what
power the poison has as i took it my self for some months and i was
so ill treated that I was quite out of my minde and in a eviel hour
i yealded to the temptation he was taken ill at the mine and came
home and quarrelled with me and satan tempted me an I gave him
what i ought not but i thought at the time that if I gave him time
to prepare to meet his god i should not do any great crime to send
him out of the World but i see my mistake now I thank god he
had time to make his peace with his maker and i hope shall meet
him in heaven for i feel that god has pardoned all my sins he has
forgiven me and washed me white in the precious blood of Jesus
i feel this evening that i can rejoice in a loven Saviour i feel his
presence here to night he sustains me and gives me comfort under
this heavy trial sutch the world can never give. Dear friend if I*

may call you so I am mutch obliged to you for your kindness to a
poor guilty sinner but great will be your reward in hevean i hope
i shall meet you their and I hope that god will keep me faithfull
to the End o may be abl to say that live is Christ but to Die will
be gain Bless the Lord he will not turn away any that come unto
him for he says com unto me all ye that labour and are hevy laden
and i will give you rest i feel i have that rest i hope to die singing
Victory through the Blood of the lamb i remain sir yours truly a
sinner saved

by grace ELISABTH LILLIAN WOOLCOCK

Elizabeth Woolcock is buried between the walls at Old Adelaide
Gaol, the site marked only with her initials and the date. But
the punishment inflicted on an already severely punished young
woman continues to send out a ripple of disquiet, and even today
fresh flowers regularly appear on her grave.

❧

The Reverend James Bickford, to whom Elisabeth Woolcock wrote
her last letter, had been a missionary in the West Indies. Towards
the end of his time there his parents immigrated to South Australia,
and in 1852 he applied for a transfer to the colony. After a return
visit to England, he eventually sailed for Australia, and during a
visit to Melbourne was called upon to administer spiritual conso-
lation to two murderers, Thompson and Gibbs, whose execution
he witnessed in the Melbourne Gaol. Perhaps this prior experience of hangings was the reason Bickford was chosen to minister
to Elisabeth Woolcock. Only two days after her death he accompanied another young man to the scaffold – William Ridgeway was
executed on 1 January 1874 on the same gallows as Woolcock for
the murder of Frederick Burt. Between them, they kept Bickford
and Benjamin Ellis busy from Christmas to New Year.

A sketch of Bickford in the newspaper portrays a man with
a long white beard below a dull and humourless face, yet poor
Elisabeth Woolcock seems to have been grateful for his presence.

He died in June 1895 and his address is Road 2, Path 21; Plot 1 is on the western side of the path in an area that seems to be home to a colony of Wesleyan clergy.

Charles Josiah Lawrence, another governor of the gaol, died in the year Elizabeth Woolcock was hanged. His address is Road 3, Path 12; Plot 40 is on the eastern side of the path. Lawrence's elaborate marble headstone is adorned with ivy leaves and features a rope with tasselled ends, and – bearing in mind his role at the gaol – a pair of sinister rope loops that remind one irresistibly of Benjamin Ellis's hangman's noose.

Ellis died from a stroke on 22 May 1881 in the Adelaide Gaol; he was sixty-eight. His address is Road 5, Path 9; Plot 62 is said to be on the western side of the path by the cemetery's southern boundary, but the site is unmarked.

⚜

Perhaps Elisabeth's Woolcock's death on the scaffold, and the public's unease over it, helped to save another young woman from the same fate. On 19 August 1879, a young single mother, Johanna Sullivan, was tried for infanticide. Sullivan had given birth to a healthy male infant, Patsy Sullivan, on 3 July 1879. Two weeks later she left her lodgings saying that she had obtained a position as a wet nurse, and that someone at Glenelg had offered to care for her child. She was seen by two ladies, Mrs Stanton and Mrs Stone, in the train that left at a quarter to four. The baby was wrapped in a heavy, red shawl, and the two women worried it was being deprived of air. Johanna uncovered the baby's face, and an hour later she was seen walking on the beach. Still later, without her child, she went into the bar of the Pier Hotel and asked for a glass of brandy. As this was an unusual occurrence, the landlord, Mr Hamlin, took particular notice, and had no difficulty in identifying her when asked.

On the following morning the baby's body was spotted by a coachman driving along the Broadway. It was lying, partially dressed, on a bank of seaweed; death had been caused by drowning, exacerbated by a head injury that might have been caused by a blow or a fall, or by the waves washing it against a stone or a piece of wood.

Johanna Sullivan was defended by Charles Cameron Kingston, who attempted to convince the jury that the child had accidentally smothered under the mother's shawl, and in a panic she had left his body on the beach. But the jury decided that she had caused Patsy's death by leaving him exposed on the beach; she was found guilty of murder, and the judge pronounced the death sentence.

⚜

What came out of this trial was an unexpected wave of empathy for Johanna Sullivan. It was clear that she had been seduced and abandoned, that she was penniless and friendless, and facing poverty and misery. It was suggested that there was a need for a foundling hospital. A member of the Destitute Board, Mr Darling, raised the Sullivan case in the House of Assembly with a view to the urgent need to establish such a place. He pointed out that Johanna Sullivan was not the only guilty party and the man who had deserted her should also be standing in the dock, which might be the first time in the colony, or anywhere, that the question of paternal accountability was raised.

A report from the chairman of the Destitute Board confirmed that in the previous three months there had been fifty-seven confinements in the Destitute Asylum, forty-seven of them to unmarried women with two of those under fifteen. The government announced they would subsidise, pound for pound, subscriptions for a foundling hospital. Fewer mothers would be driven to destroy their children, they surmised, if a foundling hospital was available.

As with the facts that came to light through the activities of Francis Sheridan, Johanna Sullivan's story is the tip of a vast iceberg of infant deaths in suspicious circumstances. If abortion was considered too dangerous, concealing the birth and dealing with it later was another option, for in an era where infant deaths were common, fewer questions were asked. Babies were despatched by every possible means, from deliberate withholding of sustenance to exposure, suffocation, and even the odd neck slashing. South Australian law did not distinguish between infanticide and murder, so a conviction meant the death penalty. But as 'live birth' had first to be proved beyond reasonable doubt, women were often charged with the lesser crime of having concealed a birth for which the maximum sentence was three years.

As late as 1906, a young woman called Emma Lydia Hoffman was observed throwing a paper parcel off the jetty at Semaphore. John Williamson, a deckhand on the launch *Petrel* testified that he watched her walk down the jetty and return without the parcel; later he saw the parcel floating in the water. When it was retrieved it was found to contain the body of a male child, along with some scraps of clothing and a lead ball. In a striking coincidence of names, a widow, Johanna Sullivan, living at 93 Flinders Street, testified that Emma Hoffman had rented a furnished room in her house on 6 June, and on 9 June said she was going away for a week or two.

Emma Hoffman returned two days later in the company of Constables Burford and Nettle. When the room she had rented was inspected it was found to contain bloodstained articles of under-wear. A post-mortem examination concluded that the child had been stillborn. Emma Hoffman refused to be admitted to hospital for medical examination; it was noted that she was 'in a melancholy condition' and in court it was stated that she was 'friendless'. By her own testimony she had come from Victoria, although it seems likely she was the daughter of a couple from Talunga in South Australia.

The post-mortem evidence saved Emma Hoffman from the more serious charge of murder, and she was found not guilty of concealing the birth. But whatever else happened to her subse-quently, enduring her labour alone and in silence in Mrs Sullivan's furnished room, the horror of cleaning up afterwards, of wrapping her newborn son in a parcel and making her way to Semaphore must have stayed with her for the rest of her life.

If Johanna Sullivan's death sentence had stuck, Ben Ellis would have had to face up once more to his terrible task. On being taken to the gaol after the trial, records show that corporal punishment was administered to Sullivan, probably a number of painful lashes. At that stage she was still under the death sentence. The following day it was reported in the newspaper that Johanna Sullivan was, unsurprisingly, in a terrible state, and had begged hard for mercy. Eventually, mercy of a kind was dispensed, and perhaps Johanna Sullivan owed this unusual leniency to the doubt that still nagged over Elisabeth Woolcock's guilt, for her sentence was reduced to life in prison, which meant fourteen years, with hard labour.

There were letters to the newspaper calling for mercy, at least one of them written by a jury member. While she was in gaol, Boyle Travers Finniss was one of those who attempted to keep track of her fate, writing to the newspaper to inquire after her whereabouts. And his letters elicited a response (from H.D. Bridle of Narridy) that Johanna Sullivan was in Gladstone Gaol and had a thoroughly good record. A further letter in 1887 revealed that she had been released and was in service in Gladstone, that she was doing well, and was in good health.

⚜

Standing in the quiet dark, it feels as if the living city encircles this space like a rowdy crowd at a football match. Its brash presence is a bit disturbing. From halfway down Road 1 the signs on West Terrace are readable: *Elephant and Castle*; *Toyota*, red, between the palms beside the curator's cottage, and I wonder, not for the first time, how those I have been visiting would react if they could see this modern city. Especially Finniss, who with William Light had known it before it was surveyed.

Boyle Travers Finniss, a graduate of the military academy Sandhurst, had arrived in South Australia with his Irish wife Anne on board the *Cygnet*. At Rapid Bay, on 31 December 1836, his daughter, Fanny Lipson Finniss, became the first white female child to be born in the colony. He was a founding member of the surveying firm of Light, Finniss & Co., which surveyed in the Lyndoch valley until Light became too ill; Finniss laid out the township of Gawler. Always a devoted friend to Light, both he and Anne were present at his death on 5 October 1839.

Finniss became the first premier of South Australia under responsible government. He was an original member of the short-lived South Australian Club, its inaugural meeting held at the office of Light, Finniss & Co. With Charles Sturt, he was a trustee of Trinity Church and responsible for offering the living to the Reverend James Farrell after the death of Charles Beaumont Howard.

Boyle Travers Finniss died at Kensington Park on Christmas Eve 1893. His address is Road 2, Path 22; Plot 17 is on the western side of the path not far from William and Julia Wyatt's tomb on Path 21. Finniss is buried here with his first wife, Anne. With them is their firstborn daughter, Fanny Lipson (Morgan), who died at twenty-eight, and two young sons of fourteen months and fourteen years respectively. A simple slab of marble on the site is a cremation memorial for Julia Howard Finniss, which dates from her death in 1918. William Charles Maxwell Finniss is buried in an adjacent plot.

15

Darkness in Daylight

From the virgin robe all pure and white
Dabbled with human gore,
And the silken tresses shred by fiends
Upon the blood-stained floor.
'The Gawnpore Massacre'
– Caroline Carleton, 1860

Aside from the ritualised mourning that has been part of the cemetery's daily life since it was established, the site has a history of dark doings and illegal activities. When the Dead House operated as the city's morgue it was often broken into. Sometimes the intrusion was relatively harmless, the work of so-called 'derelicts' entering the refrigeration engine room attached to the morgue and switching off the motor so that they could sleep there for the night. Such nocturnal incursions were mild compared to the cemetery's other troubles.

In December 1877 the body of a full-term infant was found there in a box. It had been born a few days previously, and earth had been shovelled in an attempt to cover it. This was not the first baby in a box to be discovered within the cemetery's boundaries, nor would it be the last. Then, on an April afternoon in 1911, a man whose name was believed to be Walter P. Jones fatally shot himself while in the cemetery. In November of the same year the body of another man was discovered with a wound in his forehead and a revolver nearby. A note found in his clothing read: *The suffering I get with my eyes is more than I can bear. W.M. Hewish.* A business card identified him as William Hewish, photographer, of Brown Street. In April 1945 intruders broke in and dragged a woman's body from a refrigerator onto the morgue floor. Nothing was stolen, and the body was not interfered with. While it might have been youngsters acting out a dare, the newspaper noted that the cemetery was often frequented by people overcome by grief who kept lengthy graveside vigils.

On another occasion it was reported that 'a sadist' had broken into the morgue and mutilated the body of a young woman. Entry was through a side window, and the corpse had been dragged from the refrigerator and taken outside into the grounds where, with a razor from the morgue, the perpetrator inflicted terrible wounds. Unofficially, it is said there was a sexual assault on the woman's body and that police at the time suspected it was the work of John Balaban, the man who was later tried and hanged for the Sunshine Café murders of his wife, child, and mother-in-law.

But there is, too, a long and more troubling list of activities that eventually became the focus of a government investigation. They involved the appropriation of bodies for dissection, especially from public institutions such as the gaol, the lunatic and destitute asylums, and even the Adelaide Hospital. As so often happens in life, a major event was sparked by an apparently minor one – the sudden death of a hapless fellow on a winter morning in 1903.

At Ovingham railway station north-east of Adelaide the man scribbled a few lines on a scrap of paper, then drew a revolver from his pocket, put it to his head and pulled the trigger. The note read: *Cannot get work; no food or shelter. Better give up the struggle than starve.* The body was removed to the city morgue, the Dead House at West Terrace Cemetery. A jury was sworn in over the remains and the coroner, Dr William Ramsay Smith, conducted an inquest. A pawnbroker with whom the deceased had dealt in the days pre-ceding his suicide identified the body as that of Eugene Green. To a non-medical person, what happened next is sickening, but I feel I owe it to Eugene Green, and to others who suffered a similar fate, to relate the awful details.

At the conclusion of the inquest, a group of medical students from the University of Adelaide arrived at the Dead House. Dr Ramsay Smith had ordered them to attend to hear his clinic on the body of an infant discovered in a field. The students arrived to find the baby's corpse lying on a table beside Eugene Green. Constable Sandercock, the morgue cleaner, said Dr Smith asked him to fetch a bucket to put Green's head in. The head was still attached to the body when he went for the tin and when he returned it was on the bench. He put the head into the tin, poured some water over it and put it under the bench, as instructed by Dr Smith.

When everyone had gone, Sandercock began the clean up. Pieces of Eugene Green, including a kidney and severed fingers and toes were scattered about the floor. Sandercock gathered the stray parts and placed them inside the body, then threaded a needle and sewed up the trunk. Finally he sewed the scalp, stuffing the liver into the skull cavity. The infant's corpse was put beside the mutilated remains of Eugene Green, and they were taken away together.

In Brisbane, Christina Green read a press report of the death and contacted the South Australian police. She later identified her husband from a photograph of the dead man, along with the pocketbook found on his body. Eugene Sydney Green, about forty-five, was the son of a New South Wales bank inspector. He had been travelling to look for work.

⚜

There has always been a dubious line between the medical profession's need to study the progression of diseases through dissection and the human rights of the deceased. At the time of the seemingly pointless dismemberment of Eugene Green in the Dead House at West Terrace Cemetery, in England the medical profession could look back upon a long history of grave robbing and body snatching. In Edinburgh, William Burke and William Hare raised the bar on body snatching with a gruesome series of anatomy murders. In 1829, 20,000 people watched as Burke was hanged, most of them baying for his corpse to be dissected. It seemed the fear of post-mortem dismemberment was both widespread and contagious, second only to the fear of death.

The winter months were the most dangerous time to die, and England had a long winter. Sometimes a cage was erected over a grave to protect the newly buried from being raided by so-called resurrection men. More usually, family members simply kept a graveside vigil until decay put the corpse beyond the reach of raiders.

In England the *Act for Regulating Schools of Anatomy* was passed through parliament in a bid to stem the flow of corpses supplied through 'burking'. Although it started out along ethical lines, by the time it had been debated and redrafted the Act was vague enough to allow for the wholesale dissection of the inmates of workhouses and perhaps even encouraged it. In South Australia the *Anatomy Act of 1884* included a decency clause, which required students to remain respectful, to avoid unnecessary mutilation, and decently inter human remains – although as Eugene Green's death illustrates, it was loosely adhered to, if at all.

When the Green case came to public notice, Dr William Ramsay Smith was suspended as Inspector of Anatomy as well as his coronial duties. The city was rife with rumours of his harvesting of body parts, and even entire skeletons, many of which were said to have been shipped back to Edinburgh. All Smith's books and papers were seized by the government, and hundreds of inches of column space in the *Register* followed the inquiry as it ground on through the late winter and spring of 1903.

⚜

From the outset, William Ramsay Smith's career in Adelaide had been contentious. In 1896 he had ignored a stern caution from the British Medical Association and accepted a three-year appointment as a senior physician at the Adelaide Hospital. This came in the wake of the resignations of honorary medical staff who were in a vicious dispute with Charles Kingston's government. The South Australian branch of the BMA viewed Ramsay Smith's acceptance of this tainted position as 'highly dishonourable and unprofessional'. He had crossed an invisible picket line, and on his arrival in Adelaide he was effectively ostracised. The following year he was expelled from the association, and was never readmitted; however, his contract was extended to five years, and he was appointed as medical officer for the gaol. For a time he was the hospital's honorary pathologist, but continuing dispute made life difficult and he resigned that role, ending up as city coroner, inspector of anatomy, and chairman of the Central Board of Health, though he continued at times to do pathology work.

William Ramsay Smith – physician, naturalist, anthropologist and civil servant – had been born in 1859 at King Edward, Aberdeenshire, Scotland. He was the son of William Smith, a farm servant and railway stationmaster, and his wife Mary, a domestic servant. A bright young man with an enquiring mind, William studied arts at the University of Edinburgh before taking up medicine. A natural scholar, he supported himself through his university years with scholarships and by teaching natural history and zoology. For five years he was Assistant Professor in natural history and comparative anatomy at Edinburgh University; he was also examiner for the Royal College of Surgeons and the Royal College of Physicians at Edinburgh. Subsequently, he practised for nearly three years in North Wales, where he 'passed through some vicissitudes'. At the government inquiry into his conduct, Ramsay Smith was defended by Sir Josiah Symon, KC.

※

When he testified at the inquiry, Ramsay Smith explained that students at the Medical School paid for instruction at the Adelaide Hospital, and that included attendance at post-mortem examinations. The students paid £2.2s. for six months of instruction in the post-mortem rooms, where they carried out examinations. They also rehearsed operative surgery whenever they got an opportunity, all of which, according to Ramsay Smith, was standard practice the world over. It sounds perfectly reasonable, and yet what gradually emerged was a rather different picture. Smith admitted that every body it was possible to examine was examined post-mortem, and medical staff took every specimen of interest, which amounted to whatever body part took their fancy. Further, in the interests of his frequent role as an expert medical witness, he had often experimented on dead bodies using firearms. John Desmond, the government veterinary surgeon, testified that he had been present in the mortuary at the Adelaide Hospital when Dr Ramsay Smith fired a .303 rifle into the skull of a dead patient; according to Desmond, it was not an isolated incident.

Desmond and Ramsay Smith shared a laboratory space, and following a quarrel over the signing of a pay claim, Desmond, the injured party, seems to have set his mind to bringing about Ramsay Smith's downfall. This was not all that difficult to achieve, since Smith had many enemies in Adelaide dating from his first appointment to a disputed position. Desmond took his grudge to Charles Owen Smyth, a powerful public servant and the man who oversaw Adelaide's cemeteries. John Desmond disclosed that Eugene Green's head was being stored at their joint laboratory, along with skeletons and many other specimens in jars. When Smyth procured exhumation orders, the opened coffins revealed there were many missing body parts. In some cases all that had been buried was skin and a few bits of flesh. The body of the infant was discovered bundled in beside Eugene Green, and Ramsay Smith was called to account.

In particular, he was quizzed over the bodies of an Aboriginal man, Tommy Walker, and Emmett Harris, an African American. Harris had died of tuberculosis in a strange city and there had been no relatives to claim his body. After a post-mortem examination, Harris's head was cut off and Smith had shipped it to William Turner, his old anatomy professor at the University of Edinburgh, where it joined other specimens in Turner's 'skullery'. There was no one to raise a fuss. But Tommy Walker was well-known in Adelaide, and his burial, including a marble headstone, had been paid for by a group of stockbrokers. On exhumation, the coffin was found to contain very little of Walker's corpse – the body had been intercepted between the hospital and West Terrace Cemetery and the skeleton cut out for Ramsay Smith, who sent it to Turner.

An earlier scandal at the hospital had involved a man named Morgan Gwynne. When he died there in 1895 his friends had arrived to claim the body, only to find that it had been examined without permission by the previous Professor of Anatomy,

Archibald Watson, and his students. When the friends complained, a constable arrived to investigate. What he found in Gwynne's coffin was closer to the contents of a butcher's basket than a body.

⚜

While sifting through documents at the state archives I have studied many police reports to the coroner. These routinely take the form of a letter from the City Watch House. The following is a typical example:

> *Sir, I beg to inform you Dr Lind of The Mental Hospital Parkside reports per letter which is herewith attached that a patient named James Aldridge 42 years of age who was admitted to the Institution on 15th September 1913 died 31st December 1915 from diarrhoea and exhaustion. I have the honour to be sir, your obedient servant.*

Across the report, in red ink, William Ramsay Smith has written in his small, even hand: *Inquest unnecessary. W.R.S.* The sight of that scarlet note always strikes me now with a shiver, for if it was possible to hijack a body from the relatively public Adelaide Hospital, patients who died in such closed environments as the asylum were easily spirited away to be dissected.

During the inquiry into Ramsay Smith's conduct, the vet John Desmond related how Smith had come to the laboratory and asked if he could borrow a knife.

'He said he was going to bone a Chinaman at the lunatic asylum,' Desmond said.

The man was Ah Kione Chun, a long-term inmate. Smith himself went to the asylum's mortuary with his borrowed knife and cut out the skeleton. When he was finished, skin, muscles and entrails lay in three piles on the table. An undertaker, Mr Wallman, was instructed to collect the remains. Defending Ramsay Smith against the charge of misconduct, for he was not licensed to dissect and the asylum's mortuary was not an authorised place of dissection, Josiah Symon insisted that the 'boning' had been carried out in the interests of anthropology. The intended recipient of the skeleton, William Turner in Edinburgh, was the world's most eminent anatomist. His requests to his students to supply him with interesting specimens would not be made if he thought for a moment that it involved mutilation.

⚜

The Parkside Lunatic Asylum opened its doors in 1870. People ended up there for reasons that now seem absurd – inmates included epilepsy sufferers, the vulnerable elderly, or those with undiagnosed diseases. Unmarried women with children, and prostitutes were also sometimes shuffled from sight behind the asylum's forbidding walls. Then there were dementia patients, those with senile decay, mania, or delusional insanity, and the criminally insane. So many of the final pronouncements in the aftermath of their deaths include exhaustion, and I imagine life and death at the Parkside Lunatic Asylum was infinitely exhausting.

On 27 July 1906, the *Register* published a list of people who had died in the Lunatic Asylum in the first six months of the year; they added that their relatives were either unknown or resided interstate, which would have made them fair game for dissection. The dead were:

Elizabeth Franke, 54, influenza and exhaustion; Minnie Tracey, 60, brain paralysis and decay; Mary Geelan, 50, apoplexy and brain disease; Charles Williams, 49, colitis and melancholic exhaustion; Rachel Marie Blanch, 63, diarrhoea and senile decay; Richard Savage, 23, diarrhoea and exhaustion; Christina Williams, 38, broncho-pneumonia after severe burns (verdict of Coroner's jury); Denis Maloney, 67, senile decay and diarrhoea; Mary Morgan, 43, cardiac disease and anaemia; Richard Mathieson, 33, colitis and exhaustion; Kate Talty, 28, general paralysis of insane and apoplexy: Janet Harkes, 49, entero colitis; Mary Walsh, 70, senile dementia and cardiac failure; Anders Johann Janssen, 64, brain paralysis and senile decay; and David Ross, 66, senile decay and arterial atteroma.

One of the names on that list was Christina Williams. At the time of her death she had been a patient at the asylum for eight years. According to the resident medical officer Dr Cleland, Christina was born a 'weak-minded woman', indeed the newspaper headed the announcement of her demise as 'Death of a Weak-minded Woman'. Dr Cleland said Christina was 'subject to violent passions' but she had been entrusted with domestic work in the institution. As an ordinary working patient, she had more freedom than other inmates. In the course of her duties she had access to kerosene and other supplies. Kerosene was noticed on her clothing and Dr Cleland was of the opinion that she had set fire to herself.

Henry Dodd the asylum cook said at the inquest that when returning from breakfast he heard screams and saw a flash of fire. He and others found a woman in flames, which they managed to extinguish. Though badly burned, Christina was recovering from her injuries when she contracted pneumonia and died. Bridget Schrapels, an attendant, said in her evidence that the deceased had often filled the kerosene lamps and stove, and her conduct had not been such as to make it necessary to prevent her having access to the kerosene store. A verdict was returned of death due to bronchial pneumonia, consequent upon burns, self-caused.

In March 1898, the same month and year in which Christina Williams entered the asylum, there had been another death of a young woman by fire. I cannot help wondering whether Christina, having witnessed it, saved it up as a solution for herself should the exhaustion of the asylum become unendurable.

Florence Bees was said to be a quiet patient. In her early twenties, she had been an inmate of the Lunatic Asylum for about five months. Under supervision, she undertook domestic work about the wards, until the morning she went to the store and obtained a box of matches. Margaret Kinnear, the attendant in charge of D ward, put the box of supplies on a table and left the room. Within minutes she heard screams from the ward and ran back to find Florence Bees on fire.

Lily Wark, an attendant, said she was attracted by screams from a room in D ward. The door closed with a spring and could not be opened from either side without a key. She helped Margaret Kinnear to extinguish the flames. Lily did not know whether there were any rules prohibiting matches being placed within reach of patients, but said if she were in charge of a ward she would not deem it safe.

Florence said that she had struck two matches and the second set fire to her dress. She died at about 6.30 on Sunday morning. Dr Cleland reported that Florence Bees had been at the asylum since 1897; she suffered from mild dementia, or childishness. She appears to have been one of many children of Henry Bees and his wife Julia. Florence was in the asylum because of her 'propensity to wander away from home'. She had never before been known to play with matches. She was trusted. She had never attempted injury to herself, although on one occasion she had tried to escape. Florence's death was deemed an accident. No blame attached to anyone, though a recommendation was made for the future that matches or anything flammable should be kept out of the reach of patients.

⚜

So many skulls were removed from corpses in Adelaide that it was said a supply of plaster moulds was kept at the Adelaide Hospital. Inserted into the cavity, the facial shape could be maintained in case of a protest from relatives. Yet William Ramsay Smith was acquitted. It had to be so, or else the government would have been placed in the position of taking action against other leading doctors who had aided and abetted him, and who had committed the same acts themselves.

The enquiry into the charges laid by the Government against the City Coroner, Dr Ramsay Smith, has ended, as most intelligent people expected it would, in a complete breakdown of the allegations, and consequent reinstatement of the suspended officer, who not only comes out of the ordeal fully exonerated from blame but with an independent Board's practical commendation for zealous service in public service, scientific research, and laudable

efforts in the cause of his profession and suffering humanity. It
appears to be necessary to state that his work exhibits evidence of
painstaking research and restless zeal in the cause of his profession,
as well as in the performance of his official duties, which sometimes
involved work of a most unpleasant character. He had had no gain
or personal benefit from the acts in respect of which he has been
charged; but on the contrary, he had been out of pocket.

Southern Argus, Thursday 24 September 1903

⚜

The subject of dissection commonly arouses feelings of great repugnance, even among anatomy professors, even in Robert Knox, the doctor who was at the centre of the Burke and Hare murders. Knox expressed dread of his own dissection, and other surgeons shied from imagining their loved ones under the anatomist's pitiless knife. The horror of it is the subject of a 1798 ballad by Robert Southey, 'The Surgeon's Warning'.

All kinds of carcasses I have cut up,
And now my turn will be
But brothers, I took care of you,
So pray take care of me.

And my 'prentices will surely come
And carve me bone from bone,
And I, who have rifled the dead man's grave,
Shall never have rest in my own.

Ramsay Smith belonged to the Royal Anthropological Society of Great Britain and Ireland. Alongside his dissections of Indigenous people, his avid collection of their skeletons and body parts, he also championed their rights, declaring them the 'most interesting {race} at present on earth and the least deserving to be exterminated by us and the most wronged at our hands'. It is difficult to square this with his behaviour, but this is where the line between science and human rights becomes blurred.

Smith was a lover of music and poetry, an enthusiastic cyclist, photographer, and teetotaller. With his belief in the need for dissection and his apparent ease around post-mortem procedures, you might have thought he would offer his body to science. Yet I suspect William Ramsay Smith shared Robert Knox's dread when it came to his own post-mortem destination, for when he died at his home in Belair in 1937 he was cremated.

⚜

In winter the deciduous trees down by the Jewish Section are dark and skeletal. As I meander west, pigeons rise in a startled rush into the still, cold air, their wing-beats like the sound of gloved hands, softly clapping. In the grove where the quandongs grow the fruit is flushing from green to yellow and red, and I wonder about the taste of quandong jam. I think, too, of one of the groundsmen chuckling as he told about the edible asparagus that grows throughout the cemetery: it is known as Dead Men's Fingers. I can understand anyone planting bulbs on a grave, for bulbs double and renew almost indefinitely, but who would plant asparagus? I wonder about its significance in the now dead Victorian language of plants and flowers, and resolve to look it up.

I am heading towards the southern boundary wall and a piece of rough ground where a monument commemorates all those 'persons of goodwill' interred in the cemetery who 'generously bequeathed their bodies for the benefit of medical science'. It has been erected in gratitude by the University of Adelaide and the Flinders University of South Australia, and considering the extensive use they have made of bodies, both willing and unwilling, it seems like the least they could do.

The monument is an outsized and ungainly lump of orange and gold and brown stone. I wonder what those it commemorates would have to say if they were able to make their feelings known. People like the Aboriginal man known as Copper Top, a roundabout hand from Anna Creek station who died in the Parkside Lunatic Asylum in February 1906 of heart disease and one month and two days of diarrhoea. Having died before the government inquiry into anatomy practices, the chances are that Copper Top's skull, or even his entire skeleton, found its way to Edinburgh. The place where the memorial stands, though it appears vacant, is filled with pauper graves.

⚜

There is little to see at the graves of most of the people whose stories I have just unravelled. In the cemetery's archive I can find no trace of Eugene Green, but Christina Williams is in the area designated Road 5X, Path CE. Plot 43. From the map, she is surrounded by the graves of stillborn babies. Florence Bees is on Road 3, Path 33A. The plot number is 15 – just a corner of another grave – but there is nothing to show. Even the names belonging to the surrounding sites are impossible to trace, and I fear her plot site has disappeared under the huge Greek and Italian tombs here.

Ah Kione Chun's address is R1 South, Path 22; Plot 10 is on the eastern side. The site associated with his name is almost opposite the tomb of John Monck, the first sexton of the cemetery. It is an empty space between the fenced vaults belonging to the Stocks family, and the grave of Thomas Edward Inskip.

Morgan Gwynne, who died in October 1895, has an address in the records at Road 5 East, Path Z1E, Plot 11.

16

Love Measured in Marble,
Grief Weighed in Granite

Each time I walk through the cemetery's main gates my gaze is drawn to the massive vault on Road 1 North where, in 1883, Frances Coglin was interred. It must have dominated the more sparsely populated nineteenth-century landscape, and even today its pale mass remains an enduring statement of grief and mourning.

Frances Coglin's husband Patrick spared no effort or expense to create this memorial to his life's companion. Frances was much-loved for her good deeds among the poor, especially in the neighbourhood of Brompton, so if, as Wordsworth believed, the best portion of a good man or woman's life lies in 'little, nameless, unremembered acts of kindness and love' then Frances Coglin appears to have been a very good woman whose acts of kindness are remembered here in many, many tons of marble and granite.

Patrick Boyce Coglin was born in County Sligo in 1815, the son of a well-respected Catholic family. In 1831, when Patrick was sixteen, his parents immigrated to Tasmania. There, after finishing his schooling, Patrick was apprenticed to a noted architect, Mr Biggins. After ten years he decided to try his luck in South Australia, where he arrived with a small amount of capital and boundless energy. One of his mottos was that a man would never get rich working for an employer, and so after trying a few different things he launched his own little business – a wood yard on Hindley Street in which he dealt mainly with Tasmanian timbers. It seems to have been around this time that he met and married the widowed Frances Gerrard, a farmer's daughter from Cheshire with an infant son from her marriage.

Patrick was an instinctive businessman, shifting easily from timber to property, to hotel ownership, gold, politics – in 1860 he owned the Napoleon Bonaparte Hotel and his brother James ran the Newmarket Inn on North Terrace; when gold was discovered at Echunga, Patrick Coglan took up one of the first licenses; elected to parliament, he became an energetic and diligent member.

The mausoleum he built for his wife and which he also intended to occupy is as much a testament to Coglin's determination as it is to his wealth. The highly polished top is of grey granite. The red granite die alone weighs eight-and-a-half tons, and this rests on an immense slab of Italian marble weighing seven tons. The slab is all one piece and was cut from the Carrara quarry in Italy from a forty-two-ton block. Since nothing of this size had ever been brought from the quarry, the access road had to be widened for three-quarters of a mile to accommodate its removal, and steam haulage was used in place of horses to transport the slab to the seaport. At West Terrace Cemetery the vault was dug twenty feet square, its walls shored up with two feet of concrete. This was roofed with Mintaro slate, and a kerbing of Port Elliot granite. Above the kerbing, a casket of polished red granite was lowered into place and inscribed to Coglin's wife.

In affectionate remembrance of Frances Coglin, a native of
Cheshire, England, who departed this life on 17th October, 1883,
aged 76 years.

Hear me when I call, O God of my righteousness; Thou hast
set me at liberty when I was in trouble. Have mercy on me and
hearken unto my prayer.

The heavy wrought-iron fence that surrounds the edifice was tipped with gold. Coglin had given his builders an open cheque, but I wonder what Frances Coglin would have made of this extravagance: the whole thing took around eighteen months to build at a cost of £1500.

By all accounts Patrick Coglin was an eccentric and likeable character and one of his most remarkable peculiarities was his habit of using long and complicated words. To his way of thinking 'sesquipedalion adjectives promiscuously promulgated by the indescribable intellectual advocates are an incomprehensible conglomeration of impractical ideas, and enough to create a volcanic disturbance in the cerebral region' was a perfectly reasonable sentence. He had also been a jockey, and his passion for horseracing had much to do with obtaining the lease of Victoria Park Racecourse and with building its handsome grandstand.

A story is told of Coglin being thrown while riding a favourite mare. Although he was unhurt, the horse had a broken leg. So the ever resourceful Coglin engaged the finest veterinary surgeon he could find, the leg was amputated and a wooden one attached. The horse was seen walking with the improvised leg 'for many months', though it sounds as if his attempts to save its life were ultimately in vain. But the impulse behind this makeshift medicine shows, as does the over-the-top monument to his wife, that Patrick Coglin's heart was in the right place.

⚜

Did I mention that Coglin's Catholicism had lapsed? Perhaps to smooth the path of business he had become a Freemason, an Oddfellow, and a Forrester. But a few days before his death he renounced all of these activities and, having been baptised and confirmed in the Catholic faith, chose to be buried in the Catholic Section in the smaller vault he had built for his mother, Rebecca. His brother James and sister Helena rest there with him.

⚜

I think of Frances Coglin's coffin at the centre of her vast, below-ground vault. Throughout the cemetery there are many such spaces, though few on such a scale. In places where the surface of a vault has subsided I sometimes glimpse a dark nothingness below. Groundsmen during routine maintenance and repairs have unearthed moulding copies of nineteenth-century books, and I imagine these hidden places dotted with leather-bound volumes of *Infelice*, or the *South Australian Church Hymn Book* published by Charles Beaumont Howard. In the Jewish Section, sacred texts and books bearing the Hebrew name of God occupy their own grave.

⚜

Frances Coglin's monument stands on Road 1 North on the corner of Path 4. I have seen it many times from the entrance, which means that I am to be robbed of the fun of seeking it out. But as Patrick Coglin is in the Catholic Old Area there might still be some searching, for the layout there is not so easily interpreted. The inscriptions in the red granite mark the lives of Frances Coglin and also her son, William Gerrard. The blank space between their two names was being saved for Patrick, but it will remain blank forever because of his deathbed return to Catholicism.

From here I can take the long meander down Road 1 and turn right towards the Smythe Chapel. Or I can cut across and skirt the excavated remains of the old crematorium. As I dawdle along it occurs to me that Coglin's tombs and the disposal of human remains by cremation stand on opposite sides of what was once a passionate debate, and that the logical route for this walk must take in the old crematorium.

⚜

Being so accustomed to funerals that end in cremation, it requires an adjustment in thinking to return to a time when it was seen as a radical concept. Passions ran high on the subject of burning versus burial. When cremation was first mooted in Europe its promoters stressed its sanitary aspects and the benefit to public health. Plague and cholera were widely feared, and outbreaks had been linked to old burial grounds. Medical men were at the forefront of the push towards cremation, and I wonder whether it is too cynical to suggest that many of them initially saw it as a convenient method of clearing up after the bodies they dissected so messily and in such numbers. There could be no doubt that it was the answer to grave robbing and other interferences with traditional burial grounds. Lines were drawn on the subject, with progressive, utilitarian, and secular forces on one side, and religious fundamentalism on the other. Among the pious, the crucial question concerned resurrection and whether or not a body could possibly be raised intact from an urn full of ashes. The Catholic Church was fierce in its opposition, branding cremation 'pagan', and prohibiting its use for Catholics until as late as 1964.

Queen Victoria's surgeon Sir Henry Thompson was one of the leaders of the movement to promote cremation, becoming the first president of the Cremation Society of England. The trouble was that it took a while to perfect the process, and the unfortunate use of phrases such as 'baking oven' aroused repugnance and resistance. In Adelaide, Dr Robert Tracey Wylde was an early advocate for cremation, establishing the South Australian Cremation Society and raising subscriptions to fund the building of what was to become Australia's first crematorium.

It was designed by Alfred Barham Black, engineer and architect, and the father of the printmaker and painter, Dorothea (Dorrit) Black. Both he and his more famous daughter were eventually cremated here, Dorrit following her sudden death when she was hit by a car in 1951. The design was based on the City of London Crematorium, with an English gothic-style chapel above and a furnace discreetly arranged below. The chimney was cunningly disguised as an Italianate bell tower, but I do not suppose its true purpose was ever far from the minds of the sick, the dying, and the bereaved. The smell of burning, too, was a giveaway. Wafted towards the city by the prevailing wind, it triggered renewed fears for public health and sparked calls for the cemetery's closure. Which was all very well, but although the subject was endlessly debated in parliament and elsewhere, no new site was ever settled on.

After several practice runs in which dead sheep were incinerated, the crematorium opened for business in 1903. The first cremation occurred on 4 May; the deceased, Bishin Singh, was a

Sikh, a religion that traditionally favoured cremation over burial. An extraordinary amount of fuel was needed – more than half a ton of English coke and some extra wood. In the hour-and-a-half it took to cremate Bishin Singh, journalists and even mourners were invited into the hell realm below the chapel to observe the cremation through a peephole in the furnace.

Early cremations attempted to mimic the burial process, although when the coffin was lowered into the floor of the chapel, the clanking of chains and grinding of cog-wheels is said to have traumatised sensitive mourners and next-of-kin. In the first decade of its existence, the cremation rate stood at only about five a year. Dr Robert Wylde was a man who stood by his convictions; at his death in November 1903 he became the third person to be cremated, and his remains are interred in the garden opposite the crematorium.

Until as late as 1925, the West Terrace crematorium was the only such facility in Australia. By then resistance to the process was beginning to ease, but with its outmoded equipment the crematorium soon struggled to keep pace with demand. It closed in 1959 and ten years later was demolished and the site filled in. But as history shows, being buried here is no guarantee of remaining so: in 2004 the site was excavated, exposing the remains of the old furnace and chimney. The iron pulley is in place. Rust-coloured, the sinister hook that secured the coffin still dangles on its chain, and the metal tray on which coffins were lowered from the chapel remains intact. During the crematorium's working life, 4762 coffins slid onto this tray to be lowered into the furnace.

⚜

Lapsed Catholic or not, Patrick Coglin, with his need to memorialise those he loved, would have abhorred cremation. The tomb he created for his mother Rebecca Boyce Coglin is in the Catholic Old Area, Row C9, site 20. It stands surrounded by a heavy wrought-iron fence, which makes it easy to spot; the striking design worked in iron seems to be in the shape of vine leaves, another mysterious message, perhaps, in the Victorian mourning vocabulary.

Even here, Coglin's reluctance at parting, his determination to remember and be remembered is evident in the precise measurement of his mother's life, something more usually seen on the headstones of children. Rebecca Coglin died, he wants us to know, when she was eighty-two years and ten months. He has caused to be set in stone her origins in Boyle County, Roscommon, Ireland – has insisted, too, on his own part in raising her memorial and claimed his position as her eldest son: *P.B. Coglin M.P.*

The Coglin gravesites have endured for more than a century and look as if they will survive for as long as the cemetery remains. In that time they must often have been read as a rich man's statement of wealth and status, but I feel sure they sprang from a heart that lacked a trip switch when it came to the grief of parting with loved ones. The only surprise is that he did not raise a substantial memorial for his three-legged mare.

I cannot help wondering whether this weighing and measuring of love in marble and granite means more in the grand scheme of things than some of the insignificantly endowed yet infinitely touching graves I have seen. I am thinking of a small slab of white marble close by here, with its simple inscription: *Mary – Loved.* I am also thinking of those with homely objects pressed into them, pieces that look like they were made by small hands around kitchen tables, tiny treasures that speak of love. A white wooden cross trimmed with baubles and flowers and a perpetual candle comes to mind; it is pushed into the lumpy turf beyond the Children's Memorial, where most of the graves are unmarked. Elsewhere there are hearts wrought of iron, or cut from tin. I am continually amazed by the things people offer up in grief.

My favourite is a small velvet-lined and shell-encrusted box; it contains a single shell to which grains of sand from an unknown beach still cling. Sheltered from the weather for many seasons by a wooden cross with handwritten names under plastic, I imagine that if you were to hold that shell to your ear it would roar with love. I came upon it by accident, the pale light of an overcast afternoon having snagged on one of the tiny shells edging its wooden lid. When I drew it from its hiding place it seemed to shine like the moon; I lifted the lid, but did not interfere with its cargo, for the right to touch it belongs only to the one who placed it there. As I nestled the box back into place I wondered about objects that embody strong emotion, their mysterious power to reach out to a stranger who is unaffected by the original love or grief. In the simplest, most direct way, they do what great art can do when it speaks to us. That such objects exist in the world is, somehow, oddly comforting.

17

A Ramble in the Ringing World

On 4 May 1863, the governor of South Australia, Sir Dominick Daly, laid the foundation stone for the Adelaide Town Hall. He wielded a silver trowel on which was embossed an image of the finished building, and at the laying ceremony a bottle containing coins and other souvenirs was sealed in a cavity beneath the stone. Unfortunately, the foundation stone itself was not inscribed, and its precise location is no longer known. The Town Hall took three years to build, and in June 1866 its ring of eight bells in the key of F, named after Queen Victoria's beloved Albert, were rung for the first time at a grand opening ball and banquet.

Bells of varying significance marked Daly's tenure at Government House. There were wedding bells when his daughters Joanna and Caroline were married in a double ceremony at Trinity Church. One daughter was fair, the other dark; they both married bank managers – one tall, the other thin. The story that did the rounds at the time was that as the bridal parties departed on their respective honeymoons the luggage was switched, so that the tall bank manager was left with the short bank manager's wardrobe, and vice versa.

The Albert Bells were the first tower bells in the city of Adelaide. They had been ordered from John Warner & Sons of London and arrived at Port Adelaide on the *Edinburgh* in May 1866. With the opening of the Town Hall approaching they were quickly hung, although the architect advised waiting until the mortar in the tower was properly set before they were rung.

Having been in the ringing room of the Albert Tower when the bells are rung, his anxiety is understandable: when the bellringers pull on their ropes and all eight bells are swinging, the tower sways quite alarmingly. Yet it is almost a century and a half since the architect's attack of nerves, and the Albert Tower is said to be quite sound. At the grand opening of the Town Hall those in charge must have decided to risk the mortar, and the bells were chimed for the first time at noon on 20 June 1866, and again that evening for the 800 people attending the mayoral banquet. The sound of the bronze bells no doubt gladdened the hearts of many settlers who had grown up with church bells in English church and civic life.

The artist James Shaw – born in Dumfries, Scotland in 1851 – captured the opening night at the Town Hall in an oil painting, and his 'City Ball in Honour of HRH Duke of Edinburgh' is in the collection of the Art Gallery of South Australia. It shows a lone, tartan-clad piper standing beneath a pair of grand chandeliers; he is at the centre of a circle of whirling couples, and to my eye their gaiety holds more than a hint of desperation.

⚜

Bells have a long history, with the world's oldest surviving bell thought to be around 5000 years old: it was found at Babylon. The earliest bells were small and used for everything from frightening birds from orchards to sounding warnings. In China, bells and gongs seem to have existed since the beginning of time, though they were generally struck from the outside rather than rung with a clapper. It took Christianity a while to catch on to using bells, but once it did their shape and size began to evolve and they acquired mystic qualities. A cast bronze bell, 'The Bernane', associated with Saint Fillan, was said to cure lunacy, migraine, and other ailments when placed over the victim's head. (The patron saint of mental illness, Saint Fillan must have been invoked on countless occasions at the Parkside Lunatic Asylum and other places in early Adelaide.) If anyone tried to steal his bell it would ring non-stop and draw attention to the thief. In Scotland a bell was sometimes handed over before death to a relative as a kind of title deed to their inheritance.

From about the eighth century onwards, with the mixing of copper and tin to produce bronze, larger bells began to be cast. The larger the bell, the deeper the note, and bigger bells found their way into church towers. Following on from this came the bell-founder's increased skill in tuning, achieved by paring away layers of bronze, and the evolution of change-ringing.

⚜

I am in no hurry to reach a destination today, happy to walk for the pleasure of walking in this endlessly absorbing landscape. While I intend to end up in the Catholic Old Area at the grave of Sir Dominick Daly, instead of starting at the gates on Wylde Road I set out from the curator's house at the main entrance, turning my back on the restless thrum of the living world and sauntering west along Road 1. I admit to following a loose thread here, though one that has a connection with my interest in the history of bellringing, or campanology.

On the left side of Road 1, at Path 14, I arrive at the family plot of William Flett and his wife Margaret Crear. The headstone is an understated gothic arch inscribed with their names and a simple floral motive, but the fence that surrounds it is unique, with a design that includes the shapes of bells. Each bell is suspended between two tall, plain uprights, evoking miniature bell towers of iron and air in a repeated pattern. A decorative urn and leaf medallion above each bell brings substance and weight to the overall design, and the only way it could have been improved was if, rather than flat silhouettes, the bells were hollow and had clappers.

When I first came across this fence I imagined it must enclose the grave of a bellringer, and it may be that something in William Flett's history caused his family to choose this pattern – perhaps he was particularly fond of the strange, other-worldly music made by these large and noisy instruments; perhaps he grew up close to a church with bells. We will never know, but with its frieze of silent, rust-coloured bells the design conveys both solemnity and celebration.

Since discovering this fence I have learned that William Flett and his wife were early colonists, and that they arrived in Adelaide in February 1840 on board the ship *Indus*. The *Indus* had sailed from Leith, a port north of Edinburgh, but after a collision off Montrose it was forced to turn back to Leith for repairs. The decision to leave Scotland for such a distant land was a momentous one, and I cannot help wondering whether, on the return to Leith, any of the ship's twenty-two passengers were tempted to change their minds and disembark. The *Indus* sailed again on 5 October 1839 under the command of Captain John MacFarlane.

William Flett was from Kirkwall on the main island of Orkney, the northern-most British port for early expeditions on their way to the Arctic. He and Margaret Crear were married there in 1829 and by the time they sailed for South Australia they had four children, with a fifth born during the voyage. February's heat would likely have shocked them, used as they were to cool northern summers with their soft mornings and long green twilights. What extremes of change, then, those first weeks of thudding heat and scouring light, and the scrubby plain so different to the bare, haunting hills of Orkney. We must suppose that the Fletts were hardy people.

I have also learned that Kirkwall's narrow cathedral dedicated to Saint Magnus has an ancient set of bells, which William Flett would certainly have heard being rung. The three bells were presented to the cathedral in 1528 by Bishop Robert Maxwell, and almost 150 years later the largest bell was damaged and had to be sent to Amsterdam to be recast. In 1671 the bell tower was struck by lightning and the tower was destroyed when its timber frame caught fire. To save the bells, the people of Kirkwall brought soft material into the Cathedral to cushion their fall, but even so the largest bell was cracked. The original inscription on that bell recorded that it was cast in Edinburgh Castle by Robert Borthwik. The subsequent inscription records that the 'Bell was taken to

Amsterdam by Alexander Geddus, a Kirkwall Merchant, and recast there by the City Bell-Caster, Claudius Fremy'.

⚜

The *Indus*'s passenger list included James Munro Linklater, whose wife Mary was William Flett's sister. In Adelaide, the brothers-in-law set up in business together, opening a grocer's shop in Currie Street near Light Square. In those early years Hindley and Currie streets were the city's business heart, but as the centre of trade began to shift eastwards Flett and Linklater moved to Hindley Street. Eventually they operated a remarkable combined grocery and drapery business; Flett & Linklater was on the south side, close to the corner of King William Street.

Partners in life, the Flett and Linklater families also lie side by side here, or more precisely, back to back, for James Munro Linklater's address is Road 1 South, Path 15; Plot 1 is on the eastern side of the path. This puts his headstone close behind the bell fence of William Flett. A second headstone for Linklater's children stands beside it, and from the inscriptions it appears that, of the older generation who emigrated from Scotland, Mary Linklater was the only one who lived to see the century turn. At her death in December 1904 she had outlived her brother, husband, and all of her children.

Although I pass over the same paths many times there is always something fresh to see, something new to puzzle over. For it is a site so rich in detail that it cannot all be taken in at a glance; indeed, it is not possible to notice every monument, to read every name and date at a single visit, even one that lasts many hours. In truth, the detail can be overwhelming, so that every interesting object that catches my eye slips from memory the moment something further along the path beckons. There are, though, certain small, perfect details that persist in my thoughts, like William Flett's 150-year-old fence with its frieze of iron bells.

⚜

Sir Dominick Daly died at Government House on 19 February 1868, the first death of a governor in office. As his funeral procession left St Francis Xavier's Cathedral in searing heat an immense crowd lined Grote Street, and the Murphy Memorial Bell at the cathedral was tolled. The Murphy Bell – the largest and oldest of the cathedral's bells – has a twice-earned name, being christened in honour of the St Francis Xavier's first bishop, Francis Murphy, and having also been cast in the Murphy Bell Foundry in Dublin. It was hung in 1867, just in time for the governor's funeral.

The flag-covered coffin was placed on a gun carriage drawn by six horses, with the governor's hat, sword, and gloves lying on top. The *Advertiser* reported that as the procession made its way west, 'a muffled peal was rung upon the Albert Bells'. To muffle the sound of bells, the clappers have to be covered with leather pads; there is a tradition of bells being rung this way to mark the death of a bellringer. Half-muffling, which is how they were probably rung for the governor's funeral procession, involves a leather pad being strapped to one side of each bell's clapper. This has the effect of damping alternate strokes, so the bells ring out and are immediately answered by a ghostly echo.

Along the route the Adelaide Regimental Band played Handel's 'Dead March' from *Saul*. Handel composed this oratorio in 1738 and at its earliest performance specified an orchestra that included a carillon – an instrument made up of bells that are rung by striking a keyboard. As the governor's funeral procession crossed West Terrace into the Hilton Road 'the bell at the Roman Catholic chapel began to toll'. This bell must have been at the original St Patrick's Church on the corner of Grote Street and West Terrace, for the Smyth Chapel, which is the centrepiece of the cemetery's Catholic Section, had not yet been built. It was constructed in 1871 as a memorial to Father John Smyth, who is buried beneath its floor. However, Daly's grave stands close beside it, and there is a certain symmetry to the fact that the designer of the Smyth Chapel, Edward Woods, also designed the Adelaide Town Hall, General Post Office, and St Francis Xavier's Cathedral.

Fabian Stedman, a printer from Cambridge, was the man who single-handedly changed the style of English bellringing, and with it the way we hear bells rung in Australia. Stedman wrote *Tintinnalogia, or, the Art of Ringing* with Richard Duckworth, published in 1668, and nine years later *Campanalogia*, which became a classic of the bellringing fraternity, with its precise exploration of all the possible changes that can be rung on any given number of bells.

The maths is staggering: for example, on a ring of eight bells like those in the Albert Tower, the maximum number of changes to the order in which the bells can be rung before a pattern must be repeated is 40,320. With twelve bells, like the ring at St Francis Xavier's Cathedral, the number of possible changes, called 'the extent', runs to some 480 million, which if rung non-stop would take around thirty-six years to perform.

One of Stedman's rules of ringing is that a peal must consist of 5040 changes, or the maximum number of changes that can be rung on seven bells; this takes a band of ringers somewhere between three and four hours. The physical effort and the concentration needed for this non-stop ringing explains why peals are sometimes attempted but not completed, and why those that are completed tend to be commemorated on plaques in the ringing towers. At St Peter's Cathedral a handsome wooden board notes that the first peal on the bells occurred on Wednesday 20 February 1963, and that it was 5040 Grandsire Triples. Peals had been attempted before, but on this occasion it was completed in three hours and thirty-two minutes in honour of a royal visit. The Albert Bells are notoriously difficult to ring, but the first peal was rung there on 23 April 1984.

Adelaide has four bell towers with a total of forty-three bells. At St Peter's Cathedral the tenor bell known as 'Great Frederick' weighs in at over two tons, and its octave of bells pitched in C is regarded as one of the finest in the world. St Andrew's Church in Walkerville has a set of six in F. Cast at the Whitechapel Bellfoundry in 1886, they have rung out on Saturday afternoons and Sunday mornings for well over a century. St Cuthbert's at Prospect has an octave in G; the first peal was rung there in 1975, and in 1994 a record peal was performed in just under ten hours.

The music or patterns followed by bellringers are long strips of numbers in which each ringer follows the thread of their bell as the changes are called. Compared to music written horizontally on a five-line stave, bell music looks more like a woven bookmark or a braided wall-hanging. Each bell has an identical time value, so it may be easier to read, and memorise, once you get the hang of the changes.

At the start of a ringing practice in the Albert Tower, the ringer of the treble bell leads off.

'Look to!' This is the signal to take hold of the bell ropes.

'Treble's going' announces that the treble bell has been brought up to its balance point. 'She's gone!' – the command to begin ringing.

The bell ropes creak; they scrape against the guide slots in the ceiling where a small black plastic bat has been hung – a bellringer's joke. Ringers throw their whole bodies into the pull-and-let-go-again rhythm, and soon the eight ropes are whipping up and down. Loops of rope strike the floor and bounce away; the floor creaks and shifts underfoot, and the tower rocks. The bronze voices of the bells fill the confined space of the ringing room. Their jangle resonates within the chest cavity, within the skull; it travels outwards, and inwards, back and forth, tapping lost memories, stretching through trans-generational memories to all the passings and processions, all the joyous celebrations that have ever been marked by the ringing of bells.

⚜

The freedom to wander from the subject of South Australia's seventh governor laying the foundation stone for the Town Hall into the slightly tangential territory of bellringing is one of the joys of these walks, which take place in a different register to journeys that hinge on destination. In some respects, with the site's unchanging pattern of roads and pathways, walking here has more in common with the meditative pacing of a labyrinth, or with being lost within a sizeable maze.

Mazes and labyrinths are often confused, or the terms are used interchangeably, but the two have distinct and opposing purposes: a maze is a puzzle, designed to trick a walker into getting lost, while the gentler labyrinth leads the walker towards its centre. Of the two, I prefer the labyrinth, for life already presents enough puzzles and dead ends, enough islands in the design that negate the 'hand on the wall' method of maze navigation. Like the labyrinth, walking here does shepherd one's thoughts towards a private centre, even though on each occasion what unfolds could be anything from an historic event to the cycle of endless renewal symbolised by bulbs, to the path beside the abyss that constitutes living with the knowledge of our own – and our loved ones' – mortality.

For a place where so much grief has gathered the cemetery has a palpable calm, and I wonder if perhaps this is its true function, aside from the aspect of crude disposal – as a site where grief can culminate and quietly disperse. Walking here, even while engaged in some harmless, seasonal quest – perhaps to inspect the fruit-laden quandongs or to check the progress of the pretty blue or white-flowered *Scilla peruviana* – I am unconsciously absorbing the whispered message of the physical world's impermanence.

Buddhism has a meditation on impermanence. Its aim is to encourage calm acceptance of the transitory nature of everything in the world, but also to bring about the realisation that humans have the power to change, to transform their own lives. There is an even more confronting death awareness meditation – confronting because death, although everywhere, is habitually shoved to the furthest darkest corner of our minds. Death is unmentionable; we do not want to think about it, let alone embrace it as a natural and inevitable part of life.

Buddhism teaches that by practising the death awareness meditation we learn to decide what is truly valuable. A constant awareness that life is fleeting means we will not squander time but spend it wisely. This practice involves embracing a number of difficult truths, beginning with the inevitability of death, bringing to mind people from the past who have lived and died – writers, artists, musicians, philosophers, explorers and botanists, criminals, and ordinary unknown souls. Further steps include bringing to mind all the people we know, becoming aware of their ever-decreasing lifespans and the uncertainty of the hour or cause of death, recognising the fragility of the human body and the solitary nature of the death experience. It occurs to me that walking here opens a subtle pathway through this difficult practice. Whether we know it or not, the site, like a labyrinth, guides us through all the stages of the death awareness meditation.

⚜

On a recent visit to St Peter's Cathedral I noticed that the pew at the front right-hand side of the church is inscribed in gold: *The Governor*. I am not sure how long it has been there, but Sir Dominick Daly would have attended the Catholic Cathedral. The obituary of James Munro Linklater mentions his connection with Chalmers Free Church on North Terrace, now Scots Church, which was built in 1851 by members of the Free Church of Scotland.

Scots Church was built by the firm of English & Brown; they also built the Adelaide Town Hall, General Post Office, Parliament House, National Bank, and Flinders Street Baptist Church. Like the partnership of Flett and Linklater, Thomas English and Henry Brown were brothers-in-law. They had arrived in South Australia in January 1850 on board the ship *Richardson*, which was under the command of Thomas English's brother, James. The ship had been chartered to bring out the plant and machinery and the miners for the Burra Mine and the English and Australian Smelting Works. It was said that at their arrival the only presentable building in Adelaide was the one known as 'Waterhouse's Corner', at the corner of Rundle and King William Street; there is a painting in the Art Gallery of South Australia of the three-storey Waterhouse Building by the artist J.A. Gilfillan, which shows a simple yet imposing structure with an arched entrance, and a first-floor balcony. English and Brown soon set up a builder's yard in Carrington Street and later bought a corner acre in Hindmarsh Square.

Thomas English was mayor of Adelaide from 1862–1863. Later he became a member of parliament. When he was buried at West Terrace Cemetery on Thursday 18 December 1884 five mourning coaches followed the hearse, along with a large number of private vehicles. Chief among the mourners was Thomas's brother, Captain James English, and his son, Joseph, along with elders of Chalmers Church. There are no women's names among the mourners, which probably means that in keeping with Victorian tradition women and children were excluded from the graveside rites for fear that they would not be able to control their emotions.

While he is certainly buried here, Thomas English is not listed on the cemetery's online archive, but with a bit of detective work I have discovered that his address is Road 3, Path 29; Plot 40 is on the eastern side. To locate the site it is far easier to walk down Road 4 to where the plot stands on the corner of Path 29. It is a substantial memorial, visible for some distance because of its height. The stonework bears many floral motifs, including olive and oak branches tied with ribbon, and the whole affair is crowned with an angel who stands with one graceful arm raised to heaven: miraculously, after 130 years of weather she appears intact. This site is close to the grave of John Isaacs the tiger-tamer in Path 30, and when the cast and crew of Harmston's Circus passed along this road for Isaac's funeral, this sweet-faced, impassive angel – already fourteen years on her plinth – was a silent witness to the procession.

The surrounding iron fence has a design of open lotus flowers, and its tapering corner posts are reminiscent of the supports of a four-poster bed. The gate will still allow itself to be eased open, although it needs support because its hinges have all but given up. The closing mechanism, too, has been improvised, with a cone of weathered wood to peg it closed. It is a family grave, and includes Thomas's wife Sarah and their son Joseph, as well as James English, and other family members.

On the walk from Road 4 to the Catholic Old Area I stop many times, my eye and interest captured by this detail and that. I do not resist the impulse to pause and look, to read inscriptions, or even to go out of my way entirely and cross pathways and roads, because who knows what treasures may be randomly stumbled across.

Sir Dominick Daly's grave is easy to find. On reaching the Smyth Chapel I look to the right of it, past the tall ornate obelisk to Luke Murphy that echoes the chapel's gothic architecture, and there behind an iron fence is the governor's memorial. For a site that is almost as old as the city's town hall, the stone is hardly weathered. Its base is solid, its inscriptions intact, but whatever once rested on top – at a guess it was an urn, although it might have been a statue – has been either vandalised or accidentally broken and disposed of.

The newspaper reported that the governor's relatives had erected a handsome Gothic monument. It was 'ten feet in height, and consists, including the basements, of solid blocks of freestone'. The monument weighed between four and five tons, and the stone was quarried from William Blackler's property at One Tree Hill. The enclosure is ten feet square, and the monumental mason was Mr W. Prosser of Gouger Street. William Prosser was one of the earliest of Adelaide's stonemasons and his work is found throughout the older parts of the cemetery. On other walks I have often passed Prosser's own memorial. It stands in Plan 3, and on taking the left turn from the curator's cottage it lies roughly between roads 3 and 4. A tall column surmounted with a tasselled cloth, it faces towards the road, its exact address on the map being Path 1, Plot 52.

Adelaide is famous for its 'Spanish light', the golden sunlight of late afternoon that is at its loveliest when it slants in low in autumn. More by luck than by judgment I have arrived here late in the day, and the mellow stonework of the light-soaked Smyth Chapel blazes with a holy fire. Thus gilded, it reminds me of a verse by Blake: *I saw a chapel all of gold / that none did dare to enter*

in. / And many weeping stood without / Weeping mourning worshipping.
I imagine the day of Sir Dominick Daly's funeral, the black-clad
mourners clogging the paths as far as the eye can see, mothball-
scented and sweating profusely, no doubt, in the punishing heat
of February – had women been present, their clothing alone would
have killed them. I hear the measured toll of the bell from St
Patrick's Church, the stamping hooves of waiting horses and the
swish of their tails as they flick at flies. On this autumn afternoon
the paths are empty of all but a few flittering, fluting birds.

18

The Little Knight

No bells were rung when Governor George Grey's infant son was interred at West Terrace Cemetery, for in 1841 the Town Hall had not yet been built and it would be years before the young colony could afford to buy the Albert Bells. The boy, also named George, had been born at sea about a month after Grey and his wife sailed from England in the *Lord Glenelg*. The couple arrived in South Australia on 10 May 1841, and their son died on 25 July; he was five months and nine days.

Rumour insists that Grey blamed his wife Eliza for neglecting the boy. Evidence is necessarily elusive at this distance, though there is a strong sense that Eliza resented her life in Adelaide, a city then only four or five years old, seeing it as a rough backwater. But whatever the facts of little George Grey's demise, his parents' marriage would be marred by accusation and counter-accusation for as long as they remained living together.

The two had met when George Grey was appointed resident magistrate at King George Sound, replacing Sir Richard Spencer. Eliza Lucy was the seventh child of Sir Richard and Lady Spencer – her father had served under Lord Nelson and been wounded three or four times, including a severe head wound that was thought to be the cause of his mood swings and rages. After a brief courtship George and Eliza were married at her parents' Strawberry Hill Farm; she was sixteen, barely more than a child, and he was twenty-seven.

Unfortunately for Eliza, raised within the orbit of an unpredictable temperament, marriage meant more of the same; George Grey was an impulsive and difficult man whose moods, it has been suggested by more than one source, were exacerbated by, and consistent with, long-term laudanum use. Neither was Eliza easy to get along with: a smouldering, dark-haired beauty, she was described by contemporaries as 'beautiful, fascinating and spoilt' and 'a perfect devil'.

Much has been written about the abrupt shift of governorship of the new colony from Gawler to Grey, but the most interesting opinions are those penned at the time. In his memoir *A Journey from Port Phillip to South Australia in 1839* George Hamilton describes the city as the Greys must have encountered it, with its unformed streets, its houses dotted amid the gum trees, and the River Torrens meandering through a tangle of tea-tree, rushes, and reeds. Hamilton, a congenial character, sees beauty in all of this, but it is easy to imagine a spoilt young woman concluding that she has been dragged beyond the boundaries of the civilised world. Hamilton reports, too, how in those early years the success of harvesting a strawberry, apricot, or watermelon could be cause for widespread joy among the colonists, but I imagine Eliza Grey's mouth (described as twisting about 'in a rather ugly way' as she reclined on a sofa) curling in disdain at such paltry treasures. In her defence, she had recently buried her only child.

Among the lines drawn over whether or not Gawler had brought the idealised colony envisaged by Wakefield to the brink of financial ruin, George Hamilton defended Gawler.

He was left by the S.A. Company without funds to rule over a community which could not make both ends meet. His position was a most difficult one. Fortunately the colonists had a governor of high principles and stout moral courage, and in spite of all the contumely that has been heaped upon him, he took the only course an honest man could have taken. Colonel Gawler, rather than see the colony of South Australia, deserted by its founders and ruined

by its feeble Government, fall to pieces, had the courage to plunge
it into debt, and cast it into the arms of the Imperial government.
Nothing wiser could have been done.

Hamilton's testimony communicates a sobering sense of how
precarious life was in those early years. Reading it, I consider
for the first time how the whole endeavour might have failed,
in which case I would never have had the chance to call myself
a South Australian. But Grey's austerity measures, though deeply
unpopular, succeeded, and he had almost managed to balance the
colony's budget when in 1845 he and Eliza left Adelaide following
a dispute over the payment of a government debt. He arrived in
New Zealand as governor in time to preside over the first wave of
Maori–British land wars.

Looking back over Grey's career, from two early and calamitous
explorations in Western Australia that saw him wounded by an
Aboriginal spear, his party stranded on an island without water,
and a 300-mile march back to Perth after their boats were wrecked,
to his political manipulations and unpopular governorships (he
was once described as 'the Artful Dodger of governors'), it is difficult to understand why he remained so long in favour with the
Colonial Office. It can only have been because the British Empire
was pieced together by men like George Grey: privileged; skilled; a
man with many interests, from the natural world (he was tireless in
collecting specimens for Kew Gardens, Kensington Museum and
other places) to books (he donated valuable libraries to both Cape
Town and Auckland); an elegant figure of great ability, with a dash
of the mad-dog Englishman.

His relationship with Eliza, always at the simmer, eventually
boiled over on a sea voyage from England to South Africa – it was
a roundabout route via South America. The elements of romantic
tragedy were all there: moody husband, dissatisfied wife, dashing
admiral, and adjacent sleeping quarters. Eliza was caught passing
an amorous note under the cabin door of the ship's captain, Admiral
Henry Keppel, and when it seemed Grey would either kill her, or

himself, the ship was turned around and Eliza and her maid were put off in Rio de Janeiro. The breakdown of their marriage caused a scandal in Britain, and for the next thirty-seven years, Grey would not speak her name.

The Greys were eventually reconciled, if somewhat uneasily, in 1897, reputedly due to an intervention by Queen Victoria. They died two weeks apart in 1898, Eliza first, then George. Still somehow a favoured knight of the Empire, he was buried in St Paul's Cathedral.

⚜

The site of baby George Grey's grave, though small, exudes an old-world, almost mythic romanticism. Although it is now surrounded by other headstones, when the child was interred here in the bleak mid-winter of 1841 it must have been a lonely and unpopulated spot, far from the main entrance, and I wonder why the Greys chose it. It has always reminded me of the tombs of knights found in old English churchyards, the ones where a stone figure reclines, sword on chest and dog at feet. This grave has neither figure nor dog, but it is, perhaps, the grey, horizontal form of the tomb that suggests the likeness, and the vaguely sword-like motif folded over the shallow roof-pitch of its lid.

The address is Road 4, Path 13. Plot 41 stands on the western side of the path, enclosed by a low iron railing. Around the edge is inscribed a line from the New Testament: Matthew 19:14 – *Jesus said suffer the little children to come unto me*. For such an early grave it is in remarkable order. Standing beside it, I am aware that Sir George Grey lingered on this same spot, and perhaps even Eliza in one of her voluminous, trailing dresses. The *Register* of 17 January 1914 published a piece on West Terrace Cemetery, and in it reported that Sir George Grey had made a return visit to South Australia many years after leaving it as governor. Warmly welcomed at the railway station, he postponed attending an official reception until he had made a pilgrimage to his son's grave.

One-hundred-and-seventy-three years have slipped by since the Greys buried baby George. Although physically attractive, they were flawed, unhappy people, and an ineffable grief still seems to pulse here, quietly. I think of Eliza's shipboard flirtation and Grey's cold abandonment of her in Rio, of her bitter insistence on George's infidelities and of the spite with which she once set about wrecking the romance of Edward Eyre (her husband's lieutenant governor in New Zealand) and his pretty fiancée, Fanny Ormond; I think about other verses in Matthew 19, the ones that exhort man and wife to 'cleve together' and to shun adultery. But neither George and Eliza's sexual shenanigans, nor the Bible, explain the residue of sorrow that I often feel is tethered here. The adult Greys are both buried on the other side of the world. No, I imagine the source of this strange small ache in the landscape is the abyss that opens underneath a child when, for whatever reason, and however briefly, it has not been able to secure its mother's love.

19

A Stroll to the Physic Garden

It is early June and already the first round of winter coughs and colds have surfaced in my household. Despite a flu vaccination I spent a miserable week with a respiratory infection, probably viral in nature, guzzling various soothing mixtures through long nights racked with a cough that left me with a tender ribcage. It took a few weeks to fully recover; I missed my walks here yet I still felt fortunate, for with the arrival of winter, nineteenth-century households would have faced a range of ailments they were poorly equipped to deal with. Doctors, as I discovered when tracking Francis Sheridan and even the well-intentioned Charles Carleton, seemed to be able to hang a brass plate outside their doors whether or not they had a medical qualification. Medicines were often mixed by chemists to their own recipes, and contained toxic ingredients potentially more dangerous than the diseases they professed to cure. Anaesthesia was discovered in the 1840s; in London there was a public demonstration of the effects of ether, but it was a hit-and-miss business for a very long time: God forbid you should ever need surgery.

In an age where the standard medical treatment for constipation, and much else besides, was a blue pill containing mercury washed down by a mug of the 'black draught', where blood-letting and purging were the first line of defence against violent illness, it is hardly surprising that homeopathy and herbalism gathered converts. Homeopathic remedies, especially, did no harm; patients were less likely to be killed by their treatment than those who were bled until they fainted, and homeopaths and herbalists often had better outcomes than doctors. Indeed, we still turn to them, often as a frustrated response to what the father of homeopathy Samuel Hahnemann referred to as 'allopathic' medicine, in other words mainstream Western medicine.

South Australia's first homeopathic practitioner was Samuel Kidner. Sickness in his family, especially his first wife's battle with tuberculosis, had led him to study with one of England's first homeopaths, Dr John Epps. Kidner never managed to gain a certificate of qualification due to his domestic circumstances, which included the death of his wife and all but one of his children, the latter through accidents. Burdened with so much misfortune, Samuel's own health was poor, and in 1857 in search of 'a change of air' he and his surviving daughter Albertina travelled to Australia.

Kidner did not come straight to Adelaide – he had been offered a job in the dispensary of a Sydney hospital, but due to a misunderstanding the position had been filled by the time he arrived. So he set out for Melbourne, where he established a homeopathic pharmacy in the township of St Kilda. A second business in Collins Street followed, in partnership with a Mr Gould.

Another early colonist whose life was to be profoundly affected by homeopathy was Thomas Magarey. Born in County Down, Ireland, in 1825, Magarey had been raised in the milling business and at the age of seventeen migrated with his brother James to New Zealand. There they settled in Nelson, and it was around this time that Thomas had the accident that would lead to his enduring interest in homeopathic cures. Having slipped and fallen under a cart, he sustained severe head and arm injuries; doctors treated him with the usual round of bloodletting and opiates, but nothing relieved the pain. Then, Nelson's small community of United Christians, into which the Magarey brothers had been drawn, was unsettled by the arrival of Wesleyan and Anglican clergy. Thomas and his brother decided to try Adelaide, that stronghold of Dissenters; they arrived in 1845, and after working for a few years at the Hindmarsh Flour Mill, they bought the business from the owner, John Ridley.

But Thomas continued to suffer symptoms from his accident,

and by 1858 his headaches were debilitating. Word of mouth put him in touch with a 'Dr McKearn' in Melbourne, who treated him with arnica and rhus, while prescribing less mental work, more loitering in the garden, no travelling or absences from home, and a routine of sitting baths. Magarey's health picked up with this treatment, and he returned to Adelaide a passionate believer in homeopathy.

Samuel Kidner knew both McKearn and Magarey, and his move to Adelaide followed a meeting with Thomas Magarey in Melbourne. The two had much in common, including intense religious beliefs, temperance, and devotion to homeopathy. Their familiarity with the Bible meant both would surely have known this verse from Ecclesiasticus, 38:4: *The Lord hath created medicines out of the earth; and he that is wise will not abhor them.* I imagine Thomas Magarey, especially, interpreted this as a sign from God in favour of homeopathy.

Kidner visited Magarey in Adelaide in 1860, and as there was no resident homeopath in the city he soon found himself besieged with appeals for professional help. He agreed to stay for twelve months until a qualified practitioner could be brought out from England, but in the end he remained here until his death in 1883.

⚜

At the root of homeopathy is the principle that 'like can cure like', a principle that was at variance with the Law of Contraries on which most nineteenth-century medical treatments were based. The theory of like curing like can be traced back as far as Hippocrates, who was the first to suggest that disease resulted from natural forces rather than divine influences – it is difficult now to imagine such ignorance of the workings of the human body. Compared to violent medical procedures, such as purging, venesection, and the terrifying trepanning, homeopathy was both safe and gentle.

Samuel Hahnemann was a German doctor who protested the violent methods of his era. He was ahead of his time in advocating better public hygiene, attention to diet, fresh air and exercise, but he gave up medicine in disillusion to work as a translator. It was while translating *A Treatise on Materia Medica* by William Cullen that Hahnemann came across the information that would change his life and the lives of others. It related to quinine, a substance extracted from the bark of the cinchona tree, which in Cullen's view was an effective treatment for malaria. When Hahnemann experimented by dosing himself with quinine he found that he soon developed the symptoms of malaria, although he did not have the disease. He repeated the experiment on other people in a system of tests he called 'provings' and from there he went on to test substances like arsenic and belladonna.

After six years of 'provings' Hahnemann had gathered a vast knowledge of the effects of different substances. He believed he had discovered a new system of medicine, which he described as *similia similibus curentur*: like can cure like. With many of the medicines being poisonous, Hahnemann administered them in small, diluted doses. Sometimes patients felt worse before they felt better, and to counter this Hahnemann devised a system of shaking a medicine vigorously before banging it down on a hard surface, a method he believed released the energy of a substance and avoided the 'aggravations' as he called the unpleasant symptoms.

Out of all of this came further dilutions, with solutions becoming weaker and weaker until not a single molecule of the original substance remained. In the cholera outbreak in Europe in 1831, Hahnemann recommended camphor and quarantining, and one of the many people he saved from cholera in this way, Dr Frederick Quin, went on to establish London's first homeopathic hospital. A cholera epidemic in 1854 showed that the death rate at the London Homeopathic Hospital was around a third less than in other hospitals, although perhaps the quarantining of patients had more to do with that than the camphor.

Homeopathic remedies are derived from many sources, but the fifteen key remedies include arsenic oxide (used for treating anxiety and fear, digestive disorders, and inflammation), silver nitrate, the substance used for backing mirrors (anxieties and fears, including stage fright and claustrophobia, and digestive complaints such as diarrhoea). Calcium, graphite, quicksilver or mercury, ignatia seeds, dried snake venom, salt, phosphorus, sepia, silica, and sulphur all have their uses. Plant-based ingredients like cyclamen, foxglove, and sarsaparilla overlap with herbalism.

Homeopathy's most alarming remedies call for a whole, live wolf spider, or female black widow spider. I imagine myself nursing a sorely afflicted husband or child through a long dark night while wondering where to lay hands on a black widow spider, or a gram of dried snake venom. I think of the helplessness of the times, and how in the Middle Ages physicians attempted to ward off the plague with the herb rue. In *Confessions of an English Opium Eater* Thomas de Quincey describes the toothache, the rheumatic pain of head, eye, ear, and cheek that led to his addiction. Walking here among the nineteenth-century graves, I sense the panic and desperation of many of our earliest settlers and ponder whether an understanding of medical practices, of the agony involved in everything from dentistry to childbirth, could bring us closer to the past than almost anything else.

I dip into my personal well of pain – a broken collar bone at school that hurt so much I thought I would die, a broken ankle years later that required surgery – but I find it impossible to call up the sensation of pain, to re-experience it in my body. Sure, I remember the nasty nature of the events, but the actual suffering seems to have healed along with the bones. I think of an abscessed tooth, perhaps the worst physical pain I have ever known in that the mouth's distress hammered directly up into the brain like hot roofing nails. I imagine myself back into the chair of a clumsy dentist, a man with beefy fists and impassive eyes who was determined to extract the infected tooth; I recall that I screamed out loud and frightened patients in the waiting room, but I cannot now feel in my body the agony and helpless rage of that moment.

⚜

Homeopathy and religion both require faith, and perhaps that is why this system of medicine appealed to the fiercely religious Thomas Magarey. Having mixed with United Christians in New Zealand, with a breakaway group from the Scotch Baptist Church he helped found the first Church of Christ in Australia, and later in life joined the Plymouth Brethren.

The picture that emerges of Thomas Magarey is of a severe man with a retiring nature. His last home was a farm at Enfield, where he built a telescope in the garden and studied the stars. With his wife Elizabeth he had produced ten children, but at home he kept to his own apartment, only emerging for family prayers. To his grandchildren he was an unsmiling man with intense blue eyes, his greying hair worn long to cover the evidence of his old accident. Perhaps it was the loss of his brother that turned Thomas Magarey into such a silent and formidable figure; they had been through much together, and Thomas must have been deeply affected by his death.

In 1859, James Magarey perished in the wreck of the ship *Admella*, off Carpenter's Rocks. Of 113 passengers and crew on board only twenty-four survived the ordeal. The ship also carried seven horses, some of which belonged to James Magarey. A survivor later reported that the horses swam ashore, or were drowned in the attempt, and that a grey carthorse belonging to Magarey was seen struggling in the waves towards the wreck. James Magarey behaved with great kindness to other passengers, giving away items of his clothing to those who needed them. He was anxious for the safety of a black portmanteau, to which he attached pieces of ship's furniture so that it might float; it carried important papers, and a reward of £50 was offered for its recovery. It was recovered, and inside was found a pencilled note from Magarey: *We shall all be lost unless we get God's assistance.* Upon a receipt for one of the horses he wrote, 'I think this horse got on shore'.

The victims were stranded for a week on the broken ship without food or water. On the third day, thirteen people crowded into the captain's little cabin, and James Magarey was one of those who read passages from the prayer book. Before help came, Magarey slipped and fell into the water. He was seen feebly battling the waves and when a rope was thrown to him he was too weak to grasp it; unable to swim, he drowned about 300 yards off the wreck, despite wearing a cork life belt. When his body was found it was said to have been 'terribly disfigured by sharks'. Magarey was identified by a card case and its cargo of cards inscribed with his name, and by the labels sewn inside his clothing.

In the same year his brother died, Thomas Magarey embarked on his first pastoral venture, with a lease on land at Naracoorte. It was on this property that Harry Oxley worked before the move to Adelaide that ended so disastrously on Christmas morning.

Among football fans the name Magarey is synonymous with the medal presented each year to a player in the SANFL. It was Thomas Magarey's great nephew, William Ashley Magarey, a lawyer with sporting interests, who was responsible – as the inaugural chairman of what would become the SANFL he wanted to rid the sport of rough play. The Magarey Medal rewarded the fairest and most brilliant player each season. William Magarey, nicknamed 'Beautiful Bill', personally presented it every year from its inception in 1898 until his death in 1929; the only exception to these annual awards was the period of the First World War, when the competition was suspended. William Magarey was cremated at West Terrace Cemetery.

⚜

The use of plants for healing predates written history, and botany and medicine were once one and the same study, especially during the centuries in which the great herbals were written. The invention in Germany around 1440 of printing from movable type on a printing press resulted in a flurry of herbals in Europe. In England, famous names associated with herbal lore throughout the sixteenth and seventeenth centuries were naturalists, botanists, and apothecaries – Turner, Gerard, Parkinson, and Culpeper – while Mrs Grieve's *A Modern Herbal*, published in 1931, is perhaps the last great collection of herbal knowledge and one that carried forward the spirit of past texts. But at a point between Nicholas Culpeper's *Complete Herbal* and Maud Grieve's reprise, botany and medicine parted company. After the seventeenth century, books on botany barely touched on the medicinal properties of the plants, while medical texts contained little or no botanical information.

Widespread belief and use of herbal remedies ceased with the development of modern medicine and synthesised drugs, although powerful plants such as the foxglove and poppy are still generally recognised as ingredients in the prescriptions scribbled down by modern doctors. Yet the age of home-made poultices and soothing syrups is not so far behind us. As a child, my grandmother taught me to draw out splinters with a paste of sugar and soap; she treated coughs and colds, even pneumonia, with a hot mustard plaster applied to the chest. Believing that illness entered the body first and foremost through the soles of the feet, during one bitter desert winter, she cut brown-paper templates of our shoes and soaked them in kerosene, so that friction combined with the fuel to produce heat on the walk to school. It worked, though in an era where everyone smoked it is a wonder that a stray match or carelessly tossed cigarette butt did not turn us into human torches.

Jacob Bowden was one of South Australia's earliest herbalists. His last address in England was Five Lanes, near Lanson, Cornwall, before he sailed aboard the *Royal Admiral*. His wife Anne and small daughter Lydia accompanied him; a son, Edward, was born during the voyage. They arrived at Adelaide in 1838; Jacob's brother John, a harness-maker, brought his wife and five children out on the same ship. John Bowden took up land north-east of Adelaide and named it Kersbrook after his birthplace in Cornwall, while Jacob Bowden set up in business as a herbalist, at an address in Gilles Street.

Bowden was credited with many cures and with good works among the poor. His wife Anne died in 1861 after giving birth to at least thirteen children. Jacob was married again in 1863 to a widow, Elizabeth Musson. When Elizabeth died he married a third time. The bride, Keturah Bliss, was a widow of fifty-six, and Jacob was seventy-three. Throughout all the changes that occurred in the city – and they were many, for when Bowden arrived from England William Light was still alive – and through the ups and downs of his own life, he continued to ply his trade in Gilles Street. In 1882 he retired in favour of one of his sons.

⚜

Of all the months in the year, June is my favourite time to walk here – it can be cold, but on a fair morning like this the light has great clarity and the spring bulbs are beginning to stir; some are already up, and early jonquils are flowering. As I walk from the main gates and turn down Road 2 the air is fresh with the scent of pine, and the magpies are busy crafting their songs in the treetops.

Thomas Magarey's address is Road 2, Path 12; Plot 27 is on the western side of the path. It is an easy walk to the path on the fringes of the quandong grove. Bars of light and curls of shadow are thrown down by the old ironwork, and the place I am looking for is about three-quarters of the way along. Surrounded by a simple but sturdy iron fence, Thomas Magarey's gravestone is suitably austere: a flat, polished slab has been cut from a granite boulder, and inscribed with his name and that of his wife Elizabeth. There are no flourishes, no symbols or euphemisms. Indeed, its restraint would make this stone a worthy contender for the Quaker cemetery. To one side is a smaller, much older headstone with an even simpler inscription: *TM, 1855*. From its size I guess it marks the grave of an infant, perhaps another Thomas, although I can find no record of it on the cemetery's archive. However, it was during the time of John Monck's rein when records were loosely kept, and if children were stillborn they were often buried quickly and without ceremony.

From here I walk towards Road 3, and the path I am looking for is almost opposite. Jacob Bowden's address is Road 3, Path 10, Plot 6, on the eastern side. I cross and turn in, and a few steps along is the grave of Joseph Cooke Verco, the physician and conchologist. Beside it stands the lovely memorial Jacob Bowden erected at his first wife's death. It features a circular lily motif, and records his

253

profession as herbalist and his rooms in Gilles Street. Jacob himself died in 1888 at the age of eighty, which considering the life expectancy of the times must have been regarded as unusual longevity and a testament to his herbalist's skills. The headstone is restrained without being severe, and speaks of a gentleness of temperament. In 1907, Jacob's third wife Keturah chose to be buried here with him.

The monument is signed at the foot: *Prosser*. It seems that Jacob Bowden and Sir Dominick Daly, though unlikely ever to have met in life, had in common a monumental mason.

Samuel Kidner's address is Road 4, Path 30; Plot 3 is on the western side of the path. When his funeral set out from his residence on Port Road, Hindmarsh, there were three mourning coaches and twenty-six private vehicles following the hearse. Samuel Kidner had been vice-president of the Robert Street Literary Society, and it was reported he had been looking forward to the literary competition about to take place in the Town Hall. He had attended the preliminary competition held in the Stow Lecture Hall only a week earlier, and mentioned to a friend afterwards that while there he had suffered from sitting in a draught.

Path 30 lies toward the bottom of Road 4. The deciduous trees there have dropped their leaves, and their bare branches press a dark and intricate tracery upon the sky. I turn in left, and Samuel Kidner's headstone is just a little way in on the right. It is a simple Gothic arch, with suitably Gothic lettering. Its loveliest feature is a sheaf of wheat tied with ribbon. Doubtless it is primarily religious in tone, yet it hints at Kidner's connection with the discipline of natural medicine.

*

As I make my way towards the main gates and prepare to be absorbed back into the living world, I am reminded that botanic gardens evolved out of the much earlier physic gardens, and that many such gardens were instigated by members of the medical profession. Perhaps the most famous, and one of the oldest still extant, is London's Chelsea Physic Garden, founded in 1673 by the Worshipful Society of Apothecaries for its apprentices to study the medicinal qualities of plants. Samuel Kidner, Thomas Magarey, and Jacob Bowden would all have been aware of its importance, as would John Bailey and George William Francis; perhaps one or two of them even visited it before they set sail for South Australia.

It is said that during the First World War the Chelsea Physic Garden was tended by women, since all its gardeners had gone to the war. That was a time when many English gardens fell into decline, but Chelsea hung on – as serene and beautiful as any earthly walled garden could be. Miraculously, all the men who left the physic garden to fight returned uninjured. Just knowing that fact makes my heart swell; I want to say something about it, but sometimes a beautiful truth is best left to speak for itself.

20

Depths of Emerald Green

O tell me not of the beauteous sea,
With its bright waves leaping joyously,
Of its clear calm depths of emerald green,
Where far, far down, rare gems are seen;
And floating flowers of fairy land
Gleam in strange beauty o'er silvery sand.
'The Wreck of the Admella'
– Caroline Carleton, 1860

At school I read dry accounts of shipwrecks, pages sprinkled with names and dates and numbers of lives lost. I can remember thinking how awful it must have been, how terrifying, but I never felt the terror as it deserved to be felt because those books, with their recital of what was sunk and what was saved, reduced history to a bloodless paperchase. Yet the story of a shipwreck as told by the survivors puts the reader right there beside them in their peril. The details of the sinking of the *Admella* are probably no more agonising than many another maritime calamity, yet I cannot read them without a twinge of anguish.

The steamer *Admella* sailed from Adelaide early in the morning of 5 August 1859, on its run to Melbourne. The weather was clear all down the gulf and through the passage between Kangaroo Island and the mainland, until, at about one in the afternoon, the swell on clearing the island caused one of the horses on board, Jupiter, to throw himself onto his back in his stall. While the horse was being got back onto his feet, the captain altered the ship's direction. The weather continued fine, and in the evening some of the passengers enjoyed a game of whist. Then, at around five in the morning, the *Admella* struck the Carpenter's Reef about twenty-five miles north-west of Cape Northumberland. Within a few minutes the ship had broken into three pieces; the main mast and the funnel fell, smashing the lifeboats. An attempt by the captain to launch the quarter boat ended with it being swamped.

Passengers stumbled from their cabins onto the deck, and

some were washed overboard by the rolling sea. As day broke, a great number of people clinging to the mast were thrown into the water when it fell overboard. Some were drowned while others managed to clamber back onto the wreck. The man in charge of Mr Magarey's horses was seen floating away on a horsebox, paddling with his hands, and a fireman, Adam Purdem, swam to a piece of timber in the hope of reaching the shore. Once both men were about half a mile from the wreck those stranded watched helplessly as the current carried them out to sea. Ships passed by without noticing the survivors' plight, despite a number of female passengers removing their white underwear to be waved as flags, and ringing on the ship's bell. No children survived the wreck, and only one female passenger, Miss Bridget Ledwith.

Throughout the week in which the stranded passengers clung to the wreck, there were many terrible scenes, with a few that stick in the mind as representative of the general horror.

A woman with two broken legs clung to her dead baby; when the child's body was consigned to the waves, she threw herself in after it. A lad who was on board as cabin boy, an excellent swimmer, volunteered to swim to one of the lifeboats that had floated away at a great distance. Fearful of sharks, and of the pointless loss of a young life, the passengers argued against it. But the boy insisted that he could swim the distance, and they tied a rope to him and watched as he battled towards the boat. As the boy swam further from the wreck, more lengths of rope were found and tied together. As the last piece was being added and the boy was almost in reach of the boat, the person holding the rope let it go. The boy was swept away, along with their hope of retrieving the lifeboat, and in the midst of an already dire situation, the watchers were overwhelmed by grief.

They all fought with terrible thirst, and one man persisted in lowering his boots into the sea on a rope, then hauling them up to drink seawater. He became delirious, then lost his boots, and ended by going into the water. Miss Clendinning, the stewardess, also grew delirious and insisted upon going down into the water-filled cabin to take her dinner, which she fancied was ready. A seaman, Soren Holm, undertook to swim to an upended boat. A rope was tied to him, and other ropes knotted as the need arose. The man reached the boat, though he could not right it and ended by sitting on top. When those on the wreck attempted to haul him towards them the knots unravelled and the unfortunate man was cast adrift. For the next day and a half he was seen floating about; the boat was later washed ashore.

A great number of women and children stranded on the bow section soon disappeared. Mr McNair the purser reported afterwards that those who died on the wreck were lowered overboard without ceremony, their clothing handed out among the survivors. However, one chilling detail was the exception made for the last victim, James Hare, the chief steward, 'reserved lest terrible necessity should have prompted that which a timely rescue happily prevented'.

Two men, John Leach and Robert Knapman, finally reached the shore on a makeshift raft. Exhausted by their three-hour battle in the surf, they stumbled all night through swamps and over sandhills to reach the Cape Northumberland lighthouse. From there, the lighthouse keeper set out on horseback to Mount Gambier, however he was thrown from the horse, and the journey had to be completed by a local station owner, Peter Black. When help finally arrived, the rescue effort was fraught with difficulties because of the heavy seas.

In the end, eleven passengers and thirteen crewmen survived. Hurtle Fisher a fearless steeplechase rider had been taking his horse The Barber to Melbourne for the Australian Champion Sweepstakes. His brother George was lost in the wreck, but by some miracle The Barber swam the two miles to shore and survived. After Fisher was rescued he walked the horse cross-country to Geelong; from there they travelled the last fifty miles into Melbourne by train, arriving in early September. Although The Barber appeared no worse for the experience, and was the popular favourite for the Sweepstakes, he finished the race unplaced and never won again. His owner, who had started out on the journey at a weight of nine stone seven pounds, was reduced to five stone twelve pounds when he arrived at his destination.

George and Hurtle were the sons of Sir James Hurtle Fisher the resident commissioner, and the man in whose hut the fire that destroyed William Light's belongings was started. When the *Admella* was wrecked Sir James was president of the Legislative Council of South Australia. After his experience at sea Hurtle Fisher moved permanently to Melbourne, where he established a stud farm and became a founding member of the Victorian Racing Club. His racing colours were black with a red sash, and it might have been his connection with the beginnings of the Essendon Football Club that resulted in those colours being adopted for the club's strip.

Hurtle Fisher died in Melbourne in 1905. He is buried at West Terrace Cemetery in the Fisher family vault in the Kingston Allotments, Row 4, Plot 14. The pale-yellow tomb stands isolated at the centre of a gravelled area, fenced by high iron railings. Its gate is rusted fast and it is difficult to get close enough to read the inscriptions, but Hurtle Fisher's name is there at one end, and I suspect that his brother's death by drowning is also remembered somewhere on the vault.

A little further along, in the Kingston family plot, a marble scroll records the death at sea of Sir George Strickland Kingston, in 1880. He was buried off Ceylon. *The sea shall give up its dead*, is inscribed below.

Another of the *Admella*'s victims was Henry Holbrook. Originally from near Nottingham in England, twenty-six-year-old Holbrook was an employee of F.H. Faulding. His body was recovered and brought to Adelaide, and his address is Road 1 South, Path 20; Plot 7, marked with an obelisk, is on the western side of the path.

Caroline Carleton wrote a poem about the doomed ship, and it became the subject of paintings by a number of artists. James Shaw's oil of 1858 shows the *Admella* intact, though riding a dark and terrifying sea. Black smoke pours from its short funnel; there are no sails on its three masts, and in the front left foreground is a piece of wreckage, or an anchor, in the ominous shape of a cross. He painted the ship again in 1859, although this time the wreck is all but submerged. Charles Hill's painting depicts the broken ship, some parts already underwater, and the band of desperate victims on the tilting hull. Rescue boats approach the wrecked *Admella*, but who can tell if they will be successful, for those treacherous emerald depths loom in the foreground, they shimmer beneath spray and foam to the horizon. In the left front foreground Hill has placed a small white bird, a soul, perhaps; if so, it may belong to the boy who swam so heroically towards the lifeboat.

⚜

Both James Shaw and Charles Hill recorded Adelaide's early days. Aside from Shaw's *Admella* paintings, the Art Gallery holds his 1865 view of the Botanic Garden. In it we see a man-made lake with white and black swans, a three-tiered fountain on the main walk, glasshouses, buildings that probably shelter George William Francis's collection of animals, and a view of his two-storey residence.

James Shaw was born at Dumfries in 1815, the son of James and Isabella Shaw and younger brother of George Baird Shaw who would follow him to Australia. The family lived at 28 Gayfield Square, Edinburgh; the row of grey-stone Georgian houses fronting onto a cobbled street and a grassy square is still there now. James senior had trained as a lithographer and engraver in Glasgow; he was also an enthusiastic amateur painter, so he probably tutored both boys in drawing, painting, and lithography. James went to the University of Edinburgh to study law and qualified in 1836; then, via a stint in Jamaica, around 1850 he pitched up in South Australia. His brother George was sent to the Academy of Fine Arts at Trieste, and afterwards was commissioned to engrave portraits of Sir Walter Scott and his family for John Gibson Lockhart's *Memoirs of the Life of Sir Walter Scott, Bart*. George immigrated to Dunedin,

New Zealand, and stayed five years, until in 1856 he visited his brother James, who by now was a prolific portrait painter and photographer in Adelaide. George eventually settled in Sydney, where he produced portraits of Sydney politicians and clergy. On a return trip to Adelaide he was awarded the five-guinea prize for the best South Australian oil landscape painting.

James Shaw died in Adelaide in September 1881, followed two years later by George, in Sydney. James's address is Road 2, Path 17, and Plot 28 is on the eastern side. Many graves along this path have been invaded by quandong trees; his remains intact, though its modest headstone is much weathered and has an ominous crack.

Charles Hill was born in 1824 in Coventry, England, the son of an officer of the King's Dragoons who had served under Wellington. After being apprenticed to a line engraver at Newcastle-upon-Tyne, in 1840 Hill entered the Newcastle Academy of Fine Arts. Later he studied under the well-known painter and printmaker William Bell Scott, and in London under Samuel William Reynolds the younger, whom he assisted in making a popular engraving of the opening of the 1851 Great Exhibition.

Encouraged to travel to South Australia to benefit his health, Hill arrived in 1854 on board the *Historia*. Unable to find work as a line engraver, he established an art school at his home in Pultney Street, and eventually became drawing master at various schools, including St Peter's College. In 1856 he called a meeting at his home of Friends of the Arts, a group that later became the South Australian Society of Arts; Charles Hill was its first chairman. When in 1861 the South Australian School of Design was founded, Hill became its art master.

His most ambitious oil painting, 'The Proclamation', took fifteen years to complete and includes portraits of nearly a hundred people present at the occasion. He and his wife had eight children, and perhaps his best works are the informal studies of his own family. These include 'The Artist's Wife and Eldest Daughter, Henrietta' (1854), 'Mrs Hill and Children' (1857), and 'Family Group' (circa 1870).

Although Hill brought his engraving tools to the colony and wrote a monograph on etching techniques, he is not known to have made engravings here. But as well as being an important art teacher he played a leading role in the artistic life of the new colony. A member of the Old Bohemian Club, contemporary sources noted that his habitual dress was frock coat and high hat.

Charles Hill's address is Road 3, Path 18; Plot 31 is on the eastern side. Sadly, for a man who made such a valuable contribution to early South Australian society, Charles Hill's headstone has been broken and removed. The base and concrete edging remains but his plot can only be identified by the surrounding graves. (To his right is a handsome headstone in memory of Jane Stewart and Alexander Leighton.) Hill died in 1915 at the age of ninety-one. His wife Eliza Georgia Jane died three years later, and she is buried here with him.

⚜

When the *Admella* went down she carried a number of passengers who were to sail onwards from Melbourne to Liverpool in the steam clipper *Royal Charter*. One man just missed boarding the *Admella*, and when news of its fate broke in the newspapers he wrote to his family in Scotland to say how thankful he was that he had been delayed. He travelled to Melbourne by the next boat and managed to catch the *Royal Charter*.

The newspaper clipping that records this event puts me in mind of Somerset Maugham's 1933 retelling of a very old story, 'The Appointment in Samarra', in which a merchant sends his servant to market to buy provisions, and in a little while the servant returns, white and trembling.

'Master, in the marketplace I was jostled by a woman in the crowd, and when I turned I saw it was Death that jostled me. She made a threatening gesture. Please, lend me your horse, and I will ride away from this city and avoid my fate. I will go to Samarra and there Death will not find me.'

So the merchant lent his horse to the servant, and the man

galloped off as fast as he could. Then the merchant went down to the marketplace and saw Death standing in the crowd.

'Why did you make a threatening gesture to my servant this morning?' he asked.

'That was not a threatening gesture,' Death said, 'it was only a start of surprise. I was astonished to see him in Bagdad, for I have an appointment with him tonight in Samarra.'

The *Royal Charter* sailed from Melbourne on 25 August 1859 under the command of Captain Taylor. She was the pride of the British passenger fleet, the *Queen Mary* of her day. Unfortunately for the passenger who had narrowly missed the *Admella*, on the night of 25 October the *Royal Charter* was wrecked on the rocky Welsh coastline, driven onshore by a force 12 gale that came to be known as the 'Royal Charter Storm'. It was a night in which 200 ships were wrecked in British waters, though the *Royal Charter* accounted for more than half the death toll.

As dawn broke a man who lived on the nearest hilltop to the site found his roof being stripped by the storm. Together with a neighbour, he got out a ladder to make temporary repairs, and from there looked down towards the water where 'some dark troubled object' lay close to land. With others, he ran to the shore, where they watched 'the sea beating mercilessly over a great broken ship'.

Of the roughly 480 on board, only forty-one were saved, and most of those owed their lives to the courage of a Maltese-born seaman, Guzi Ruggier, also known as Joseph Rogers, who volunteered to swim ashore with a line. Hailed afterwards as a hero, even portrayed the following year by Henry O'Neil in his painting 'A Volunteer', Ruggier's bravery enabled a few people to struggle to safety through the surf. Many passengers went down with the ship; others were smashed against the rocks, stunned to death before they could be drowned. The total loss came to more than 450 lives. As with the *Admella*, all the women and children on board perished.

In the second chapter of *The Uncommercial Traveller*, Charles Dickens paints a vivid picture of his visit late in 1859 to the site of the wreck. The other hero of the hour was the rector of Llanallgo, the Reverend Stephen Roose Hughes, who with his family worked tirelessly to identify and bury the dead. Dickens met Hughes and saw the church where the flagstones were still damp from the laid-out bodies of the drowned, and where pitch had been burned as an improvised disinfectant. Dickens saw, too, the great numbers of coffins being made and graves being dug – so many that the local community began to worry that there would be no room left in the churchyard for them and their descendants. Bodies that could not be identified were described, numbered, and buried four at a time. The rector's task was a gruesome one, but he never complained. Dickens had nothing but the highest praise for this compassionate man who wrote 1075 letters to bereaved relatives.

What has kept the wreck alive in the public imagination for more than a century – so much so that the *Royal Charter* has its own Facebook page – is the large quantity of gold on board from the Victorian goldfields. Many of the passengers were new 'gold millionaires' on their way home after having made their fortunes. There were reports of men tying quantities of gold around their waists, but on that doomed ship they only sank all the quicker. The bullion room was broken up by the sea and its contents scattered, but at the time of Dickens's visit divers were already working to recover the treasure.

Today the site still attracts divers who come in the hope of scooping up a stray gold sovereign from beneath the sand. What they find are knives and forks, pieces of broken crockery, and barnacle-encrusted chains.

⚜

In 1859 the colony of South Australia was still in its infancy, and two such significant shipwrecks would have sent out ripples of grief that touched many families. One early colonist who perished off the coast of Wales was Robert Forsythe MacGeorge, and it is likely he was the passenger who missed boarding the *Admella*. MacGeorge, his wife Elizabeth and ten children, had arrived in South Australia in 1839 aboard the *Ariadne*, and by 1846 had established a home, which MacGeorge named Urrbrae, in the foothills south of the city. 'Urr' was his home parish in Scotland, and he added 'brae', meaning a slope near a creek or river. Their large, single-storey house was later over-built by Peter Waite, who turned it into the thirty-five-room, two-storey mansion that today forms part of the University of Adelaide's Waite campus.

Elizabeth MacGeorge's address is Road 1 South, Path 19; Plot 2 is on the eastern side of the path. Her husband may be one of those buried by the Reverend Hughes in the churchyard at Llanallgo, but his death in the *Royal Charter* is remembered here with an impressive marble obelisk. It stands at the corner of Path 19 under the sheltering boughs of a large pine, and its low iron fence is remarkable for the small wing-like shapes at its corners, or perhaps they represent waves. The monument, with its discreetly carved decoration, is signed by William Prosser, and unlike Governor Daly's memorial is in perfect condition. It is also within sight of the last resting place of Henry Holbrook, who perished on the *Admella*.

⚜

Thirty-two years after the *Admella* and the *Royal Charter* went down on opposite sides of the world, the sinking of the steamship *Gambier* off Queenscliff at the entrance to Port Phillip brought distress to local families, since most of those who lost their lives had been bound for Adelaide. The *Gambier*, a passenger vessel, was travelling from Sydney on 28 August 1891 when, just after midnight, it was struck at right angles by the collier *Easby*. The *Gambier* sank within seven minutes. Most of the twenty-one lives were lost when a lifeboat capsized.

Passengers John and Clarinda Trewenack had been visiting their children in Sydney. John Trewenack had arrived from England in 1849 and set up in business as a blacksmith in Wyatt Street, Adelaide. Later he was head of the blacksmith's department at the Wallaroo mines; at his death he was retired, and a resident of Norwood.

When the body of a woman was found partly embedded in the sand near Queenscliff it was identified by William Henry

Trewenack as being the remains of his mother, Clarinda. The corpse was brought to Adelaide, where Clarinda's daughters were unconvinced that it was their mother. The clothes she had been wearing when found were brought for them to examine, and on seeing them the two women were even more certain of the mistake. They telegraphed to William in Sydney, and William replied that if the clothes did not belong to his mother then it was not her body. The discovery of five teeth in the corpse's jaw confirmed the daughters' suspicions. Their mother, they said, only had one. An examination of the feet seemed to seal the matter: a deformity of one toe, peculiar to Clarinda Trewenack, was not present.

The undertakers, Pengelley and Knabe of Rundle Street, passed on these identification doubts to the police. Inspector Sullivan was ordered to view the body and reported that the woman was about five feet in height, although her face was entirely gone, with only the bare skull remaining. There were two grinding teeth on the upper right jaw, and a fourth tooth on the right. The toenails were very long and looked as if they had not been cut for some time; the lady had small feet, he said. She wore a red flannel petticoat under a black lustre skirt, quilted about eight inches from the bottom, and yellow stays, drab-coloured body, trimmed with pure velvet, a pair of grey woollen stockings, and elastic-sided leather boots. A red-and-blue silk handkerchief, white cotton drawers with the legs trimmed with deep embroidery, and a hand-sewn chemise. The policeman took possession of the clothing, and the undertakers were ordered to bury the body.

The remains were interred at West Terrace Cemetery on a Tuesday afternoon at the expense of Clarinda Trewenack's friends, who followed her to the grave. It was said that the 'unfortunate mistake in identity' not only entailed a great deal of trouble upon the undertakers, but also considerable expense to the relatives of Clarinda Trewenack, as the cost of carriage and other necessary mortuary arrangements fell to them.

Lacking a positive identification, the unnamed victim appears to have been buried as Clarinda Trewenack. Her address is Road 2,

Path 11, and Plot 31–32 is on the eastern side. The verse chosen by the children for their parents' headstone evokes a metaphorical rescue from the terrors of the sea.

We are resting so sweetly in Jesus now,
We sail the wide sea no more.
The tempests may sweep o'er the wild stormy shore,
We are safe where the storms come no more.

The gravesite was first established at the death of Henry Trewenack in 1853, and Jane, his widow. Clarinda and John Trewenack were sixty-one and sixty-two respectively, and from the headstone, the family had its roots in Penzance, Cornwall. The stone with its decorative floral motifs is still readable, but the iron fence surrounding the plot has lost its gate and all that remains is the lock, the keyhole, and the rusted knob.

❦

West of the Kingston Allotments and on their northern side, a tree-less expanse is flooded with pale cold light. It is wintry June, and I stand for a few minutes watching pigeons flutter against the pearl-coloured sky. Higher up, swallows fling their tiny bodies into wild, swooping flight patterns. I am looking across a landscape peopled with seamstresses, harness-makers, and English ploughmen, people whose skills have all but vanished from contemporary life. It is this view of mostly nineteenth-century headstones that reminds me how often people remark that they love old cemeteries. 'There are so many stories,' is the most common reason given, but as I found when I first came here, the stories have to be teased out. I too love a good story, but I wonder if the widespread fascination with old cemeteries is actually a veiled fascination with life and death and our human lifespan. Sites like this one offer a sideways glance at our own mortality, with the need for misdirection perhaps based on an unconscious belief that if we are not caught looking we will escape Death's return gaze. 'Death? Oh, all in good time,' we say, when what we really mean is 'Never!'

In an interview, Woody Allen once pointed out that if we were told that on a certain day, at a certain hour, a man with a gun would burst through the door and shoot us dead, we would never be able to think about anything else. Forgetting is a survival mechanism; with death, and even with losses like emigration, forgetting is a necessary kindness. But here, as far as the eye can see, I am surrounded by signs of the stubborn struggle to remember, for humans are contradictory creatures. And yet, in the choice between compassionate forgetting and painful recall, I too favour remembrance, which is why – although almost half my life has been lived away from Australia – I never made a satisfactory migrant.

21

In Deep Water

Beneath the surging wave,
There lie the young and brave –
God rest their souls and save!
'The Rescue'
– Caroline Carleton, 1860

I have been walking in this city of stories, city of stone and iron,
for almost three years, following its crisscross of grief lines with
undiminished enthusiasm. It is a city of inexhaustible mystery, a
contrary city that sometimes holds its secrets close. On ordinary
days in the living world I often pause in the midst of some busy-
ness and remember its lack of flurry, for quiet hour falls upon quiet
hour here. Or I find myself gnawing at the problem of one of its lost
stones, some deteriorating slab of sandstone or limestone or slate,
its engraving indecipherable. A number of these stones haunt me,
for their wind-smoothed faces are almost, but not quite, readable;
curiously, these nearly all relate to death by drowning. They slip
into my thoughts at odd hours, mutely teasing; they reproach me as
I pass along the paths. One ancient and disintegrating tomb in particular calls me back again and again in a voice that is now barely
even a whisper. It has a compelling story to tell, but no matter
how I stare at its scoured surface – and I have photographed it in
different lights hoping for clarity – I have not been able to harvest
more than a few fragments: *in the same grave; drowned; Frederick;
28th November 1847; Aged 34.*

But I have salvaged one story that was, perhaps, only a season
or two away from eternal obscurity; I have heard its faint voice, and
written down its words. I was drawn to it by its symbol of a heart
pierced by an arrow. *Man proposes, God disposes* encircles the heart.
The stone is simple in shape, and its size hints at a child not fully
grown. The lettering is hard to read on its weather-blasted surface,

but when photographed and blown up I could see that it was the grave of James Harry Barkly Horton, second son of Joseph Walter Horton, and that information released the story.

Joseph Horton was one of Adelaide's early veterinary surgeons with a practice in Currie Street. As the headstone notes, he was a member of the Royal College of Veterinary Surgeons, although until I knew that I could not make sense of the letters on the stone: MRCVS. On 27 March 1874, Joseph and his two sons drove to the North Arm Bridge on the Port River to hire a boat. Finding no boatman, Joseph went to the bridge to fish, while the boys undressed and went into the water in search of crabs and cockles. The water being low, Joseph Horton fastened his line to the bridge and got into a dingy; he rowed further along the shore to look for cockles. When he returned the boys asked him for a row, and he pulled along the shoal line so that they could reach the cockles. He then took the boat back to where he had found it, ran it aground and told the boys to get dressed and take the cockles to the trap.

Meanwhile, Horton's fishing line had become entangled on one of the piles of the bridge, so he returned to the boat with the intention of rowing out and disengaging the line. The boys had not dressed, as ordered; instead, they were playing with the boat, pulling it this way and that. Joseph told them to jump out, and the younger one did as he was asked, but the older boy, James, hesitated. How often would Joseph Horton look back upon that moment and wish it otherwise, for in that instant of hesitation his son's fate was sealed. Joseph recognised the boy's desire to go with him in the boat, and he relented. The two rowed out under the bridge to the spot where the line was tangled. But when James stood up to reach for it, his father saw he was in danger of falling.

'Catch hold of the pile,' he cried.

But instead the boy leant against it, pushing the boat off, and fell headlong into the river.

In trying to reach him, Joseph Horton let go of his oars, though he recovered one, which he pushed towards his son. It was not long enough, so he leaned over. Now the boat capsized, and both father and son were struggling in deep water. Joseph called to the younger child to run for help. He tried to shed some of his clothing. Mr Kewblet the magazine keeper came to help with a boat, but Joseph Horton was unable to get into it, so Kewblet towed him ashore. Ely Turner arrived on the scene and he and Kewblet went in search of the boy, but the water was so dark that they could see nothing.

Kewblet took Joseph Horton to his house and gave him dry clothes, while Ely Turner continued to search the river. Kewblet went to the Port and returned with two constables and drags, to begin the grim task of recovery, but by the time they reached the bridge Turner had discovered the drowned boy. James Harry Barkly Horton was twelve-and-a-half; the water at the place where he fell was around fourteen feet deep.

⚜

The names of people who drowned in the River Torrens would fill a book. Many of them were children, and although few could swim they found their way towards the water. On a Sunday afternoon in November, Henry Charles Etheridge, aged nine, and his brother Edward, seven, left their home on the Parade at Norwood and went to the river near Hackney Bridge. Neither boy could swim. The younger boy entered the water and at once sank to the bottom. His brother jumped in to save him, and he, too, disappeared.

Some small boys who were on the riverbank noticed what had happened and raised the alarm. Three lads of about eighteen rushed to assist – Charles Veitch, Clem Hill, and Herbert Leslie. They stripped off and leapt into the water, and after several dives the body of the older boy was found, soon followed by that of his brother. Charles Veitch brought them both to the surface; they had been in the water for twenty minutes. Three medical students came upon the scene, along with Dr Brummitt. Resuscitation was attempted for almost an hour, without success. The boys were the sons of Henry (Harry) Joseph Etheridge, a bootmaker, and his wife Mary Frances (Minnie).

Money to fund a headstone was collected by a Mr Blunt, and in February 1903 it was unveiled by the mayor of Norwood. The monument of white marble stood seven-and-a-half feet high and was surmounted by a cross; the grave was enclosed by an iron fence. At the unveiling ceremony much was made of the older boy's heroism in sacrificing his life to try and save his brother. It was good to die for another, the mayor said, but he hoped everyone would remember that it was good to live for each other, hence the sympathy and goodwill evident in the memorial designed by Mr Blunt.

The cross is gone, as is the iron fence. A graceful Gothic arch features a pair of small flying angels, and above their heads a dove clasps a trailing shamrock plant in its beak. The carved part of the stone has been broken and mended; perhaps this repair marks the point at which the cross was lost. Or perhaps the headstone, signed by Mr Draysey, is a combination of the original and later additions. The choice of a shamrock, and the plot's site in the Catholic area, suggests the family may have been Irish.

The site stands in the Catholic Eastern Ground, Row G, Plot 47, and as with most gravesites in this area the headstone has a north–south orientation.

⚜

Thomas Lincoln Ware of the Torrensville Brewery, Hindmarsh, was the second son of Fanny Ware, well-known proprietor of the Exchange Hotel in Hindley Street. Tom and his brother Arthur were pigeon-shooting champions, but Tom was also an ardent cricket fan – not a player, but a great barracker. When the Australian cricket eleven toured England in 1893 Tom went with them. One of the team, Arthur Coningham, told how the cricketers were treated to a picnic lunch aboard a steam launch by the head of a great firm of bat makers, Mr Ayers. They were going up the Thames when one of the boatmen, a lad of seventeen, fell overboard, and Tom Ware, who weighed around fifteen stone, jumped in to save him. Coningham, who hadn't realised that Ware was in the water, also dived in. The lad was rescued from drowning, and the plucky pair were presented with gold medals, suitably inscribed, to mark the occasion.

Three years later, Tom Ware left the Adelaide Oval after watching an inter-colonial cricket match and headed to his home at Grange. At about eight o'clock he went down to the beach for a swim, but soon cried out for help. People hastened to assist, but although Thomas Ware was pulled from the water, he did not survive.

Described as 'bluff, hearty, and genial', Tom Ware was a friend to all, 'liberal-handed, honest, and brave'; he was said to be a great raconteur and 'no mean vocalist'. When the news of his death broke, the Exchange Hotel closed its doors.

The life of the Wares in Australia had begun with ownership of World's End Station, near the Burra. Thomas's father, Charles, also conducted a brewing business at Kooringa, but the severe drought of the mid 1860s forced him to sell the station, and the Ware family began their new life as hoteliers. Ware's Exchange Hotel was described as 'a place that Dickens would have loved. Antiquated, full of comfort and tradition'. It had been that way ever since Charles and Fanny Ware took possession of it in 1868. Built along the lines of inns in the Old Country, its small drinking parlours were reminiscent of the English 'snug'; substantial meals were served in patriarchal style, with 'imposing sirloins of beef, lordly turkeys, and inspiring hams' carved by the proprietor at the head of the table, in sight of all. Everything was of the best. 'Good was not good enough; the best was not too good.' After five-and-a-half decades in the Wares' ownership the story of the hotel and the people whose lives revolved around it would make its own book, and perhaps one day it will be written.

Thomas Lincoln Ware died on 22 December 1896 at the age of thirty-two. Although he got into difficulties in the sea, a later report suggested his death could have been caused by 'heat apoplexy'. His headstone forms part of a substantial memorial Fanny Ware erected in 1871 on the death of her husband. The verse she chose for Charles Ware is a touching one, finishing with the lines:

still live the fine, fond ties that bind / the heart to heart, the mind to mind.
Thomas's inscription is simpler, as if Fanny had already said all she
had to say of grief and loss. The address is Road 1 North, Path 21;
Plot 2 is on the eastern side of the path.

⚜

On a Sunday morning in February 1860, George Debney set out
for a sail at Glenelg. With him were his wife Susanna, daughter
Matilda and his three sons, along with sixteen-year-old Annie
Attwood, and Mary Godlee. It was perfect weather; I imagine the
measureless blue sky, the diamante-sparkle of the water.

George Debney was one of Adelaide's earliest and best known
cabinetmakers. From 1847 to 1875 he traded from premises in
Rundle Street, where he may have supplemented his furniture business with undertaking work. Debney had owned the eighteen-foot
boat for some time and often sailed. They had passed the pier head
and were about two miles offshore, when a sudden puff of wind
rose. The ladies were all sitting on the leeside; they did not move
over quickly enough and when Debney tried to put the boat about,
it capsized.

Frederick Debney was a lad of almost thirteen years. He tried to
save his mother, and for half an hour held her up while clinging to
an oar. But Susanna fainted and became too heavy for him. Frederick
left her holding onto the oar; he gave his sister a loose seat from the
boat, and then set out to swim towards the shimmer of the distant
sand. It was a long swim, but Frederick managed it and landed near
Oyster Point. Too exhausted to run, the boy walked to raise the
alarm. The mail boat was despatched and all who were still afloat
were picked up. Unfortunately, Susanna Debney, Matilda, and
Annie Attwood had vanished; with their already heavy clothing
water-logged, they might as well have been carrying rocks in their
pockets.

Boats combed the ocean for the missing women. At about four
o'clock that afternoon a fisherman picked up the body of Matilda
Debney and a little later found her drowned mother. They were

taken back to the house they had 'shortly left in such health and happiness' and an inquest was held the same evening at six o'clock. As was the custom, a jury was sworn in over the bodies, with Charles Francis Heath as its foreman. The women presented a sad sight – although Susanna Debney's expression was one of repose, Matilda was said to have been frozen in the act of struggle. George Robert Debney's hair, it was said, went white overnight.

At the time of the inquest, Annie Atwood's body had not been recovered; Annie was the daughter of Mrs Hornabrook, formerly of the York Hotel, the child of her first husband.

⚜

George and Susanna's marriage began and ended on water. They were both passengers on the ship *Lloyds*, and their romance had blossomed during the long voyage to South Australia. George, who travelled with his parents and siblings, was listed as a cabinet-maker and timber mill worker; Susanna Woodward was in the company of her brother, Leonard. The ship arrived on 1 December 1838, and George and Susanna were married at Trinity Church in March 1839.

Susanna's address is Road 3, Path 11; Plot 20 is on the western side. The plain dark slate headstone with its severe design records the details of the accident; George Robert Debney's parents are also buried here.

George and Susanna had five sons, of which the youngest was only nine at the time of the boating accident. Sixteen months later, George married Ellen Elizabeth Turner at the Union Chapel in the Lyndoch Valley. A son was born to the couple in 1862, but George Debney had no luck when it came to daughters, for in 1870 just a few weeks after the birth of a girl, Maud, his wife Ellen died. She is buried here in the family plot, which extends through to Path 12 and is surrounded by a low iron fence.

Frederick, the boy who was so brave and resourceful in the moment of crisis, was destined to have a life-long relationship with the sea. At fourteen, still nursing his sorrow, he left home

281

and signed on board a ship bound for foreign lands. Years later he returned to Port Adelaide, where he gained his Master Mariner's Certificate. In 1875 Frederick married Emily Stanford, whose mother had also died when she was a child. The couple had nine children, and their firstborn, a daughter, was named Ellen Susanna in remembrance of Frederick's mother and stepmother. Frederick worked as a ship's captain, but around 1883 he bought a farm at remote Point Morrison on Kangaroo Island.

In 1889, Frederick happened to be at home when the wooden schooner *Maldon Lewis* ran aground on the coast in front of his house. A line was thrown out from the ship, and Frederick Debney, perhaps driven by a memory of the moment years earlier when he had tried and failed to save his mother and sister, plunged into the surf and made it fast. All hands from the ship were safely guided ashore. Debney entertained the survivors at his farmhouse, and was later commended for his great kindness to them, but the sea had done its work. Frederick had caught a chill, which developed into pneumonia; tuberculosis followed. He died in 1891, and is buried with his mother and sister.

Meanwhile, George Debney was married a third time to Mary Watson, a fifty-one-year-old widow, at the Congregational Church, North Adelaide; George was fifty-seven. When he died in May 1897 at the age of eighty, Mary chose to bury him beside the rest of the Debney family. While his name is still clear on the headstone that stands beside Susanna's, the verses and other details are now difficult to read. Mary is buried with him.

Their address is Road 3, Path 11; Plot 20 is on the western side of the path. This area has a messier feel than some other parts of the cemetery, with many of the old graves invaded by plants and trees, in one place even a tall palm. Every time I walk here I think of the dangerous decades during the twentieth century when there was no interest in the cemetery and little money for its upkeep; a period when the history held here stood in danger of being lost. At one time there was even a plan to return the site to parkland, and that was when many of the destructive trees were planted. During those wild and weedy years the long grass was often cleared by fire, and wooden artefacts – headstones carved from wood, simple crosses, and picket fences – almost all went up in smoke.

James Harry Barkly Horton's grave is close by. The address is Road 3, Path 12; Plot 23 is on the eastern side, just a little further on beyond the Debneys'.

Annie Atwood is listed as having been buried at West Terrace Cemetery, but in 1860 Charles Carleton, the sexton, was dying of tuberculosis and unfortunately the location of her grave is unknown.

A hall table and a pair of chairs made by George Debney are on display in the Art Gallery of South Australia. Made sometime between 1860 and 1865, they are of English oak and oak veneers on Australian red cedar. Both the table and chairs have small blank shields incorporated into their design, as if the owner might have wished to engrave or paint his initials. The chairs, Elizabethan in style, have decorative carved backs and the corkscrew legs that were a feature of seventeenth-century furniture.

A postscript to Frederick Debney's story is that after his death his widow Emily struggled to support their children on the farm. Although warned against it, Emily was so desperate to survive that she married Jack (James) St Pier. Jack had worked on board ships with her husband. But the marriage, which took place at the farmhouse at Point Morrison on 1 March 1894, cannot have been happy, for Emily left St Pier, sold the farm and returned to the mainland. When she died at eighty-five she was living at Trinity Gardens, and her plain square headstone records her name as Emily Debney, although the cemetery archive shows that she was Emily Harriet St Pier (aka Debney). The stone is inscribed with her name and the date of her death and gives no hint of the dramatic history unfolding back through time.

Her address is Flinders North, Path 3; site number 5 is on the western side of the path. It is just west of the Baby Memorial and not far from the western boundary. Her lawful husband, James St Pier, was buried in the cemetery in 1915, but Emily clearly chose not to be buried with him.

The one thing the deaths by drowning have in common is that they were sudden and unexpected: the Debney family and friends were on an outing in perfect weather; Thomas Ware was a strong swimmer who had once rescued another man from drowning; the Etheridge boys were just kids out playing; Joseph Horton had taken his boys fishing. But once a certain point of danger had been overstepped, nothing would ever be the same again, as the arrow-pierced heart so graphically communicates. I am glad to have deciphered its story before it is erased.

But I have not quite given up on the other poor Frederick, drowned in 1847 at the age of thirty-four. I have fallen to pondering whether the only way to release the tale so closely guarded by that old stone is with a graphite-rubbing, when an email unexpectedly supplies me with the unreadable surname. Alerted to my interest in the tomb, one of the team of committed volunteers at West Terrace Cemetery has, by careful cross-referencing of site maps, identified the names associated with the two plots: Thomas Bailey, and Frederick Henry Handcock. Armed with these pieces of the puzzle, the story cracks open.

Handcock's life is as dashingly colourful as one could wish for, but although its tragic end is indeed a drowning, its glamorous high points properly belong with the subject matter of my next walk – horse racing, steeplechasing, and the madcap pursuits of a small band of stylish young bachelor colonists.

22

A Tour of the Stables

Adelaide's streets and squares may have taken time to materialise, but horse racing got off to a galloping start. In 1838 the first event was held on an improvised track at Thebarton with a two-day meeting that began on New Year's Day. Its instigator was James Hurtle Fisher, a keen horseman and the resident commissioner. Colonel William Light, who in the Peninsula War against Napoleon had performed a heroic ride across enemy lines and was known as a skilled horseman, was an enthusiastic supporter. The other names associated with the event read like a roll call of old colonists, with John Morphett, Samuel Stephens, and Dr Cotter the colonial surgeon.

A shortage of horses was the immediate difficulty, but eventually ten were nominated to compete in the four events of the first day of racing. They were described as having 'no aristocracy of blood or looks. They were innocent of pedigree'. But around 800 people assembled to watch them race, and as the population of Adelaide was only around two-and-a-half thousand, the organisers were more than satisfied. One of the riders, mounted on a brown mare called Taglioni, was Frederick Henry Handcock, the man whose almost illegible name on a slab of stone has nagged at me for the last two years.

Handcock was a native of Athlone, County Westmeath, a member of a landowning family associated with the Irish peerage. He had arrived in Australia in July 1837 by the *Africaine* from Launceston, and he became the original holder of Town Acre 629 on the southern side of Gilbert Street. While he never held public office, Handcock quickly became a notable young bachelor about town, and with his 'charming and high-spirited' character he was doubtless the target of much flirtation and matchmaking.

Fred Handcock accompanied Colonel William Light on his expedition to the Barossa Valley and his name appears in Light's *Diary of a journey to Lynedoch Valley, January 1839*. Early in the previous year, he and James Fisher had established a sheep run near the junction of the Little Para River and Gould Creek; it was known as Fisher and Handcock's Station. While camped there Light sketched their little homestead, and the watercolour he later painted from this sketch is in the collection of the Art Gallery of South Australia.

One of the most interesting discoveries about Handcock is that in September 1846 he and his friends, all with a passion for horses and racing, were present at the First Grand Steeple Chase ever staged in Adelaide. It was held at Glen Osmond in front of an excited crowd, and the race became the subject of a painting attributed to George Hamilton, police commissioner, scourge of sparrows, poet, essayist, and very close friend of Julia Wyatt.

There were seven starters, and the race was won by a bay gelding named Stranger. Second was Forrester, a grey ridden by Charles Fisher. In Hamilton's painting the two are seen taking the last fence with the rest of the field a short distance behind. The painting has had some restoration work, and its gold and green foreground and background strip of turquoise sea are vivid beneath a clouded sky.

The inaugural Grand Steeple Chase caused quite a stir and was reported in the newspaper as a day 'devoted to pleasure'. Many people took the day off work, and the road to Glen Osmond was packed with horses and vehicles, with much jostling for a good view of the race. Although Fred Handcock was not one of the nominated riders, he seems to have leapt on board when Mr Stein lost his seat.

'Highflyer' fell at the third jump, unhorsing his rider, Mr. Stein, who was an invalid, and apparently much exhausted.

*Mr. Hancock, who happened to be at hand, backed him, and
followed in the 'ruck' about a section behind the rest. He pulled
up, however, upon the leading horses, 'Stranger', 'Teazer', and
'Forrester', but, unfortunately came down at the last jump.*

In November 1847 a pastoralist neighbour of Handcock's,
twenty-five-year-old Thomas Frederick Bailey, went missing.
Handcock went out searching for him and eventually both men
were found dead at Limbra Creek. Bailey had apparently fallen while
crossing the flooded waterway and had been struck on the head
by his horse's hoof. Although Handcock was an expert horseman,
he could not swim, and he had drowned while crossing on horseback to reach Bailey's body. The two were encased in expensive lead
coffins and escorted back to Adelaide for burial by fellow pastoral-
ists James Fisher and Edward Meade Bagot. Their joint funeral was
postponed for over a year, perhaps to allow time for their relatives
to make the journey to South Australia, eventually taking place on
7 December 1848.

Handcock's address is Road 2, Path 21; Plot 13 is close beside
the handsome marble tomb of William Wyatt, which straddles
the pathway. Its slab of now almost illegible stone is signed in the
bottom right-hand corner by the cemetery's colourful first sexton,
John Monck. While Handcock's name is all but lost, and Bailey's
tomb is destroyed, after more than a century-and-a-half Monck's
signature is still legible.

⚜

In 1869 the inaugural Hunt Club Races were held on the old
Thebarton racecourse. By the following year the Hunt Club had
rented the horseboxes at the Britannia Hotel and used them for
housing dogs and horses. The chief difficulty of cross-country runs
was the cost of repairing damaged fences, for sometimes upwards
of a hundred riders followed the hunt mounted on anything from
rundown hacks to thoroughbred steeplechasers.

In the early 1870s a man called William Blackler imported a

stag from England to give the Hunt Club's hounds a good run. It was drawn by horses in a closed van to Fulham Park and there released. When the hounds gave chase the stag rushed straight to the sea at Henley and plunged into the water up to its neck. Unfortunately, the poor confused creature was recaptured and taken back to Fulham Park 'for a further adventure with hounds'.

Dingoes were also kept for hunting purposes. In one hunt at the Reedbeds a dingo was lost before finally being chased out over the sandhills and along Henley Beach. Like the stag, it was driven into the sea before being captured. But when the dingo was released a second time it ran for home and survived, thanks to the superior cunning of the native Australian dog.

Blackler allowed the club's hounds to roam around Fulham, and the residents naturally became agitated. The naturalist Samuel White had established a sanctuary for kangaroos, emus, and other native animals in a secluded part of his property, and on one occasion the dogs broke in and killed many of them. Still Blackler took no steps to control the hounds, so on their next raid White retaliated by destroying some of the dogs. This led to litigation and a win for the naturalist.

All this racing and hunting, though colourful, was wildly dangerous; it led to human deaths as well as the barely remarked upon deaths of animals. The memorials to fallen riders tend to be extravagant, probably because they involve the sudden loss of young men in their prime. The grief that ensues is intense, and is often accompanied by guilt on the part of racing officials. Pockets are dipped into, both for the cost of burial and to provide something for the poor prostrated widow.

One such death was reported in the newspaper in the winter of 1879. The fatal accident was said to have cast a gloom over the hunt at Stepney. James Breen, a twenty-seven-year-old jockey, was riding a horse called Trump and jumping in company with James Watson on Smoker. They got over five or six fences together, but at the jump into the Payneham Road at the Buck's Head Hotel, Breen was slightly ahead of his companion. Trump struck the fence with his knees and Watson saw him fall on Breen, who was not able to get out of the saddle. Breen was picked up by a bystander, but showed no signs of life.

Watson told the inquest that Trump had showed bad temper that day and had baulked at fences. He had ridden the horse himself in a hunt at Laura and had been thrown. A subscription in aid of the widow was started that evening, with £70 collected at Tattersall's Rooms, and £60 at the Adelaide Club.

James Breen is buried in the Catholic Old Area and this walk begins at the gates on Wylde Road, once called the Old Catholic Road in the days when the Catholic burial ground was a separate, fenced-off section of West Terrace Cemetery. James Breen's address is B8, Site 23, and although the Catholic Area can be difficult to navigate, his grave is visible from the main roadway; it is a little west of the Smyth Chapel, and on the same side.

The headstone bears a beautifully executed carving of a horse and man rolling in front of a broken fence. A verse beneath it mourns the tragic events of a summer's day in which a young man in youth and health rode off and never returned.

⚜

In the Art Gallery of South Australia, 'In The Starter's Hands' by John Michael Skipper, circa 1850, shows two horses lining up to race at the Adelaide Racecourse near Victoria Park, where races were first held in the 1840s. The red monogrammed letter P on one of the saddlecloths suggests the horse is 'Highflyer', owned by Mr W. Paxton. Highflyer was the horse Frederick Handcock attempted to get over the finish line in the First Grand Steeple Chase. In Skipper's painting the jockey is probably Charles B. Fisher, son of James Hurtle Fisher the resident commissioner. There are four other small figures in the background, three of them with horses, and I like to imagine that one of them is Patrick Coglan with his much-loved mare.

The first Adelaide Cup was run on 21 April 1864 at Thebarton, and despite wet weather more than 7000 people turned out to watch. Twelve horses out of a nominated sixteen lined up at the starting post; the race was won by Falcon. From that time on, riders have lost their lives on all the main racing tracks in South Australia, and their graves are scattered throughout the cemetery.

James Power, a twenty-four-year-old jockey, was accidentally killed while riding Pendulous at Snowtown on 4 February 1914. His address is Catholic Western Ground, Path I, plot 142. To locate it, look for the tall statue of a man on the eastern side of the path: this is Joseph Regis Cooney, First Chief Scout Commissioner of Australia. Further along on the western side, Power's memorial – erected by his sporting friends – is elaborately decorated with horseshoes and stirrups carved into the marble corner posts; there is a carving of a horse, and the whole monument is surmounted by a broken column and wreath.

Another gravestone adorned with a horse belongs to young Thomas Driscoll. It is in the Catholic Eastern Ground and the address is Path A, Plot 123. I follow the Old Catholic Cemetery Road towards Sir Donald Bradman Drive and at the boundary gate look right to where Driscoll's headstone is about 150 metres along in the shelter of a stand of olive trees. Its horse and jockey are beautifully carved, as are the two small shamrocks that show his Irish origins. Driscoll likely came from County Cork to Western Australia with his family, and from there drifted to Adelaide. Just a couple of rows east, and almost directly behind Thomas Driscoll, is the grave of Lance Pile who 'met with an accident while riding Nicotine in the Hurdle Race at Strathalbyn' on 6 April 1903. He was twenty-four. The marble cross that once topped his memorial now lies flat in front of it. Lance Pile's address is Catholic Eastern Ground, Path E, Plot 122.

Described as 'the crack jockey of South Australia', twenty-nine-year-old Sid Willis met with a fatal accident while riding The Bird in the Welter Handicap at the Port Adelaide course at Cheltenham on 25 October 1903. Halfway through the race, Willis guided the horse into an opening, but the field closed and The Bird trod on another horse's heels and stumbled. Willis was thrown and landed on his head. He was described as 'a bold rider, a fine judge of pace, and could finish with the best'. His address is Road 3, Path 5; Plot 1 is on the eastern corner, where the white marble obelisk erected by his wife Elizabeth is elaborately adorned with a wreath of marble flowers and a rose.

An elaborate memorial close to Sid Willis's grave belongs to another crack jockey, Edwin (Teddy) Hodgkins. His address is Road 3, Path 1A; Plot 1 is on the western corner. Teddy Hodgkins died on 13 April 1901 when the river-bred gelding Corral fell with him at Victoria Park. The broken column, with cloth and tassels was erected by his widow Ethel, and his sporting friends.

⚜

John Michael Skipper's paintings and drawings would become a valuable historical record of early life in Adelaide. A passenger on the *Africaine*, Skipper met his future wife Frances Amelia Thomas on the outward voyage; Frances's parents Robert and Mary brought the first printing press to South Australia and established the *South Australian Gazette and Colonial Register*, the colony's first newspaper.

Skipper died in Adelaide in 1883, and his address is Road 4, Path 26; Plot 23 is on the eastern side of the path. His and Frances's son, Spencer John Skipper, is buried here with him. Frances Skipper's health was never strong, and indeed, one of the reasons given by her mother Mary for her willingness to leave England was her hope the South Australian climate would benefit her daughter. But Frances died in 1855 at only thirty-six. John Michael Skipper later married her younger sister Mary. Frances's address is Road 1 South, Path 20; Plot 6 is on the eastern side of the path. Having been unmarked for many years, the site has recently been renewed by descendants of the Thomas family, and Frances Skipper is buried here with her parents.

⚜

As I end this round of visits to those who loved their horses, and to the Skippers who loved to paint and draw (and who are themselves the subject of a painting by John Michael Skipper 'Artist and his wife Frances Amelia on horses') I pause beside the first of two large blocks of stone on Road 1 and run a hand over its rough surface. This one is at the entrance to Path 16, and the other is by Path 25. They are mounting blocks, installed here in the days of horse-drawn carriages, and I only wish they could tell of all the people whose boots passed over them.

23

The Little Soldier

On a winter's afternoon in August 1916, two boys were playing in the breakfast room of a boarding house at 1 Royal Avenue, off Gilles Street. The landlady, Mrs Thistleton, was keeping an eye on them while the rest of her family were in the front room playing the piano.

Allan Strang, aged nine years and seven months, and his friend Jack Mallinson were pretending to ambush German soldiers. In the midst of the First World War, it was a game played in homes and schoolyards across Australia, but it had special significance for young Allan, whose father had been killed the year before at Anzac Cove on the first day of the Gallipoli campaign.

Private William Andrew Strang of the 10th Battalion, known to his family as Arthur, was from Broken Hill. His wife Rose announced his death in the *Advertiser*.

We mourn for you, dear Arthur
No eyes may see us weep,
But many a tear we shed for you
While all are fast asleep.
But it does not matter how we weep,
No matter how we call,
There's nothing left to answer
But your photo, on the wall

Still grieving the loss of her husband, Rose supported her son by working as a domestic servant.

Jack Mallinson, eleven, also boarded at Mrs Thistleton's house with his family. His parents were out that afternoon, and when he went to their bedroom, ostensibly to look for some allies, he opened his father's chest of drawers and found a revolver. Although he had been told never to touch it, the temptation was too great. Jack slipped the gun into his pocket and returned to the breakfast room.

Jack and Allan resumed their game of soldiers. The room was chilly, but the boys – absorbed in their game of attack and counter-attack against imaginary Germans – did not notice. They had arranged furniture to form a bunker. When Mrs Thistleton left them to go into the front room, Allan picked up a chair and pre-tended to play the kettledrum.

'Here comes a German,' he shouted. 'Fire!'

Jack Mallinson pulled the revolver from his pocket and lifted it towards the door. The gun went off and Allan fell. To his alarm, Jack saw blood running from his friend's head, and ran into the parlour where the family were still thumping out popular tunes on the piano.

'I have shot Allan,' he cried.

Mrs Thistleton ran to the breakfast room, and found Allan Strang on the floor, bleeding. A neighbour, Mr Matthews, came in and bathed the boy's head. Doctor Lynch was sent for and arrived a few minutes later.

Allan Strang was taken to the Royal Adelaide Hospital, but died after two hours. His body was identified by Mrs Thistleton. The city coroner, Dr Ramsay Smith, declared the death an acci-dental shooting, and commented that rather than prohibiting the use of weapons, everyone should be taught to handle them safely, beginning with toy guns.

Jack's father, Thomas Sutcliffe Mallinson, had been on the police staff of the Military Department and carried the gun during escort duty. He had not used the revolver for five or six weeks and thought he had unloaded it when putting it away. However, he might have left a cartridge in it.

Young Jack Mallinson told Constable McCabe he did not think

the revolver was loaded. Rose Strang confirmed that the two boys 'really loved each other' and she was satisfied the shooting had been an accident.

Even after almost a century Rose Strang's grief endures in the memorial she created for her only child, and Allan Strang's grave is watched over by one of the loveliest small angels in West Terrace Cemetery. Born in Jamestown in about 1884, Rose was eighteen when she married Arthur Strang and we can only hope that she had some happy years before the terrible events of her later life unfolded. Two deaths within sixteen months were bound to take a toll, and in the year following Allan's accident Rose contracted tuberculosis. She died in 1925 at the age of forty-one, and was buried with her son.

⚜

Perhaps Allan Strang's death should be read as a war story. It certainly connects Gallipoli in a shocking way with life in Adelaide at the time of the First World War. During the Gallipoli campaign, 8141 Australians were killed, and Allan's death is a small sad echo that attaches to that figure, increasing it by one more very young life. Yet his was just one of the unacknowledged losses of the war, and there is no knowing how many other civilian deaths could trace similar connections.

If the Strang family's story is one of terrible loss, the Mallinsons, too, moved from one misfortune to another. The boy who pulled the trigger, known as Jack and described at the inquest as 'a chubby little youth', was John William Mallinson. His father, Thomas Sutcliffe Mallinson, a Yorkshireman from Halifax, had come to Australia in 1907 aboard the *Orient*. His occupation at that time was listed as 'butcher'. The ship docked at Fremantle, and from there Thomas found his way to South Australia's Mid North, where he established a butcher's shop in the town of Terowie.

But the business struggled, and the climate did not agree with Thomas's wife, Charlotte. In 1911 she travelled to Adelaide for two months 'for a change and for medical advice'; the following year she went again and stayed longer. By 1913, Thomas's business had folded, and after the family had moved from Terowie to Victoria Terrace at Glenelg he made an appearance in the Insolvency Court.

After Terowie, he had bought a boat in Glenelg in partnership with a man called Herbert Hunter. The two planned to set up pleasure trips on the bay, but before they could begin they were both struck down with typhoid fever and could do nothing at all for four months. Their boating business, finished even before it was begun, ended with a debt of £40. In court, the commissioner commented that Mallinson, though honest, seemed to be dogged by misfortune.

In 1914, Charlotte Mallinson gave birth to a girl, Rita Rose Marie – Rita was two at the time of the shooting, and its implications were probably lost on her, but the horror of Allan Strang's death doubtless made a deep impression on young John William. There was to be no respite from sorrow, for the following year the family was once again plunged into mourning. Charlotte's trips from the Mid North in search of medical help had been a portent of what lay ahead, and that April she died of a cerebral haemorrhage. At the time of her death, Thomas was listed as a hospital attendant, and the family had moved from Mrs Thistleton's house to Glen Osmond Road at Frewville.

The months after Charlotte died must have been tough ones for Thomas Mallinson and the children. In November 1917, Thomas enlisted as a cook in the 3rd Light Horse Brigade, 9th Light Horse Regiment. But with a twelve-year-old son and a three-year-old daughter to care for, he needed a new wife, and in January 1918, Thomas Mallinson married Rosey Young. Rosey also lived in Frewville, so perhaps she had been engaged to care for the children and Thomas decided to make it permanent. At twenty-one, she was sixteen years his junior, and we must assume she was prepared to take charge of young Rita, and John William who was entering his teenage years.

Fortunately the war ended before John Mallinson was old enough to enlist or he might have added to the death toll. He grew up to become a fisherman who steered clear of marriage until he was thirty-six, and for many years lived in Capper Street at Kent Town. On 29 November 1952, he died at sea on board a boat between Whyalla and Cowell; the cause of death was acute myocarditis. John Mallinson was still a relatively young man of forty-seven. He was buried at Cheltenham Cemetery.

Allan Strang's address is Road 1 South, Path 4; Plot 43 is on the eastern side and it only takes a minute or two to walk here from the main entrance. Its child-sized angel clasps a wreath to its chest, and in the fingers of the right hand a flower is poised to drop in perpetual remembrance. The statue's perfection is marred only by a missing little finger, struck off by a blow of some kind in the recent past, for the broken edge is still sharp. Soft folds of cloth on the angel's dress, its patterned hem, evoke a child's nightdress. The softly weathered stone is probably more beautiful now than when it was new, and the verses chosen by Rose Strang wring one's heart.

Thomas Mallinson survived the war only to die suddenly in 1935. His last address was 25 Cypress Street, Adelaide, and he is buried in the AIF Section of West Terrace Cemetery. Thus, a few fragments of life and death in Adelaide on a winter's afternoon in 1916 are gathered here, to be pieced together, wondered at, and remembered.

24

Remembrance Walk

Whenever I watch a match of Australian Football, especially one between two strong sides, it strikes me that if the players were wearing khaki I could be seeing something that resembles hand-to-hand fighting. I am not alone in this, for recently I heard a commentator describe a run of play as 'trench warfare'. I am reminded of Gallipoli and other battles, and as the fans cheer for goals I look with horror upon a field of young men in their absolute prime who had they lived in a different era would certainly have been lost to war. The career span of football players is roughly the same as that of foot soldiers; by the time they reach their thirties their powers are reckoned to be on the wane. In August 1914, men between eighteen and thirty-five were eligible to enlist, although within a year the upper limit would be raised to forty-five.

Thomas David MacKenzie was a football star in what was, at the turn of the century, known as the South Australian Football Association. He was the first player to win the coveted Magarey Medal three times, and it was presented to him by 'Beautiful Bill' Magarey in 1902, 1905, and 1906. Thomas MacKenzie played around 200 games for the West Torrens and North Adelaide football clubs, and captained West Torrens from 1911 to 1913. He was an outstanding and versatile rover, a great possession-getter and a fine pass; he could kick with either foot and was – that great thing in Australian Football, with its contrary oval ball – a pinpoint-accurate kick.

In July 1915 he enlisted in the 32nd Battalion raised as part of the 8th Brigade at Mitcham. Like the 27th Battalion known as 'Unley's Own', it was largely composed of South Australian enlistees. They sailed from Adelaide on 18 November 1915, and by June of 1916 were in France and destined for the Western Front. Their first major battle was fought at Fromelles on 19 July after only three days in the front-line trenches. It was a disastrous introduction to the battlefield, with casualties of almost seventy-five per cent.

I have never seen a photograph of a First World War soldier that was not beautiful. Youth in itself is beautiful, I think, but being identically dressed the eye is compelled towards the faces and they seem to shine with the luminosity of doomed youth. Thirty-three-year-old Tom MacKenzie, fairest and most brilliant on the football field, was one of the doomed, and family and friends were shocked when he was reported killed in action. He had been wounded by shellfire and left among the dead on the battlefield. But a stretcher-bearer who happened to be a West Torrens supporter recognised his club's captain, and on closer inspection discovered that Tom MacKenzie was still alive. The football fan carried him to safety, and in 1919 MacKenzie was able to return to Adelaide, where he supported his old team and held a Player Life Membership in the SANFL. But like so many other returned soldiers his experience in France eventually caught up with him, and his death of war-related injuries came in 1927.

His address is Light Oval, 8N, Plot 3, on the eastern side, where his white marble headstone bears the rising sun, and his unit badge – vertical white and yellow stripes. In 1996 Tom MacKenzie was inducted into the Australian Football Hall of Fame.

⚜

The military burial ground here was the first of its kind in Australia, and it was the return of men like Tom MacKenzie, terribly injured after the First World War, that prompted its establishment. Many returned soldiers ended up in the Repatriation Hospital at

Keswick, and ultimately in plots in the main part of the cemetery. At least 150 were interred in unmarked graves, and it was this lack of recognition and respect that moved community groups, like the League of Loyal Women, to lobby for a dedicated military cemetery. The first land grant was for half an acre, although it has now been extended to four acres and holds the graves of more than 4000 ex-servicemen and women.

It is the only truly ordered part of the cemetery. Even the surrounding hedges are tightly clipped. The uniform headstones stand to attention, their shadows moving around them as the sun travels across the sky. Husbands and wives are not buried together here if one is a civilian, which may explain why many servicemen and women preferred family plots elsewhere in the cemetery.

In the heavy silence at midday, when the shadows are short and the hedges and trees marinate in pools of their own shade, there is a starkness and a solemnity here that makes me catch my breath, makes the insides of my eyelids prickle.

⚜

Perhaps the saddest of all stories connected with Australia's war history belongs to the Indigenous men and women who volunteered to fight for a king and country that refused to recognise them as citizens. It is even difficult to gather precise statistics on how many Indigenous Australians fought in the First World War, since ethnicity was rarely recorded: in an era when the *Defence Act of 1909* prohibited those not of 'substantially European' origin from serving in the armed forces, this was a strange omission. But many were deemed 'white-enough'; they enlisted and saw active service.

If there is a positive here it is that racism largely disappeared in the trenches and that for perhaps the first time in their lives Indigenous soldiers experienced a sense of equality and comradeship with their fellow Australians. But it was a different story on their return to Australia, if they did return. Although some were decorated for outstanding courage, winning the Distinguished Conduct Medal and the Military Medal, there was a widespread lack of recognition of their sacrifice and few were granted a block under the Soldier Land Settlement scheme.

Private Miller Mack was a Ngarrindjeri man, raised at the Point McLeay mission on the River Murray. After successfully enlisting in 1916 he left Australia, and in England spent much of his training in Wiltshire incapacitated with influenza. He fought at the battle of Messines, before being returned to England with bronchial pneumonia, and at that time diagnosed with tuberculosis. Private Mack returned to Australia, where on 3 September 1919 he died of consumption at the Bedford Park Sanatorium.

He was buried just outside Light Oval in an unmarked grave, and when Bedford inmates heard of this they donated money for a memorial; Miller Mack had endeared himself to his fellow patients, who testified to his 'kindly' nature. But the site still has no head-stone, only an Australian War Graves marker.

Private Miller Mack's address is Road 5, Path 29; Plot 15 is on the eastern side of the path. It lies under the canopy of an ancient pepper tree, on the edge of the AIF cemetery.

⚜

On Anzac Day on North Terrace, crowds gather beneath a light-ening sky with its fingernail moon. There are more young people than I expected; they have brought their dogs and small children, and while they continue to turn out in the dark for the dawn service we remain a society that remembers. The words of the 'Ode' never grow tired, no matter how many times they are said. Dawn gradu-ally flushes the old stonework of the Institute, the Museum, and the Art Gallery, and soon the light-streaked sky is full of birds.

Afterwards, the Austral Hotel is open for business. It is 7 am, and even the chilly outside tables have customers. Inside, medals firmly pinned, the drinkers prime their legs with beer for the long march to the Cross of Sacrifice, while I pass on to return to West Terrace Cemetery.

Here the roads and paths are striped with long shadows. Night lingers inside the boundary walls and in the scented pines. There is bird sound. Wood pigeons perch on the headstones, indistinguishable from the stone doves until one spreads his tail into a fan and dances to impress his lady love.

In the AIF cemetery, the flag stands at half-mast and there is a single wreath at the foot of the Cross of Sacrifice. The light is soft and beautiful, as a lone bagpipe starts up far away at another wreath-laying ceremony; it is an old, old sound, a keening voice that generates nostalgia, even though I am not a Scot.

It reminds me of the contingent of young boys who in 1913 arrived in South Australia on the farm apprenticeship scheme. Seventeen of them were from the Kibble Reformatory School in Paisley, Scotland, sent there for a series of petty crimes. But in the record drought of 1914 the apprentice scheme came undone, compelling the boys to seek other work. All but one of the Kibble boys joined up – perhaps it was the prospect of returning to their own side of the world that propelled them towards the enlistment office, for the drought had convinced them they had not come to a better life in Australia. Most saw action on Gallipoli before they were sent to the Western Front. What they saw there, according to one boy, was 'enough to last me the rest of my life'.

The proximity of home would prove too much and five of the boys took unauthorised periods of leave, for which they were court-martialled. Four of the five were picked up in their home town of Glasgow.

Not all of them survived the war, but those who did were cruelly not repatriated to Scotland but to South Australia. Joseph McQueen, James Pettigrew, and Robert Watson are buried in the area designated as Kendrew Oval. Their respective addresses are Row 23A, Plot 42; Row 3A, Plot 35; Row 21A, Plot 17.

⚜

Down in Light Oval the shadows are tall. Anzac Day here is the same as all other days; that is both the beauty and the horror of this place – its indifference, its enduring silence. Those of us who live see the flag standing at half-mast; on an ordinary day we hear the metallic clang as its halyard rattles against the flagpole. We witness the white cockatoos as they rise in a cloud from the viridian pine. We feel the grass underfoot, how damp and spongy, how richly green it grows here.

As I walk back towards the entrance gates, the plaint of the bagpipe mingles with the distant, oceanic roll of traffic, and the sharp, intermittent cries of the birds. I breathe in and out and tip my face to the sun, grateful not to have had to live through those years of war.

25

A Last Ramble
in the Quiet City

Enough – let commune with the dead
Inspire our hearts with quicken'd zeal;
Enough – for on our ling'ring path
The lengthen'd shadows silent steal.
'Fragmentary Lines Written in the Cemetery'
– Caroline Carleton, 1860

After three years of walking these pathways I have not run short of stories, indeed, there are so many more I would like to tell – like the story of the bootmaker, the ballerina, the bird-stuffer, the explorers and surveyors, even the man who fell to his death from the hayloft at Mrs Ware's Exchange Hotel. But it is time to write of other things, at least for a while. While I will miss my walks here I will often return to seek a few moments of respite from the living world.

As so often happens, it can take more than 80,000 words before I begin to understand what is in my mind, and what I have been thinking about in an oblique way on these walks is human life-spans and mortality. For not one person in these stories gets out alive – they leave the stage by various exits, but they all go. None of us gets out alive, and living with this knowledge calls for a balancing act worthy of 'The Wizard of the Wire', the great Con Colleano.

Colleano was a circus performer during the golden era of trav-elling circuses. He gathered his extraordinary tightrope skills on the rough tracks of Outback Australia where, whenever the circus pitched camp, a wire would be improvised between a couple of trees. The dashingly handsome Colleano disguised his Aboriginal heritage with a Spanish performance persona complete with matador costumes, much as I imagine John Isaacs the tiger tamer masked his African roots as a Mexican.

In Colleano's day the forward somersault was thought to be impossible on a tightrope; backflips were relatively easy, but with the forward roll the acrobat lost sight of his feet and could not safely land. Colleano discovered that if he slackened the tightrope he could achieve a higher bounce, one that allowed him a split-second of vision to position his feet. By trial and error he perfected the forward somersault, only to find that on the slackened wire all his hard-won balance skills were useless for other tricks. So Con Colleano set himself to practising on the slack wire until he was as steady on it as he had ever been on the taut wire. Then he took his extraordinary act to America, where he became a tightrope legend.

Humans live on a wire tensed between remembering and forgetting. It is a delicate performance – if there is too much forgetfulness we lose our grip on the world; too much remembering can be equally disturbing. Most of us choose to walk on the tautened wire, more comfortable with not seeing our feet, not looking down. Even the presence of this old cemetery here on the flank of the living city exactly reflects our relationship with death: it is close beside us, night and day, yet we habitually hurry on past. But those like Con Colleano find a new way of seeing; they persevere, and adjust. Perhaps the death awareness meditation and acceptance is part of this, deliberately passing through the shadows to become more alive in our brief moment of sunlight.

People speak of being drawn to old cemeteries, though never to new ones. New cemeteries are too raw; their pathways are riffs on unhealed grief. But old sites give us the separation we need, that buffering distance, before the split-second glimpse of the landing place. Walking here with the birds and plants for company it is possible to calmly contemplate lifespans, to experience joy in the living moment, even though it may not be perfect. The surroundings can jog us out of our self-hypnotised conviction that, come what may, death will not touch us; we will always be alive. With constant reminding, perhaps we can choose to spend our hoard of time more wisely and live, as Caroline Carleton advised, 'with quicken'd zeal'.

᠅

This old cemetery is a liminal space – not quite in the world, but not quite out of it. Hours flow by like a river here, until I begin to experience time as something like the Wilhelm Hammershøi painting of dust motes in the stream of light in an empty room. Looking across this field of weather-bleached stones my perception of time is altered: either it slows, or it stops, or it is all time, all at once. As the writer Anne Michaels observed, 'The present is just the accumulation of a huge amount of time'. You can press down anywhere, and here, pressing down, find the stories out of which our own stories unfold.

I remember the night walk during history month, and how I wished I could be transported to an earlier Adelaide. And now I find that I have been, for that is what walking here can do in a vivid way. Over many hours spent rambling the cemetery's roads and paths I have been immersed in the city of Ben Ellis the hangman, of the Reverend Bickford, and Winnie Goater, and poor Johanna Sullivan. And each time I leave here to resume my daily life I move about a city that is so much richer for these earlier presences.

I think of George William Francis each time I pass the gates of the Botanic Garden, and look upon his pepper tree with special fondness; I recall his practical wisdom and boundless energy, even in difficult times, and I fancy that some of it rubs off on anyone who takes the time to enter into his story. I never round the western corner of the city without holding in my mind's eye the image of a young woman slouching comfortably on a horse. I see there, too, an exhausted man take a moment's pause from his task of dreaming a city into being, to sit and sketch one of the few people who understood him.

Places like the Adelaide Arcade, though lovely, are now clouded in certain spots like the silvered patterns found on old foxed mirrors. As I rattle along George Street on the 172 bus I pass a certain house with a shiver for the lost girls who put their lives into the hands of Francis Sheridan, and I am thankful beyond measure for my own time, with all its threats and promises.

⚜

There is a photograph I love to look at: it shows the entrance to the Adelaide Hospital around 1880. The hospital's wrought-iron gates stand open; the pillars on either side are crowned with elegant gas lamps and the drive is broad and sweeping. A four-wheeled carriage stands before the gates, and a group of people, three black-suited men and a child, linger inside the grounds, their features indistinct. The original hospital buildings loom, solid yet serene, a place of refuge and also of tremendous suffering. What I love about this photograph is its visual quietness: there are two signs, one on each of the pillars – I cannot read them but I imagine they list consulting times and visiting hours – otherwise there is a complete absence of clutter.

I envy people who were able to live free of the graphic cacophony that clogs our own century, and I wonder whether it was easier to think, back then, easier to plan and see clearly what needed to be done. Is that why some of these earlier lives, though short, appear so intense: there was little to distract them, other than birth and sickness, love, and death?

Sometimes I look at twenty-first-century Adelaide and try to imagine how it would appear to people raised with the symmetry of Georgian architecture. I conclude that the city has gradually lost its elegance, the poise conferred by spareness and simplicity; modern signage alone has produced great ugliness, yet we do not suffer helplessly, as we once did, for want of a qualified doctor, and I feel certain that most of the people I have visited, if they had been able to choose, would have swapped any amount of elegance for that one luxury.

History strikes me as something like the dark matter of our universe – invisible, but known by astrophysicists to exist because of the weight of its gravity. Absorbed in our own lives and times, still we spin history for future generations. On a warm autumn night, as I cross the river by the Adelaide Bridge and pause to lean on the parapet, I come face to face with the city bequeathed to us out of the muddy struggle with disease and loneliness and lack; its spangled beauty is doubled in the black mirror of the river. History is the old light that falls on us, and sometimes, strolling through the quiet city, I peer into it and wonder what we will hand to our great-great-great-grandchildren.

Author's Note

Change is unavoidable, even in a cemetery, so while the site details included in this work are, to the best of my knowledge, correct at the time of writing, they may not remain so for the life of this book. All of the graves visited were approached with immense respect, and I urge readers who may follow in my footsteps to be mindful of the often fragile state of the old monuments. While walking, and writing, I was conscious of the private nature of death and grief, however the stories gathered here offer remarkable insights into life in the young colony of South Australia and they were written in a spirit of wanting to understand the past. In most cases the lives represented here have been pieced together from many sources, and it is inevitable that other versions and interpretations exist.

Acknowledgements

Thanks to Arts SA for the grant that supported the early research work. Gratitude is also due to Jude Aquilina, Anne Bartlett, Jill Jones, and Annette Willis. The volunteers at West Terrace Cemetery were endlessly generous, especially Philippa King, Bob Sutherland, and Trevor Peart, and Tony Amato at the Adelaide Cemeteries Authority shared valuable research. Thank you to Rosalie and Emily Harding, Geoff Francis, Kesta Fleming, Matthew Sorrell, Provenance Indigenous Plants, Elspeth Grant, Rowena Holloway, the volunteers at the South Australia Genealogy Centre, and staff at State Records.

Index

Ashton's Hotel

The journal of William Baker Ashton, first governor of the Adelaide Gaol

Rhondda Harris

South Australia was meant to be the perfect colony: free settlers, no crime, and no mental illness. But good intentions go awry. Within three years plans for a permanent gaol were well established, along with a governor to oversee it: William Baker Ashton.

Researcher Rhondda Harris came upon Ashton's long-lost journal by happy accident, and was soon absorbed by 'The Governor's' handwritten pages. They told a hidden story of early Adelaide and its underbelly, of crashes and crises and crims. 'Ashton's Hotel', the colonists called their prison. His kindness of spirit, under nigh-impossible circumstances, shines through in this first published edition of his journal, expertly contextualised and introduced by Rhondda Harris.

For more information please visit wakefieldpress.com.au

Awakening
Four lives in art

Eileen Chanin and Steven Miller

When Ibsen's controversial play *A Doll's House* opened to packed audiences at Melbourne's Princes Theatre, the slam of the door as Nora left her husband in the final act echoed in the minds of thousands of young Australian women. This book is about four of these women, born in Victoria between 1867 and 1893, who lived through the changes which swept across life, culture and art during the early twentieth century. Four short biographies trace their parallel lives.

From Rome, Dora Ohlfsen established a career as a celebrated sculptor. With Mussolini's support, she became the only expatriate sculptor in Italy commissioned with a national war memorial. Significantly, her Anzac medal was the first commemorative work of art memorialising the Anzacs. From Paris, Louise Dyer invigorated music publishing and recording, helping to transform musical culture world-wide. Her label *Les Éditions de L'Oiseau-Lyre* laid the foundations of the modern early music revival and helped shape the notion of 'authenticity' in musical performance. From London, Clarice Zander promoted cultural understanding as a curator and as the publicist for the Royal Academy. She pioneered the modern marketing of art and curated Australia's first important exhibition of contemporary British art. From New York, Mary Cecil Allen, painter, critic, and educator, working at the centre of modern art, inspired many. She ran the first touring exhibition of contemporary Australian art in the United States.

Modern women of the arts, they awoke to their full potential and created opportunities for others to do likewise.

For more information please visit wakefieldpress.com.au

Wakefield Press is an independent publishing and
distribution company based in Adelaide, South Australia.
We love good stories and publish beautiful books.
To see our full range of books, please visit our website at
wakefieldpress.com.au
where all titles are available for purchase.
To keep up with our latest releases, news and events,
subscribe to our monthly newsletter.

Find us!

Facebook: facebook.com/wakefield.press
Twitter: twitter.com/wakefieldpress
Instagram: instagram.com/wakefieldpress

www.ingramcontent.com/pod-product-compliance
Lightning Source LLC
Chambersburg PA
CBHW051950270326
41929CB00015B/2606